MONOGRAPHS OF THE CENTER FOR SOUTHEAST ASIAN STUDIES
KYOTO UNIVERSITY
ENGLISH LANGUAGE SERIES, NO. 18

DEMOCRACY AND LEADERSHIP:
THE RISE OF THE TAMAN SISWA MOVEMENT
IN INDONESIA

MONOGRAPHS OF THE CENTER FOR SOUTHEAST ASIAN STUDIES
KYOTO UNIVERSITY

English-language Series:

1. Takashi Sato, *Field Crops in Thailand*, 1966
2. Tadayo Watabe, *Glutinous Rice in Northern Thailand*, 1967
3. Kiyoshi Takimoto (ed.), *Geology and Mineral Resources in Thailand and Malaya*, 1969
4. Keizaburo Kawaguchi and Kazutake Kyuma, *Lowland Rice Soils in Thailand*, 1969
5. Keizaburo Kawaguchi and Kazutake Kyuma, *Lowland Rice Soils in Malaya*, 1969
6. Kiyoshige Maeda, *Alor Janggus: A Chinese Community in Malaya*, 1967
7. Shinichi Ichimura (ed.), *The Economic Development of East and Southeast Asia*, 1975
8. Masashi Nishihara, *The Japanese and Sukarno's Indonesia*, 1976
9. Shinichi Ichimura (ed.), *Southeast Asia: Nature, Society and Development*, 1977
10. Keizaburo Kawaguchi and Kazutake Kyuma, *Paddy Soils in Tropical Asia*, 1977
11. Kunio Yoshihara, *Japanese Investment in Southeast Asia*, 1978
12. Yoneo Ishii (ed.), *Thailand: A Rice-Growing Society*, 1978
13. Lee-Jay Cho and Kazumasa Kobayashi (eds.), *Fertility Transitions of the East Asian Populations*, 1979
14. Kuchiba, Tsubouchi and Maeda, *Three Malay Villages: A Sociology of Paddy Growers in West Malaysia*, 1979
15. Cho, Suharto, McNicoll and Mamas, *Population Growth of Indonesia*, 1980
16. Yoneo Ishii, *Sangha, State and Society: Thai Buddhism in History*, 1986
17. Yoshikazu Takaya, *Agricultural Development of a Tropical Delta*, 1987

Japanese-language Series:

Available from the Center for Southeast Asian Studies, Kyoto, Japan.

1. Joji Tanase, *Primitive Form of the Idea of the Other World*, 1966
2. Toru Yano, *Modern Political History of Thailand and Burma*, 1968
3. Takeshi Motooka, *Agricultural Development of Southeast Asia*, 1968
4. Yoshihiro and Reiko Tsubouchi, *Divorce*, 1970
5. Shigeru Iijima, *Social and Cultural Change of Karens*, 1971
6. H. Storz (trans. by H. Nogami), *Burma: Land, History and Economy*, 1974
7. Shinichi Ichimura (ed.), *Southeast Asia: Nature, Society and Economy*, 1974
8. Yoneo Ishii, *Thailand: A Rice-Growing Society*, 1975
9. Yoneo Ishii, *Political Sociology of Theravada Buddhism*, 1975
10. Shinichi Ichimura (ed.), *The Economic Development of East and Southeast Asia*, 1975
11. Takeshi Motooka, *Rice in Indonesia*, 1975
12. Kuchiba, Tsubouchi and Maeda, *The Structure and Change of Malayan Villages*, 1976
13. Masashi Nishihara (ed.), *Political Corruption in Southeast Asia*, 1976
14. A. Eckstein (trans. by S. Ichimura, et al.), *Economic Trends in Communist China*, 1979

MONOGRAPHS OF THE CENTER FOR SOUTHEAST ASIAN STUDIES
KYOTO UNIVERSITY

DEMOCRACY AND LEADERSHIP: THE RISE OF THE TAMAN SISWA MOVEMENT IN INDONESIA

KENJI TSUCHIYA

Translated by Peter Hawkes

UNIVERSITY OF HAWAII PRESS

HONOLULU

Library of Congress Cataloging-in-Publication Data

Tsuchiya, Kenji, 1942–
  Democracy and leadership.

  Translation of: Indonesia minzoku shugi kenkyū.
  1. Nationalism—Indonesia—History.   2. Taman
Siswa (Organization)—History.   3. Indonesia—History—
1945–1949.   I. Title.
DS643.T7913   1988   959.8′035   87-23783
ISBN 0-8248-1157-7
ISBN 0-8248-1158-5 (pbk.)

Filmset in Hong Kong by Asco Trade Typesetting Ltd.

To Nobue and Kenichiro

CONTENTS

TRANSLATOR'S NOTE

In June 1985, Professor Tsuchiya became the first recipient of the Ohira Prize, a newly instituted award in memory of the late prime minister of Japan, Ohira Masayoshi, for outstanding scholarship on Asia and the Pacific region. The prize-winning work, which is based on his doctoral thesis, is a book entitled *Indoneshia minzokushūgi kenkyū* (A Study of Indonesian Nationalism) (Tokyo: Sobunsha, 1982); and it is this work, unfortunately abridged of certain sections for economy's sake, that is here translated.

Aside from the problems of Indonesian orthography that must be all too familiar to scholars studying this area, the treatment of which Professor Tsuchiya explains in his introduction, translating this work raised one significant problem of which the reader should be aware: my own lack of competence in Indonesian, Javanese, and Dutch—languages in which Professor Tsuchiya makes extensive use of primary materials for his research—coupled with the fact that, in places, passages from these primary sources are quoted in Japanese. For some passages I have been able to locate existing English translations, and these I have used and acknowledged in a note; but for the vast majority, no such translations were available. My recourse, therefore, was to translate into English the Japanese translations of these passages and, as far as time allowed, to check the results against the original materials by questioning the author and referring to dictionaries. While the results yielded by this rather unsatisfactory method may not always be precise, they do appear, at least from their context, to contain no serious inaccuracies; but I would recommend that anyone intending to quote any of this material directly should return to the sources, which are amply documented herein.

ACKNOWLEDGMENTS

The publication of this book was financed in part by a Grant-in-Aid for Publication of Scientific Research Results from the Ministry of Education, Science and Culture, Japan.

The map on the cover is part of the Map of Asia by Cornelius de Jode, 1593, and is reproduced by courtesy of the Kobe City Museum.

INTRODUCTION

The Task and the Method

In July 1922, a private school called the Taman Siswa National Education School was founded in Yogyakarta in Central Java. Taman Siswa meant roughly "Garden of Pupils." The leading figure in this event was a thirty-four-year-old Javanese noble named Raden Mas Soewardi Soerjaningrat.

At that time, the Netherlands Indies was experiencing a remarkable uprising of nationalism, which focused on the Partai Komunis Indonesia (PKI; Indonesian Communist Party) and Sarekat Islam (SI: Islamic Association).[1] Under Tan Malaka, the PKI was leading a series of labor strikes across Java. At the same time, more and more labor unions of various types were being organized, and SI and the PKI remained locked in a struggle for the leadership of the labor union movement. It was also at this time that the word "Indonesia" became more than just a technical term, for it was adopted in the nationalist movement in place of "Netherlands Indies" as a general term for this area and its people.

Founded quietly in Yogyakarta, the Taman Siswa school at first attacted little attention from either the nationalist movement or the colonial government. By the early 1930s, however, when the Dutch colonial government began to suppress the radical movement led by Sukarno, Hatta, and other advocates of anticolonialism and independence, Taman Siswa had established branch schools in various parts of Java and the outer islands. Throughout the decade it strongly resisted all of the government's attempts to interfere in its affairs, and gradually the government came to recognize Taman Siswa as a powerful adversary. Most notable was its fight against the enforcement of the "Wild Schools Ordinance" in October 1932, when virtually all of the leaders and organizations of the nationalist movement rallied around in support, making it the focus of the nationalist movement. Later, in the process of the Indonesian revolution (1945–1949), Taman Siswa continued to show unreservedly anti-Dutch and self-reliant qualities.

The leader of Taman Siswa was Raden Mas Soewardi Soerjaning-rat, the principal founder of the original school, who in 1928 took the name Ki Hadjar Dewantara. During the 1930s his reputation grew, and during the Japanese military administration he was recognized, along with Sukarno, Hatta, and the Muslim leader Kyai Haji Mansur, as one of the four outstanding leaders of the Indonesian people. With the establishment of the independent Republic of Indonesia, Dewantara became minister of education in the first cabinet, and to later governments he served as chief adviser on educational matters. He died at age seventy on 26 April 1959; in November of the same year he was proclaimed a national hero, and a month later his birthday, May 2, was declared National Education Day (Hari Pendidikan).

The people of the Republic of Indonesia were clearly proud of the educational system they had in Taman Siswa and of their educational leader, Dewantara. Born in opposition to the colonial government's educational system, not only had Taman Siswa spread to a wide area, it had endured and enjoyed the highest reputation. Second, as a wing of the national independence movement, not only had it fostered many of the nationalist leaders, it had itself, as in its struggle against the Wild Schools Ordinance, persistently offered stiff resistance to the colonial government.[2]

Taman Siswa has naturally attracted the attention of researchers. In addition to the monographs written by Le Febre, McVey, Soekesi Soemoatmodjo, Surjomihardjo, Meijers, and others, several pages devoted to Taman Siswa may be found in the prewar works of Brugmans, Blumberger, and Bousquet, and the postwar works of Kahin, Wertheim, Van Niel, and Pluvier.[3]

Soemoatmodjo and Surjomihardjo, both historians who graduated from Taman Siswa schools, attempt to clarify the role that Taman Siswa played in the struggle for independence by stressing its anticolonial character. Kahin, Pluvier, and Van Niel similarly emphasize Taman Siswa's role as an anticolonial movement, but at the same time they note, though with varying degrees of concern, another side to Taman Siswa: that of a unique cultural movement whose goal was the cultural integration of East and West. This aspect of Taman Siswa is examined further by Blumberger, Le Febre, Bousquet, and others. Whether emphasizing the political or cultural side of Taman Siswa, these studies concur in assigning Taman Siswa a unique place in the history of the Indonesian nationalist movement.

At the same time, with the exception of Le Febre's work, none of these studies deals strictly with Taman Siswa per se. And only McVey's study attempts to analyze the reasons for Taman Siswa's success in the context of Javanese culture.[4]

Since staying in Yogyakarta from 1968 to 1970, I have also been interested in the role the Taman Siswa schools have played in the rise of Indonesian nationalism. My conclusions can be summarized as follows.

The roles that were uniquely Taman Siswa's were to show the cultural side of nationalism, to shape nationalist education, and to attempt to reconcile and harmonize Eastern and Western cultures. This multiplicity of roles made Taman Siswa the most self-aware of the movments that created a counterinstitution to the institution of colonial society. The workings of Taman Siswa in the first half of the twentieth century clearly revolved around the axes of opposition between colonialism and nationalism, the West and Asia, order and counterorder, and tradition and modernity. And thus it was that Taman Siswa came to conceive and expound the legitimating principle on which the nation-state of Indonesia was founded, the principle that came to fruition in the Guided Democracy advocated by Sukarno.

Underlying the legitimating principle of Guided Democracy is a common motif that runs through and interlinks the images of Sukarno, the national movement, and Javanese culture. This is the concept of *kebidjaksanaan*. This concept held the key to the success of Guided Democracy as a legitimating principle.

Ultimately, three mutually different legitimating principles were established (and still operate) in Indonesia. The first is Islamic, typified by the Natsirist Islamic view of the state (an extreme example of which appears in the Dal ul Islam movement). The second is the Western democratic principle typified by Sjahririst democracy. And the third is Sukarnoist democracy. The two democratic principles stem from the idea that "the People's voice is the voice of God;" but they differ crucially in the ways and means the People's voice is heard.

To understand how Sukarnoist democracy is constituted, we must first trace within the nationalist movement the process by which the idea that "the People's voice is God's voice" gained legitimacy; and second we must trace the process by which the Sukarnoist means of allowing the People's voice to be heard came to be accepted as the most legitimate. This will require us to explain how the fusion of two such basically divergent concepts as "guidance" and "democracy" came to be regarded as legitimate. The key to this lies in the concept of kebidjaksanaan, which we shall identify in the contexts of Javanese culture, the nationalist movement, and Sukarno's ideology, and about which we shall present structures of understanding.

In tracing the processes just described, I have kept in mind the special importance of the roles Taman Siswa played. To approach Taman Siswa from this angle means looking at the movement solely in relation to Javanese culture. In defining culture, I here follow Geertz: culture is "the structures of meaning through which men give shape to their experience."[5] By this definition, Javanese culture is the "structures of understanding" shared by the group of people who think in the mother tongue of Javanese; through these structures people perceive, evaluate, and give meaning to a particular event or circumstance; and by these structures their conduct is guided and formed.

Such structures of understanding, while basically transmitted from one generation to the next of the society that bears the culture in question, at the same time constantly reflect the particular forms of their own age. Consequently, while culture is constantly being relocated, redefined, or even revived in the light of the new common experiences of its bearers, the basic forms of its structures of understanding are maintained.

In examining the Taman Siswa movement, therefore, it is necessary to consider how Javanese culture was revived, and how it was received in the midst of the common experiences of the age in which the movement was born and developed. This in turn means considering what the age was like and what kind of experiences were common.

Chapter 1 of this book examines the concept of kebidjaksanaan, particularly in connection with Javanese culture and the ideology of institution and counterinstitution. This provides a framework within which Taman Siswa is examined in the subsequent chapters.

Chapter 2 looks at the prehistory of Taman Siswa and the background to its establishment; chapter 3, its founding and early development; chapter 4, its institutionalization and the problems involved; chapter 5, its ideological development; and chapter 6, its character as a counterinstitution to the colonial system, as displayed in its struggle against the Wild Schools Ordinance. The period covered by these chapters spans approximately two decades, from 1913 to early 1933. Lastly, as a form of response to chapter 1, chapter 7 discusses briefly the political ideas of "democracy and leadership" and Guided Democracy in the light of the intervening chapters.

The Taman Siswa movement itself has a rich and varied history to which many people, both famous and obscure, have contributed, some having devoted their lives to the movement. This book examines how Indonesian nationalism was expressed in Taman Siswa, and at the same time attempts to present a detailed history of the movement. No full-scale study of Taman Siswa itself has yet been reported; and only by reconstructing as fully as possible its rich and varied history can I fully develop my argument.

The spelling of Indonesian words herein generally follows that of the sources in which they appear, which is basically the old *edjaan lama* that was in use until 1970. The "oe" spelling of colonial times is standardized to the later "u" in the name of *Pusara*, the Taman Siswa organ, and elsewhere, while in personal names, the form used in the contemporary literature is retained. Place names are all transcribed in the current orthography.

NOTES

1. See the following on the contemporary situation: G. M. Kahin, *Nationalism and Revolution in Indonesia* (Ithaca, N.Y. and London: Cornell University Press, 1952); Ruth McVey, *The Rise of Indonesian Communism* (Ithaca, N.Y. and London: Cornell University Press, 1965); Robert van Niel, *The Emergence of the Modern Indonesian Elite* (The Hague: van Hoeve, 1960); J. Th. Petrus Blumberger, *De nationalistische beweging in Nederlandsch-Indie* (Harrlem: Tjeenk Willink und Zoon, 1931); A. K. Pringgodigdo, *Sedjarah pergerakan rakjat Indonesia* (Jakarta: Pustaka Rakjat, 1960).

2. See the following for this kind of appraisal of Taman Siswa in the Republic of Indonesia: Sukarno, "Sambutan," *Taman Siswa 30 Tahun, 1922–1952* (Yogyakarta: Madjelis Luhur Taman Siswa, n.d.) pp. 20–21; Mohammad Hatta, "Perguruan Nasional," *Taman Siswa 30 Tahun, 1922–1952*, pp. 23–28.

3. W. le Febre, "Taman Siswa," *Orientatie*, No. 43 (1951): 348–391; idem, *Taman Siswa ialah Kepertjajaan kepada kekuatan sendiri untuk tumbuh*, trans. P. S. Naipospos (Jakarta and Surabaya: Penerbitan dan Balai Buku Indonesia, 1952); Ruth McVey, "Taman Siswa and the Indonesian National Awakening," *Indonesia*, No. 4 (October 1967): 128–149; Soekesi Soemoatmodjo, "Taman Siswa adalah salah satu Aspek dari Perdjuangan Nasionalisme" (B.A. diss., University of Gadjah Mada, Yogyakarta, 1966); Abdurrachman Surjomihardjo, *Taman Siswa didalam Arsip-arsip Hindia Belanda* (Jakarta: LIPI, 1971); C. H. Meijers, "De Taman Siswa en het regeringsonderwijs, Ontwikkelingen in het Indonesische onderwijs vanaf 1945" (M.A. diss., University of Amsterdam, 1973). Other studies on Taman Siswa include: David Radcliffe, "Ki Hadjar Dewantara and the Taman Siswa Schools," *Comparative Education Review* (June 1971): 219–226; N. van der Kooi, "Over de Taman Siswa als poging tot synthese en over het begrip compatibility" (Amsterdam, n.d.); Lee Kam Hing, "The Taman Siswa in postwar Indonesia," *Indonesia*, No. 25 (April 1978): 41–59. Taman Siswa is also mentioned in the following: I. J. Brugmans, *Geschiedens van het onderwijs in Nederlandsch-Indie* (Groningen: J. B. Wolters, 1938), pp. 354–356; Blumberger, *De nationalistische beweging*, pp. 33, 254; G. H. Bousquet, *La Politique Musulmane et Coloniale de Pays-Bas* (Paris, 1938); Kahin, *Nationalism and Revolution in Indonesia*, p. 88; W. F. Wertheim, *Indonesian Society in Transition: A Study of Social Change* (Bandung, 1956), pp. 257–258, 260, 266; Van Niel, *The Emergence of the Modern Indonesian Elite*, pp. 220–222; J. M. Pluvier, *Overzicht van de ontwikkeling der nationalistische beweging in Indonesie in de jaren 1930 tot 1942* (The Hague and Bandung: van Hoeve, 1953), pp. 52–57, 65, 130, 141.

4. McVey, "Taman Siswa and the National Awakening." In this context, it has been aptly noted that Soetatmo Soeriokoesoemo's ideas on "democracy and leadership"

came, through the Taman Siswa, to influence political thinking in independent Indonesia: Herbert Feith and Lance Castles, eds., *Indonesian Political Thinking, 1945–1965* (Ithaca, N.Y. and London: Cornell University Press, 1970), p. 483.

5. Clifford Geertz, *The Interpretation of Cultures* (New York: Basic Books, 1973) p. 312; in line with this definition of culture, Geertz defines politics as "not coups and constitutions, but one of the principal arenas in which such structures publicly unfold."

KEBIDJAKSANAAN

This chapter, as mentioned in the introduction, discusses the concept of kebidjaksanaan in order to establish a framework within which to examine the establishment and development of Taman Siswa in subsequent chapters. The first of its two sections defines the word kebidjaksanaan and points out its diversity of meaning and the way its usage has changed over time. The second examines how the word was originally placed in Javanese "structures of understanding," defining as it were the original concept of kebidjaksanaan.

DEFINITION AND USAGE

Definition

Kebidjaksanaan is an abstract noun formed by attaching the prefix *ke* and the suffix *an* to *bidjaksana*, which is said to derive from Sanskrit and Kawi (ancient Javanese). In Javanese it is spelled *witjaksana* or *witjaksuh*.

According to various dictionaries, the word *bidjaksana* is used in four situations.[1] First, it is used to mean "wisdom" or "insight." Second, it is an attribute of a great person and an honorific title for a king. Third, it means to deal with a certain situation (usually one perceived by those involved as difficult) by use of wisdom or insight, or to establish prospects or frame a course for resolving that situation. Fourth, it is used as a contrastive to external controls (for example, articles of law), or to express the principle behind the exercise of power that goes beyond such controls.

Examples of Usage

THE FIRST SENSE

From 1918 to 1923, Raden Mas Soetatmo Soeriokoesoemo (1888–1924) published a monthly magazine in Dutch called *Wederopbouw* (Reconstruction), first from Weltevreden (now central Jakarta), and from

1922 from Yogyakarta. The cover of each edition carried a formula evoking the Wisdom-Tradition in Theosophy: "Beauty, which controls Power. Power, which possesses Beauty. Wisdom, which brings Justice" (*Schoonheid, die Macht beheerscht. Macht, die Schoonheid bezit. Wijsheid, die rechvaardight*).[2] Ki Hadjar Dewantara (1889–1959), just before his death, talked about his friend Soetatmo, whose ideas had provided one of the principles on which the Taman Siswa was founded. He mentioned this formula and translated the last phrase as: *Kebidjaksanaan jang membawa keadilan.*[3] As in this instance, then, kebidjaksanaan is used to translate *wijsheid* or "wisdom."

THE SECOND SENSE

Examples of this usage found in the dictionaries include, in the Javanese-Indonesian dictionary edited by Prawiroatmodjo, "Ingkang Witjaksana" as the title of King Sunan of Solo, and, in Horne's Javanese-English dictionary, the phrase *penggedé sing witjaksana*, translated as "a wise leader." Another example is *Tuhan jang Maha Bidjaksana* (God the Omniscient), an Indonesian epithet for God, like *Tuhan jang Maha Esa* (The One God) and *Tuhan jang Maha Kuasa* (God the Omnipotent).

In this second sense, as in the first, kebidjaksanaan is used to express wisdom of a high degree of abstraction, beyond ordinary human wisdom. The third and fourth senses concern the use of this wisdom in society.

THE THIRD SENSE

The most typical use of kebidjaksanaan in the third sense is to indicate official policy. *Kebidjaksanaan pemerintah* means "government policy" and *kebidjaksanaan ekonomi* means "economic policy." Such usage in connection with the government has become increasingly common in recent years.[4]

In addition, the word kebidjaksanaan is widely used in connection with public institutions and officials in the sense of dealing wisely with a difficult situation or exercising proper concern. It appears in such phrases as *kebidjaksanaan panitia* ("the wisdom of the committee") and *kebidjaksanaan saudara* ("your good offices"). The examples of this usage given in Poerwadarminta's *General dictionary of Indonesian* are: *Berkat kebidjaksanaan beliau, terlepaslah kita dari bahaja besar* ("Through his kebidjaksanaan, we escaped great danger"); and *Perkaka ini terserah kepada kebidjaksanaan panitia* ("This matter was left to the kebidjaksanaan of the committee"). Typical of the style of written usage is the following example from an official document (a letter of request) from one governmental department to another: *Sehubungan dengan hal itu maka bersama ini kami mohon bantuan serta kebidjaksanaan saudara kiranya* . . . ("In relation with this matter, we request your assistance and your kebidjaksanaan so that . . . can be accomplished").

The above examples all show that kebidjaksanaan carries the implication of wit and wisdom to deal skillfully with a real situation. The administrative processes of making and implementing policy are understood as being inseparable from the workings of wisdom in the form of "good offices" or "careful consideration." What policy is implemented, namely, the substance of policy, and how policy is implemented, namely, "implemental skill," are regarded as one. Policy is expressed by the word kebidjaksanaan as the wisdom, skill, and concern of those implementing the policy; in other words, policy is no more than another expression for the exercise of their skills and talents by the policy makers. This is true whatever the level of the policy-making body, be it the government, a committee, an individual in an official position, or an individual belonging to a particular group who is able to influence the members of that group; in each case, kebidjaksanaan is manifested as the "implemental skill" exhibited by the particular group or individual.

THE FOURTH SENSE

The fourth sense of kebidjaksanaan expresses the conceptual antithesis to "laws" and "regulations," of which it is understood that their written stipulations should be implemented "without anger or excitement" strictly according to the letter, and which consequently allow no scope for the exercise of "implemental skill" based on wit and wisdom.

A typical example of this usage appears in th title of the article "Antara Rule of Law dan Rule of Kebidjaksanaan" (Between the Rule of Law and the Rule of Kebidjaksanaan), in which "law" and kebidjaksanaan are grasped as contrasting concepts, and kebidjaksanaan is understood as complementing law in specific instances when implementation of law would be inappropriate.

The article in question appeared in 1969 in *Pusara*, the organ of Taman Siswa.[5] Sumarno, the law graduate who was its author, cites the example of a foreman in charge of roadworks in Yogyakarta who had diverted part of the funds allocated for the work to the repair of another road which, while not covered by the original plan, he considered vital to the lives of the local inhabitants. For this, the foreman was being held responsible by the legal authorities. Sumarno argues that while this act was against the principle of "rule of law," it accorded with the principle of "rule of kebidjaksanaan," and should therefore be recognized as being in the Indonesian spirit of government. The article originally appeared in the daily newspaper *Kompas*, but was reprinted in *Pusara*, revealing the special interest that Taman Siswa took in the matter.

Sumarno's article suggests that, in parallel with the system of external restraints made up of laws and regulations, there exists what might be called a system of kebidjaksanaan. His use of the English phrase "rule of law" may imply, moreover, that the system of laws was introduced from outside. This would suggest that laws and regulations—although expressed by such Indonesian words as *hukum*, *undang undang*, and *aturan*—were understood as originally being no more than different expressional forms of kebidjaksanaan; only with the imposition of law from outside did the dualism of "rule of law" and "rule of kebidjaksanaan" arise.

In considering this dualism it is, of course, particularly important to investigate Dutch colonial rule. But before so doing, I would like to look at an example in which the relation between the two elements is discussed. This is an article that appeared in *Pusara* in 1936, in which Ki Hadjar Dewantara discusses the relation between regulations (*peraturan*) and leaders (*pemimpin*).[6]

> When a "regulation" does not describe what it is meant to accomplish, a leader can often do nothing at all. If you remember that no regulation whatsoever is completely perfect, you will see that Western "democracy" is often totally ineffective. It is for this very reason that I am proposing that leaders should inquire into ways and means to achieve *keselamatan* [tranquility] without being shackled. A leader can be regarded as a wise man by virtue of his being a leader, and he should also be regarded as more perfect than any *reglement* [regulation]. When a regulation cannot spell out some particular action or stance it is the leader who must use his own *fikirannja dan rasanja* [ideas and intuitions] to determine that action and stance. A leader should be given the right to make additions, deletions, or alterations to every regulation. He should be regarded as the equal of regulations, not subordinate to them.

Here, in general terms, Dewantara is claiming specifically that by virtue of being leader of the Taman Siswa, he should not be tied by the Taman Siswa's regulations—which he acknowledges as being established by Western "democratic" procedure—but rather should have the right to revise, cancel, or alter them.

Although this article does not once mention the word kebidjaksanaan, its substance sheds light on the relation between "rule of law" and "rule of kebidjaksanaan." The statement that "a leader can be regarded as a wise man by virtue of his being leader" is tantamount to saying "a leader is a man of *bidjaksana* by virtue of his being leader;" and a "leader. . . must use his own ideas and intuitions" might well be stated as "a leader must use his own kebidjaksanaan."[7] And lastly, despite the statement that a leader "should be regarded as the equal of regulations, not subordinate to them," the burden of the article overall is that a leader should stand above regulations. In other words, it advocates the principle that kebidjaksanaan transcends regulations.

Another notable point about Dewantara's article is the strong sense of distrust in Western "democracy" that pervades his views on the rights of leadership. The concept of kebidjaksanaan is portrayed as running counter to that of Western democracy.

Having examined the concept of kebidjaksanaan by looking at examples of the usage of the word, we have found that the word has broad scope of meaning and content, ranging from an attribute of God and a kingly title to an expression for "implemental skill" in daily life. In particular, kebidjaksanaan expresses the principle behind the exercise of authority, including the implementation of government "policy."

We would expect, for example, the feeling conveyed by such phrases as kebidjaksanaan permintah, that is, the kebidjaksanaan deriving from the person or agency issuing orders (*pemerintah*), as expressions for "government policy" to differ from that of the word "policy." Because the word "kebidjaksanaan" derives from *witjaksana* or *witjaksuh*, we would expect it naturally to reflect its "original meaning." Kebidjaksanaan pemerintah would thus carry the connotation of expressing "supreme wisdom."

On the other hand, we can postulate that the concept of witjaksana has itself been reconstructed through the historical expansion of its sphere of usage and the revival of its original meaning. Of the four senses of kebidjaksanaan we have just examined, the third and fourth can be understood as offshoots of the first and second. How this derivation took place and was accompanied by the reconstruction of the concept show clearly one aspect of the relation between politics and culture in Java—the mode of interaction of ideology and culture—in the time since the upsurge of the nationalist movement. In short, the concept of kebidjaksanaan was reconstructed in the movement against colonial rule and was presented as an ideology for the ordering of a nation-state.

In the following section we shall consider the original meaning of kebidjaksanaan that predated the rise of the nationalist movement.

THE TRADITIONAL CONCEPT OF KEBIDJAKSANAAN

Witjaksana

We have seen that the word *witjaksana* or *witjaksuh* was used as a title for kings of Solo. We now turn to what this meant for traditional Javanese kingship and, consequently, how the concept of witjaksana was understood in the culture that supported the kingship.

In discussing the picture of the ideal king embraced by the Javanese, Soemarsaid Moertono makes the following statement concerning *kawitjaksanan*.[8]

> The [ideal] king's power was understood as unlimited. He could not be regulated by wordly means, but within himself there was a force reflecting, or higher still, identical with the Divine Soul (Hyang Suksma Kawekas), which checked his individual will. The Javanese thought of the ideal king as one constantly seeking for this internal divine guidance. In a *wajang-lakon* [shadow play], the *dalang* [narrator] never fails to relate... that the king retires into the inner chambers of the palace after holding an audience, changes into the plain clothes of a *pandita* (sage), then enters the... chamber of worship to "acquire knowledge of God's will." And the required presence of three important officials at court, one of which was the astrologer, [the others being a sage and an ascetic] undoubtedly also served the king's need for divine guidance.
>
> Divine guidance expressed itself in the *kawitjaksanan* of the king, ... which not only endowed [him] with the widest possible range of knowledge but also the deepest awareness of realities and a sense of justice. That there is a wide range of meaning in the word *witjaksana* is illustrated in... Javanese dictionaries and word lists where it is explained as "highly excellent," as "wise, experienced, skillful, intelligent," or "learned,"... as "with clear insight,"... [and as] "practical wisdom or skill." The Sanskrit original of the word, *wicaksana*, denotes sagacity, experience or familiarity. A Javanese, Poerwadarminta, attaches two meanings to this word; first, being "aware, *waskita* (able to see into things kept secret, like man's thought, etc.)" and, secondly, "able to use one's *budi* (thinking ability, reason) rightly." *Kawitjaksanan* denoted the greatest skill not only in weighing subtly the possible advantages or disadvantages of one's decision but also a keen sense of judgment in the handling of situations, primarily to preserve the cosmic order. In practice this amounts to a policy of checking and balancing; that is, avoiding those disturbing open clashes that were not absolutely necessary. Significantly, Paku Buwana X (1893–1939) was called by the Javanese of his own time the *ratu panutup*, "the last king," for he was the last king who lived according to the tradition of grandeur and royal serenity. He had acquired the surname "*witjaksana*" because his reign was marked by tranquillity; it was irrelevant that

this tranquillity was . . . the result of . . . helpless obedience to the wishes of the Netherlands-Indies government.

Moertono concludes that "the concept of *kawitjaksanan* was a surprisingly comprehensive tool for statesmanship in traditional Javanese society," and that consequently it emphasized "the king's absolute and lone power of decision over all matters." In this explanation of the concept can be found several indicators of its traditional usage and function in Java and how it has changed in recent times.

First, witjaksana was originally "divine guidance" that overrode and checked the king's individual will. Second, it was nevertheless internal: within himself the king had the Divine Soul, Hyang Suksma Kawekas. By becoming one with the Divine Soul, he would naturally receive divine guidance. And to this end, he had to become a *pandita*. These two mutually contradictory features of witjaksana were simultaneously realized in the ideal king, the power-wielding monarch who was simultaneously a "seeker after truth."

Third, the king relied on internal divine guidance over and above his individual will in order to bring about on earth the cosmic order that was symbolized by the motions of the heavenly bodies. (This was also a central feature of the Hindu concept of kingship, which Heine Geldern has described.[9]) The practical means by which the cosmic order was realized and preserved was, according to Moertono, kawitjaksanan.

The fourth point concerns Buwono X of Surakarta. For this king, kawitjaksanan was merely a means of preserving colonial peace and order; following internal divine guidance meant nothing more than following the wishes of the colonial government. By so doing he maintained the peace and order of the kingdom; and for this he was called "the last king" and accorded the title Witjaksana.

Witjaksana and Kasektèn

The "unlimited power" of the ideal king was, according to Moertono, believed to be evident in his physical countenance.[10] Here we shall examine the Javanese conception of the "power" that underpinned kingship and attempt to locate within this structure the concept of kawitjaksanan.

In his essay entitled "The Idea of Power in Javanese Culture," Benedict Anderson focuses on the key concept of *kasektèn* in interpreting the relationship between culture and politics in traditional Javanese society.[11] With this concept he elucidates the Javanese political paradigm, that is, the structures of understanding that relate to the social behavior and social phenomena of individuals and groups with respect to power and legitimacy. The points of his argument pertinent to our task here can be summarized as follows.

(1) The Javanese concept of kasektèn differs radically from the Western concept of power, and the word is mutually untranslatable with the English word "power" (for convenience, Anderson uses the capitalized word "Power" in the Javanese sense).

(2) Kasektèn is real, a divine creative force that animates and orders everything in the universe, both in the world of man and in nature.

(3) Like ether, kasektèn pervades the universe. Its total quantity is fixed, and it is intrinsically neither good nor evil.

(4) Kasektèn is the sole source of power. Legitimacy thus derives from this single source and not from a diversity of sources. (Anderson contrasts this with the Western view of power as the result of various social phenomena and relationships.)

(5) The order of the cosmos, both in nature and the world of man, is determined solely by the distribution of kasektèn: the establishment or collapse of order is seen as the direct result of the concentration or diffusion of kasektèn. As long as the ruler preserves the kasektèn he has concentrated within himself he will continue to hold power, the ideal state of *tata tentrem karta rahardja* (order, tranquility, prosperity, and good fortune) will be maintained, and a "golden age" (*djaman mas*) will continue. But once the accumulated kasektèn begins to diffuse away from the center, order will begin to disintegrate, and an age of madness (*djaman édan*) will follow until a new ruler accumulates sufficient kasektèn to found a new kingdom.

(6) Kasektén is accumulated through meditation and ascesis (*tapa, yoga,* and *samadi*), and it is preserved through the suppression of *pamrih* (selfish motives). Visible proof of the ruler's accumulation of kasektén is seen in his possession of the *wahju* (divine radiance).

What relates this structure to the concept of witjaksana is the equivalence of accumulating kasektèn and "becoming one" (*manunggal*) with the Divine Soul, the Sang Hyang Tunggal or Sang Hyang Wenang of the wayang. We have seen that the king had also to be a pandita in order to "acquire knowledge of God's will;" and at the same time, by suppressing pamrih, he would accumulate kasektèn. The king's witjaksana, therefore, was not only the wisdom that embodied the divine will, it was also the expression and the confirmation of his concentrated kasektèn, which is essentially indiscernable to the five senses.

The king's unity with the Divine Soul also demonstrates the principle of *Manunggal Kawula lan Gusti* (unity of master and servant) upon which Javanese patron-client relationships stand. The relationship that obtained between God and king was also understood to obtain between the king and his highest officials, and in turn, at every rank, between higher officials and their subordinates. Through this nexus of Manunggal Kawula lan Gusti relationships order was established in the kingdom.

This nexus of bonds which constituted the hierarchy of the "patrimonial bureaucracy" was in fact a hierarchy of witjaksana. Witjaksana, as the passage cited in previous section notes, is related to the idea of being "aware, . . . able to see into things kept secret": in short, it is the capacity for feeling or perceiving (*rasa*). In the hierarchy of state, witjaksana thus meant the capacity to "rasa" one's distance from the king, who occupied the center and the apex of this structure, to "rasa" the witjaksana of the king, and to "rasa" the scope of authority deemed to have been vested in one by the center. When such capacities were realized, witjaksana had fulfilled its primary function.

The Counterinstitution

Together with the ideology of kawitjaksanan and the resulting emphasis on "the king's absolute and lone power" as the principle of government, Javanese culture also embraced a counterprinciple which provided the basis for opposition to the ruler. In other words, institution and counterinstitution shared a common paradigm. This point has a close bearing on the modern revival of witjaksana.

Anderson indicates that it was in the traditional schools, the *pondok*, *asrama*, and *pesantren*, that the counterinstitution was given concrete form.[12] The ideological structures supporting the counterinstitution were as follows.

(1) The ideological structures of the counterinstituton stood in opposition to those of the institution, in which the kawula, through his own witjaksana, perceived the witjaksana of his gusti, which was the expression of the gusti's kasektèn. A sympathetic resonance was thereby set up between the witjaksanas of gusti and kawula (their mutually equal responses were expressed by "rasa"). As a result they became one (Manunggal Kawula lan Gusti), and order, tranquility, prosperity, and good fortune were realized and preserved in the kingdom headed by the gusti.

At the same time, there existed in Javanese society people, called *pandita*, *adjar*, *guru*, and *kijai*, who were believed to be able to give decisive answers to a group of important questions concerning the kingdom.

Three interrelated questions concerned its spatial structure: (a) whether the gusti's grasp of kasektèn (and thus his witjaksana) truly expressed the will of Sang Hyang Tunggal; (b) whether the gusti definitely retained the wahju, the token of legitimacy given him by Sang Hyang Tunggal; and (c) whether the gusti was jeopardizing his hold on the wahju by giving expression to his pamrih.

Four more interrelated questions concerned the temporal progress or fate of the kingdom: (d) whether there were portents of natural disaster, epidemic, or unrest among the people that would threaten order and tranquility; (e) what bearing such portents would have on the king and kingdom; (f) whether they signaled the emergence elsewhere of someone able to concentrate and preserve kasektèn, be he another divine king (one possessing the wahju) or a demonic *raksasa* (a destroyer of peace and order through his enormous concentration of kasektèn, and sometimes the creator of a demonic order that was not guided by the wahju); and (g) whether they signified that the wahju had begun to drift away in search of a new resting place.

(2) The pandita, adjar, kijai, and guru (hereafter, for convenience, I shall refer to them collectively as pandita) were regarded as being able to test the truth of the king and of the order and tranquility of the kingdom and to foresee the destiny of the kingdom, for they were able to perceive directly the will of Sang Hyang Tunggal without the mediacy of the gusti's witjaksana. Because their judgment of the king and kingdom was based on their direct perception of divine will, and was made in terms of the king's digression therefrom, the king stood under the constant scrutiny of these people. Even if he killed them all, his behavior would not alter the changeless will of Sang Hyang Tunggal; as a revelation of his pamrih, it would do no more than invite a further collapse of the order and tranquility of the kingdom and show plainly that the kingdom was doomed.[13]

(3) The pandita were the leaders of the pondok, asrama, pesantren, and other types of "residential" school, which normally were located in mountainous regions away from habitation. There, as teachers (*guru*), they lived with their pupils (*murid*) in self-sufficiency. In these remote locations, which were often considered holy places (*tempat sutji*) conducive to communion with the Divine Soul, they remained independent of the ruler of the kingdom. Through a variety of ascetic practices they sought the esoteric knowledge (*ilmu*) of how kasektèn was concentrated in the gusti, and at the same time themselves finally accumulated enough kasektèn to be able to perceive directly the will of Sang Hyang Tunggal.

Their pupils, who may have come from all over Java to be with them, were also seeking to raise their own perceptive powers; and to this end many of them made pilgrimages (*samadi*), traveling on foot

from school to school. The schools thus became forums for the exchange and accumulation of information, not only on other schools and
their teachers, but on the present state of the kingdom, recent natural
phenomena, and the mood of the people.

(4) The pandita constantly played a dual role that made them the
intelligentsia of Java. This dualism, which was never ambiguous but
always clear-cut, had several aspects.

First, though men of flesh and blood, they constantly sought to
approach spirituality by rejecting as far as possible their corporeal
existence.

Second, though physically they lived apart from society, their sole
concern was with society's fate; they withdrew from society for no other
reason than to understand it totally and accurately. These schools and
their teachers were thus part of the same conceptual system as secular
society. And for this very reason, society watched with awe their every
move.

Third, the pandita were at the same time the supreme embodiment of order and tranquility in their own schools and the impartial
judges of the truth of society's order and tranquility. The mercilessness
of their judgment (as the embodiment of divine will) was in exact pro-
portion to the supremacy of the order and tranquility realized in their
schools.

(5) The dualism of the pandita's role could disappear at a stroke.
This happened when Javanese society stood at a critical juncture in its
history. At these times, the pandita appeared in the flesh in the center
of the political arena and announced publicly that the king and kingdom were doomed. Their schools were abandoned and their order
collapsed.

The leaving of their schools by the pandita struck terror in the
"secular world." Inside and outside the palace the cry echoed and
reechoed, "*Mereka bergerak!*" ("They are moving!"); and as the cry rose
to the heavens, order and tranquility disintegrated. Their physical entrance into the political arena was not, however, deemed responsible
for the collapse; rather, it was considered to be the ultimate and defini-
tive sign that the king had lost his grasp of kasektèn. Their appearance
thus acted like the seeding of a crystal in a supersaturated solution,
immediately destroying its fragile equilibrium.

When the gusti could not perceive the witjaksana of Sang Hyang
Tunggal, the means was lost for gusti and kawula to become one, and
order, tranquility, prosperity, and good fortune could no longer be
maintained. What ensued was an age of madness, in which the all-
pervading kasektèn flowed without direction, having no natural peak

on which to converge. The natural mode of existence of all creation was disturbed, and all kinds of madness (*édan*) prevailed, from natural disasters, epidemics, starvation, and war, to murder, theft, adultery, and fraud.

At this time groups of raksasa might appear who were able, either by the sword or by flattery, to win over the people and enforce their own "order and tranquility." This had no relation to true order and tranquility, however, and people eventually awakened to the fact that the raksasa did not understand the human tongue (Javanese) and were ruling only as their own selfish desires dictated.[14] The situation was recognized as *salah tatanan* ("a misordering"). The age of madness would continue until there emerged a gusti who could concentrate in himself the kasektèn at large and secure the wahju.[15]

(6) The relationship between the gusti and the adjar, pandita, guru, and kijai, that is, between the head of the kingdom and the heads of the schools, can be understood in terms of a dialectic tension between coexistent dissimilative and assimilative actions. In that he could perceive the will of Sang Hyang Tunggal, as signified by his possession of the wahju, the gusti resembled the pandita. Indeed, as Moertono notes in the passage cited earlier, the ideal king donned the clothes of a pandita when he stood alone before Sang Hyang Tunggal. It follows that if a gusti were simultaneously an unrivaled pandita, he would be able to guide his kingdom to prosperity. But at the same time, he stood at the apex of a cone of authority that extended indefinitely outward, at the origin of the gusti-kawula bonds that supported his kingship; and as such, he was obliged to maintain order and tranquility.

Added to this immense responsibility of the gusti was the question of succession. It was believed that the wahju was transmitted only to the seventh generation, and that with each generation the king's pandita qualities receded. In the course of this recession, however, the kingship equipped itself with the forms of a patrimonial state, Manunggal Kawula lan Gusti became institutionalized, and the king gathered around himself panditas of the highest spiritual perceptiveness.[16]

These panditas not only revealed to the king the will of Sang Hyang Tunggal, they also counseled him on matters contributing to the maintenance of kingship (and thus the order and tranquility of the kingdom). In the bureaucratic system, they were the king's gurus (and the king, as the head of "secular" society, was regarded as a *satria* ("knight"). But at the same time, they stood as impartial judges of the kingship. The result was a constant dialectic tension between gusti and pandita. In the most important matters of the will of Sang Hyang Tunggal, the gusti's kawula could rally not around him but around the pandita.[17] Should they perceive a discrepancy between the witjaksana shown by the gusti and that of the pandita, they could respond directly to the pandita. And because the esteem of a teacher was determined by the number of pupils who came to lodge with him, not even the king could deny that the direct response of many kawula to the pandita who served him was proof that the pandita was true and excellent.

(7) Through its tendency toward institutionalization (and in practice it normally was institutionalized), Javanese kingship came to involve within itself a counterprinciple which could support opposition to the kingship. This principle functioned in two situations.

When gusti and pandita stood together at the apex of the palace in a state of constant dialectic tension, their kawula shared this tension by becoming one with both. For this reason, Javanese court nobility and patrimonial officials attached great importance to inspiration acquired through asceticism and pilgrimage. If they thus perceived that the king was greatly removed from the witjaksana shown by the pandita, they would start action of find another, true gusti. Such was the ideology that underlay wrangles over succession in various Javanese dynasties and supported palace coups d'etat.

The second situation arose with the elaboration of the kingship, when (as was again the usual situation) the functions of the palace pandita became formalized and his post became stylized as a symol of the kingship. Then the function of counterinstitution was assumed by the pandita and the schools that isolated themselves from the kingship. People of any social origin could become pupils of a pandita, and each had the potential himself to become a pandita. Sometimes a true pandita was born in the guise of the humblest of men. And if, as happened on occasion, such a pandita acquired for himself the wahju, he could overthrow the ruling monarch and become the new gusti.

When the order and tranquility of the kingdom began to collapse, the schools became charged in readiness for the final act. People rallied around the pandita and pledged their support. One consequence of this is that almost all revolts in Java were led by men bearing such titles as guru, kijai, or pandita.[18] And if the revolt was successful and a new kingdom was created, a situation was reproduced in which the gusti was simultaneously a pandita. In this way, "golden ages" and "ages of madness" followed in succession through the functions of the institution and counterinstitution.

Not only was witjaksana the manifestation of kasektèn, the source of all creation, it was the agency through which gusti and kawula became one and order, tranquility, prosperity, and good fortune were realized in the Javanese kingdom. Witjaksana was manifested in each of the bonds between gusti and kawula, and at the same time it was the "blood" that sped through the kawula-gusti nexus. This "blood" sustained the life (*urip*) of the organism that the system constituted, and it was purified by the intelligentsia concentrated around the pandita and their schools. This purifying apparatus, however, worked constantly towards the replacement of the whole organism.

These, then, were the "structures of understanding" about power and legitimacy that were established in traditional Javanese society. In the following chapters, we shall consider how such unprecedented states of affairs as the colonization of Java and the growth of the nationalist movement affected these structures. The answer, in short, is that the basic form of these structures was maintained by replacing old concepts with new: witjaksana was reborn as kebidjaksanaan in the age of democracy, Sang Hyang Tunggal was reborn as *Rakjat* ("the People"). And these were fused in the concept of "*demokrasi dan kebidjaksanaan.*"

NOTES

1. The following dictionaries were consulted: Th. Pigeaud, *Javaans-Nederlands* (Groningen and Batavia: J. B. Wolters, 1937); S. Prawiroatmodjo, *Bausastra Djawa-Indonesia* (Surabaya: Penerbit Express & Marfiah, 1957); Poerwadarminta, *Kamus Umum Bahasa Indonesia* (Jakarta: Balai Pustaka, 1961); and Eleanor Clark Horne, *Javanese-English Dictionary* (New Haven, Conn. and London: Yale University Press, 1974).
2. On the Wisdom-Tradition in Theosophy, see *Encyclopaedia of Religion and Ethics*, s.v. "Theosophical Society."
3. Ki Hadjar Dewantara, *Demokrasi dan Leiderschap*, (Yogyakarta, 1959), p. 7.
4. Besides the reasons described hereafter, the use of kebidjaksanaan to denote "policy" can be ascribed to a growing tendency in recent years to use Indonesian terms rather than foreign loan words, and to the fact that were the English word adopted it would be spelled "polisi," like the word for "police."
5. Sumarno P. Wirjano SH, "Antara Rule of Law dan Rule of Kebidjaksanaan," *Pusara* (June 1969): 203–205, and (July 1969): 238–241, 249.
6. K. H. Dewantara, "Keterangan 'Rentjana' Perubahan," *Pusara* 6, no. 6 (April 1936): 111.
7. *Rasanja* (here translated "intuitions"), like *perasaan* ("feelings"), derives from the word *rasa*, "to feel;" and these, in the sense of "empathy," are instrumental in the understanding of an individual's feelings and volition by others.
8. Soemarsaid Moertono, *State and Statecraft in Old Java: A Study of the Later Mataram Period, 16th to 19th Century*, Cornell Modern Indonesia Project Monograph Series, rev. ed. (Ithaca, N.Y.: Cornell University, 1981), 39–42.
9. Heine Geldern, *Conceptions of State and Kingship in Southeast Asia*, Southeast Asia Program Data Paper no. 18 (Ithaca, N.Y.: Cornell University, 1956).
10. Moertono, *State and Statecraft*, p. 39.
11. Benedict R. O'G. Anderson, "The Idea of Power in Javanese Culture," in *Culture and Politics in Indonesia*, ed. Claire Holt, Benedict R. O'G. Anderson, and James Siegel (Ithaca, N.Y.: Cornell University Press, 1972), pp. 1–69.

12. Ibid., 52–57. In this work, Anderson calls those involved simply "critics" of the ruler or regime. It is in his discussion of *pesantren* in idem, *Java in a Time of Revolution* (Ithaca, N.Y.: Cornell University Press, 1972), p. 10, that he applies the term "counterinstitution," which I here adopt.

13. In the nationalist movement, the arrest and exile of nationalists by the colonial government can be understood in the same context as this.

14. The fact that many of the "social reform movements" in Java have had "magical formulae" known only to participants is indicative of a structure in which their own world is sharply differentiated from the world of people who do not understand these (Javanese) formulae, and in which such people are regarded as raksasa. An excellent analysis of this subject is given in Takashi Shiraishi, "Saminisumu to rayatto radikarizumu" [Saminism and Rakjat radicalism], *Tōyōbunka kenkyūsho kiyō* [Bulletin of the Center for Oriental Cultural Studies] vol. 77 (1979): 137–156.

15. In the following analyses of Javanese agrarian movements, the structures described can also be understood in terms of what has been discussed in this section: Sartono Kartodirdjo, *Religious Movements of Java in the 19th and 20th Centuries* (Kuala Lumpur: Oxford University Press, 1968), pp. 1–35; idem, *Pergerakan Sosial dalam Sedjarah Indonesia* (Yogyakarta: Gajah Mada University, 1967), pp. 3–19; Kenji Tsuchiya, "Samin undō to Indoneshia minzokushūgi" [The Samin movement and Indonesian nationalism], *Tō nan Ajia Kenkyū* [Southeast Asian Studies] 9, no. 2 (1971): 236–253.

16. On the patrimonial character of Javanese dynasties and the related arguments, see B. Schrieke, *Indonesian Sociological Studies*, vol. 1 (The Hague and Bandung: van Hoeve, 1955), pp. 169–221; Anderson, "The Idea of Power," pp. 33–38.

17. It is widely reported that, in the first half of the twentieth century, noble officials (*prijaji*) of various ranks employed gurus for various purposes. Numerous episodes are also told about similar groups of "teachers" behind leading figures in the republic both in the Sukarno era and even in the present day.

18. Kartodirdjo, *Religious Movements*, p. 24; idem, *Pergerakan Sosial*, p. 90.

2

THE PREHISTORY OF
TAMAN SISWA

The central figure in the founding and development of Taman Siswa was Soewardi Soerjaningrat, later known as Ki Hadjar Dewantara. This chapter focuses on the years before the first Taman Siswa school opened in July 1922. It deals with the ideas and actions of Soewardi and the group of Javanese aristocrats around him, and it considers the impact of their emergence on affairs in the Netherlands Indies in the twentieth century. First I shall attempt to clarify Soewardi's situation in those years, primarily by examining the activities of the Native Committee, through which he first attracted attention as a nationalist.

THE NATIVE COMMITTEE INCIDENT

In 1913 the Dutch colonial government held celebrations in Java to mark the centenary of Dutch liberation from Napoleonic rule. The plans for this ceremony were criticized by a group of native intellectuals who had formed a Native Committee around two young men, Tjipto Mangoenkoesoemo and Soewardi Soerjaningrat. By arresting them and banishing them from Java, the government quashed the spread of antigovernment sentiment; but as a result Tjipto and Soewardi, along with Dekker, who had been exiled with them on a charge of anti-government activities, registered in the memories of later nationalists as pioneers of the resistance movement. In fact, in the history of the Indonesian nationalist movement that began in Java early this century, this was the first time that colonial rule was openly declared to be unjust.

The incident was triggered by an article Soewardi wrote in July 1913. Scrutiny of the government's treatment of this article and of the substance of the article itself will reveal the mode of Dutch colonial rule and of Javanese resistance thereto. These are matters with an essential bearing on the history of the nationalist movement and nationalist thought in Indonesia.

We shall first look briefly at the careers of the major figures involved in the incident, then outline the incident itself. Finally, we shall examine the government's response and the substance of Soewardi's article from the standpoint of the modes of rule and resistance.

The Personalities

DOUWES DEKKER, 1879–1952

Douwes Dekker was born in the port city of Pasuruan on the north coast of East Java in 1879, the son of a Dutch father and a mother of mixed German and Javanese blood.[1] He was a great-nephew of Eduard Douwes Dekker (1820–1877), whose novel *Max Havelaar* (1860), written under the nom de plume Multatuli, had shocked Holland by exposing the realities of the *cultuurstelsel* (cultivation system) that had been developed, principally in Java, since the 1830s.[2]

After graduating from the Dutch high school in Batavia (Jakarta), Douwes Dekker worked for a while on a coffee plantation and a sugar refinery, but with the outbreak of the Boer war he left for South Africa to fight as a volunteer against the British. Subsequently captured and imprisoned for two years in Ceylon, he returned to Java in 1903 and worked on various parts of the island as a newspaper reporter and editor. Besides working for such newspapers as *Soerabajaasch Handelsblad* (Surabaya Commercial News), *Locomotif* (the Semarang daily), and *Bataviaash Nieuwsblad* (Batavia News), he wrote a novel, *Het boek van Simon de Javaan* (The book of Simon the Javanese), and contributed a series of articles to the *Nieuwe Arnhemsch Courant* (New Arnhem News) under the provocative title "Hoe kan Holland het spoedigst zijn kolonien verliezen?" (How can Holland most speedily lose her colonies?).

Dekker's ideas were grounded in strong anti-Western sentiments. He advocated that the only way the Dutch could avoid chaos in the Indies was not by furthering the Ethical policy, under which educational opportunities were to be expanded, roads and irrigation facilities provided, and power decentralized, but by agreeing to an autonomous government for the Indies.

In the early years of the twentieth century, young intellectuals from across the Indies would gather together to discuss matters at STOVIA, a school in Batavia for the training of native doctors. In 1906, the school was visited by Dr. Mas Ngabehi Wahidin Soedirohoesodo (ca. 1857–1917), who left a strong impression on two of its students, Dr. Soetomo (1888–1939) and Dr. Goenawan Mangoenkoesoemo (1890–1929).[3] Within walking distance of STOVIA lived Dekker, who was so frequently visited by students seeking his advice that his house became a "clubhouse as well as a reading room and library."[4] Looking back at those years, Soetomo wrote:[5]

> At the time Budi Utomo was established we were helped and influenced in no small measure by Mr. Douwes Dekker. As the editor of *Bataviaas Nieuwsblad*, he propagated our ideas. My relationship with him was intimate and friendly, and therefore his house was always open to me. Mr. Douwes Dekker remained a constant and loyal friend in giving us support through his newspaper, even though his ideas, which were later incorporated into his party, did not take hold in our circle.

Though in a different way to Dr. Wahidin, it is clear that Douwes Dekker had a definite influence on Soetomo, Goenawan, and other students who were central in Budi Utomo at the time of its formation.[6]

On returning to Java in 1910, having left for Europe the previous year for court hearings concerning his inheritance, Dekker settled in Bandung and directed his energies into political rather than literary activities. First he joined the Bandung branch of the Indische Bond, a friendship association for Eurasians, and laid plans to remodel it as a party organization. He advocated the formation of an Indische Partij (Indies Party), which all residents of the Indies would be free to join, and the acquisition of independence of all native inhabitants of the Indies.[7] To this end, in March 1911 he published the first issue of *De Expres*, in which he argued for the reorganization of the Indische Bond as a political party; and in mid-September of the same year he left Bandung to rally and organize support across Java.

On 25 December 1912, in Bandung, he formally inaugurated the Indische Partij. His advocacy had won strongest support among Eurasians, but had elicited little sympathy from the Dutch or Chinese; and by March 1913 party membership stood at 7,000, of whom 5,500 were Eurasians and 1,500 Indonesians. Ultimately, what Dekker envisaged was an independent Indies led principally by Eurasians. Consequently, his only sympathizers in native society belonged to his limited circle of personal friends and acquaintances. Among them, however, were Tjipto and Soewardi, two young men with major parts to play in the subsequent history of the nationalist movement.

The government was quick to respond to the Indische Partij, which Dekker and his associates had set up as a means to extend their political activities and which the government regarded as a threat to the peace and order of the colony. It thus refused to recognize the party as a legitimate association, and from April 1913, the party was obliged to suspend its activities.

In July of the same year, as will be described shortly, Soewardi and Tjipto formed the Native Committee, by which time Dekker had left for travels in Europe, not to return to Java until early September. It was during his absence that the Native Committee incident occurred.

TJIPTO MANGOENKOESOEMO, 1886–1943

Born at Ambarawa in northern Central Java in 1886, Tjipto Mangoenkoesoemo was the eldest of eleven siblings.[8] His father was a low-ranking government official whose posts had included those of Malay teacher in a native primary school, primary school headmaster, and adviser to the city of Semarang, while his paternal grandfather had been an Islamic teacher.

Tjipto's parents both valued education, and their children were all talented: Tjipto, Goenawan, Budiardjo, and Syamsul Ma'arif all attended STOVIA; their seventh child, Darmawan, studied chemistry at Delft Technical College in Holland; Kartono also completed higher education; while their youngest son, Sujitno, graduated from Batavia Medical School. Goenawan was a lifelong best friend of Soetomo, whose sociopolitical activities he supported; Darmawan and Kartono joined the Algemeene Studieclub (General Studies Club) formed by Sukarno in 1926. Later, Kartono taught at a Taman Siswa school.

Tjipto, who from early childhood had shown an independent spirit, graduated from STOVIA with flying colors. Since his student days he had spent much of his time alone reading and thinking, and he distanced himself equally from the lifestyles of the Dutch and the Javanese noble officials (*prijaji*), constantly asserting that he was "the child of a *kromo* [pauper]." Prastiti Scherer, in an outstanding comparative study of three early nationalists—Tjipto, Soewardi, and Soetomo—characterizes Tjipto's ideological stance as that of a "dissenter."[9] Indeed, he harbored a burning hostility toward both the colonial government and Javanese nobility, feelings which were shared by Dekker. Soetomo recounts in his memoirs that people who knew Tjipto were always awed by his acute sense of justice and his bitterly critical mind, and had the impression of him as being solitary and uncompromising.[10]

On graduating from STOVIA, Tjipto became a doctor. When, shortly thereafter, the plague broke out in the Malang region of East Java, Tjipto volunteered his services to fight the disease; and for this he won acclaim from the Dutch in Java.

When Budi Utomo was founded in 1908, Tjipto joined and was elected to its committee; but in October 1909 he vacated his seat, because he was opposed to the transfer of leadership to older members of the Central Javanese nobility. Thereafter, he strengthened his ties with Dekker.[11]

SOEWARDI SOERJANINGRAT, 1889–1959

Soewardi was born on 2 May 1889, the second son of Pangeran Soerjaningrat.[12] During his childhood, like most Javanese children, Soewardi spent his time playing in the world of the wayang. Of the several characters he admired who embodied his own ideals, he particularly liked Yudhistiro, whom the Javanese regard as the ideal virtuous king, and the resourceful Kresna, an incarnation of Vishnu. At the age of twelve he composed a poem in praise of Yudhistiro.[13]

Although the nephew of Paku Alam V, the ruler of the House of Paku Alam, Soewardi's father was too poor to enroll either Soewardi or his elder brother Soerjopranoto in the elite course for prijaji at an HBS (Dutch-style high school). Instead, in 1905, Soerjopranoto went to the agricultural school at Bogor, while Soewardi entered STOVIA.

Two years after his marriage to Soetartina Sasroningrat in 1907, Soewardi was forced by financial hardship to abandon his studies. For a year he worked as a clerk at a sugar refinery in Probolinggo, Central Java, then in 1911 he moved to Yogyakarta, where he found employment in a pharmaceutical factory. Around this time, he began submitting articles to magazines and newspapers, some of them commissioned; and these articles attracted the attention of Dekker. In 1912, at Dekker's request, he moved to Bandung to take up full-time editorship of *De Expres*.

Soewardi's association with Budi Utomo resembled Tjipto's: he was active in the founding of the organization in 1908, serving as its first secretary, but resigned the following year. After moving to Bandung, he was persuaded by Dekker to join the Indische Partij; and at the same time he became head of the Bandung branch of Sarekat Islam.

The Native Committee Incident

THE INCIDENT IN OUTLINE

Early in July 1913, a committee was formed in Bandung styling itself the Inlandsch Comité tot Herdenking van Nederlands Honderdjarige Vryheid (Native Committee for the Commemoration of One Hundred Years of Dutch Liberty), or Comité Boemi Poetra (Native Committee). Its inauguration was announced in *De Expres* on July 8, and four days later, on July 12, the committee's first pamphlet was published, naming the members of the committee and outlining their proposed activities.[14]

According to the pamphlet, the committee consisted of seven members: Tjipto Mangoenkoesoemo as chairman, Soejatiman Soeriokoesoemo as vice-chairman, A. H. Wignjadisastra as treasurer, Mrs. Soeradja (née Oneng), Roem, Abdul Muis, and Soewardi Soerjaningrat as secretary.[15] The committee announced its intention on the day of the centennial celebration to send a telegram congratulating Queen Wilhelmina and petitioning her for the abolition of Article 111 of the Constitutional Ordinance (*Indischestaatsregering*) and for the establishment of a parliament of the Indies.[16]

Pamphlet number two followed on July 19. It carried an advertisement for another pamphlet, of which, that same day in Bandung, at least five thousand copies were printed and distributed.[17] Written by Soewardi Soerjaningrat, it was entitled *Als ik eens Nederlander was* (If I were a Dutchman). Appended was a translation into Malay by Abdul Muis.[18]

The colonial government had been watching the Native Committee's movements closely, and when the Resident of Bandung, T. J. Janssen, read Soewardi's pamphlet he reported immediately to the authorities in Batavia. On July 25, a justice official, H. V. Monsanto, arrived in Bandung from Batavia. Judging the pamphlet to be dangerous and in contravention of Article 26 of the Press Regulations, he interrogated the author and committee members on that and the following day and ordered that the pamphlet be confiscated.[19]

In response, the Native Committee published in *De Expres* of July 26 an article by Tjipto entitled "Kracht en Vrees" (Power and fear). This asserted that the more pressure the authorities applied, the stronger the resisters would grow, and for this reason, however bitter the consequences might be, the Native Committee would continue its struggle.[20] Two days later a second article by Soewardi, entitled "Eén voor allen en allen voor één" (One for all and all for one), was published in *De Expres*.[21]

When, despite the interrogations and warnings of July 25 and 26, Tjipto, Soewardi, and other members of the Native Committee failed to cease their "dangerous writing activities," Janssen deemed these to be seditious acts intended to disrupt "public order and peace," and in the afternoon of July 30, Tjipto, Soewardi, Abdul Muis, and Wignjadisastra were arrested and held in custody.[22]

In an official letter to Governor-General Idenburg, Janssen justified the arrests by claiming that strong measures were necessary to restore order. He went on to point out the danger in the close links between those arrested and the leadership of the Indische Partij (namely Dekker) and Sarekat Islam. Of the four arrested, he did not consider

Abdul Muis or Wignjadisastra dangerous enough to warrant long-term detention and would release them after further interrogation. Tjipto and Soewardi, he claimed, had been "blinded" by the model of the far more radical Dekker, and therefore he requested the governor-general to have Dekker, who was due shortly to return from Europe, detained on arrival at Batavia port in order to achieve a complete restoration of order.[23]

Dekker landed in Batavia on August 1, and on learning of the arrests he immediately sent a telegram addressed to Tjipto in Bandung prison: "Bravo! We are all proud of you."[24] In *De Expres* of August 5, he published an article entitled "Onze Helden: Tjipto Mangoenk-oesoemo en Soewardi Soerjaningrat" (Our Heroes: T. M. and S. S.), in which he praised them as heroes, martyrs, and pathfinders, who had set an example for those who would come after.[25] Having watched Dekker quietly since his return, the authorities now pounced upon this article as a cause to arrest him.

Article 47 of the Constitutional Ordinance[26] allowed for those whom the governor-general judged to have disturbed the order and peace of the colony to be exiled solely on the resolution of the Council of the Indies (*Raad van Nederlands-Indië*)[27] without recourse to the normal courts of law. Governor-General Idenburg had decided to apply this legislation to those arrested in connection with the Native Committee incident, and to this end convened the council on July 31 to consider first the punishment of Tjipto and Soewardi. Following debate on the course of the incident and the threat these two posed to "public order and peace," the council recommended the invocation of Article 47.

After his arrest, Dekker was interrogated several times. Then, on August 18, the council reconvened and recommended that Article 47 be invoked against him as well. Later that day Idenburg announced the banishment of all three from Java.[28] His original intention was to exile Dekker at Kupang on Timor, Tjipto on Banda Island, Ambon, and Soewardi on Bangka Island, but he later relented, offering them the option of leaving the Indies should they so request within thirty days.[29] On August 27, having received their requests, he gave permission for all three to go to Holland, and on September 6, they left Java for a life of exile abroad, which for Dekker lasted about five years, for Tjipto about one year, and for Soewardi about six years.

GOVERNMENTAL COUNTERMEASURES

The fuse that ignited the Native Committee incident was the publication of two articles by Soewardi, particularly the first, the pamphlet, *If I were a Dutchman*. This contained a scathing attack on the anomaly of

Dutchmen celebrating Holland's independence in a land that remained a colony. The second, "One for all and all for one," pointed cuttingly to the confusion and shock among Dutchmen that the first article had generated. Indeed, in the course of the incident, the colonial government displayed an uneasiness verging on neurosis about the influence that the articles might have on native society.

Especially disturbing to the administration was the fact that translations into Malay were appended to the Native Committee's propaganda literature, which was written in Dutch. At the July 31 meeting of the Council of the Indies, Governor-General Idenburg stressed this point:[30]

> The major difference between the situation today and that of six months ago [when the Indische Partij was formed] is that then activities were confined to the newspapers in Dutch, whereas now everything is also published in Malay.

This was the major reason that the members of the Native Committee were indicted under not only the Press Regulations (particularly Article 26)[31] but also Article 47 of the Constitutional Ordinance, which vested "exorbitant rights"[32] in the governor-general. Aboard ship bound for exile in Holland, Soewardi himself guessed correctly the intentions of the colonial authorities when he reminisced:[33]

> When the legal authorities said I would not have been punished or exiled if only my articles had not been translated into Malay, it can only have meant that it would not be permitted for the people to know or be told about that [the anomaly of the liberation centenary].

The authorities were particularly wary of the influence the Native Committee's publications might have on the membership of Sarekat Islam (SI). Of those involved in the incident, Soewardi was chief of the Bandung branch of SI and Abdul Muis was its secretary. On July 31, therefore, the governor-general straightaway ordered D. A. Rinkes, an adviser on native affairs, to investigate the movements and, in particular, the relationship with the Bandung branch of Tjokroaminto, the central figure in SI, who resided in Surabaya.[34] As a result, in his report of 25 August to the Minister for Colonies, De Waal Malefijt, the governor-general was able to state that SI appeared to have been uninfluenced by the incident and to reassure the minister that no such danger existed.[35]

The governor-general referred in his report to "that danger" (*het gevaar*), a warning that Dekker's "dangerous ideas" might be implanted in the minds of the people by way of Tjipto and Soewardi. From Idenburg down, the colonial authorities not only regarded Dekker as a dangerous agitator whose ideas threatened the peace, they also harbored strong doubts about his personal character.[36] In several reports to the mother country, Idenburg communicated his impression that Dekker was "totally untrustworthy" and "a liar."[37] The colonial government feared that this "anarchist"[38] would extend his influence through Tjipto and Soewardi to the lower reaches of native society; they believed that, as Janssen had so aptly put it in his communication to the governor-general, Tjipto and Soewardi had been "blinded" by Dekker[39] and were being forced to act as "intermediaries" (*tussenpersoon*) between him and the people.[40]

This same view was explicitly stated at the July 31 meeting of the Council of the Indies in the speeches of the two officials most conversant with the inner workings of native society, namely, the adviser Rinkes, and G. D. Van Ravenswaay, a controller from the Bandung area.[41] In their analysis of Soewardi's second article, they lighted upon two Javanese phases with connotations that made this article far more likely to strike home with the Javanese than the first, which had "virtually no impact on the natives."[42] They pointed, in effect, to how brilliantly Soewardi had played the role of "intermediary."

The colonial government thus regarded the incident as a seditious plot by Dekker, whom they saw as a heretic within the colony's ruling group, an alien element who intended to destroy the framework of the Ethical policy. They handled it by removing Dekker and his handful of native intellectual followers from the scene as speedily as possible in order to prevent the spread of the incident and the infiltration of his ideas into the local society.[43] This was achieved by exercise of the "exorbitant rights" vested in Idenburg by Article 47—the right of the governor-general to be sole judge of whether "public order and peace" was threatened.

There was, of course, not a shred of concrete evidence that Dekker participated directly in the formation or the activities of the Native Committee or that he was behind Tjipto and Soewardi steering their actions. It is also clear from the course of the incident that during Dekker's absence the Native Committee was managed exclusively by Tjipto and Soewardi, and that on hearing of their arrest, Dekker did no more than support their actions through his praise. But concrete evidence was not very important. The governor-general and his colleagues were concerned solely with the "crimes of conviction" of Dekker, Tjipto, and Soewardi, whose writings had been based on the belief that colonial rule was unjust.[44] This reaction alone tells of the force of their impact and the degree of confusion these writings caused within the government.

Modes of Rule and Resistance

THE MODE OF RULE

The striking feature of the various governmental documents relating to the Native Committee affair is the extremely frequent reference to the title of Soewardi's *If I were a Dutchman* coupled with the almost total lack of reference to its content. Aside from Idenburg's reference to "this lampoon" (*dit schotschrift*)[45] at the July 31 sitting of the Council of the Indies, comment on the substance of Soewardi's article was couched entirely in the phraseology of an article of law: "holding Dutch authority in contempt" and "promoting discord between different social groups." The same dossier, on the other hand, records repeatedly that an article written by Soewardi was published in both Dutch and Malay, and that its title was *If I were a Dutchman*. Clearly, it was the very title of the article that was called into question.

While there is no doubt that Soewardi's first article had satirical qualities, as indeed Soewardi himself mentions in the article, in no sense was its purpose solely to ridicule. The "I" of *If I were a Dutchman* was ultimately none other than Soewardi, a Javanese. In the latter part of the article he casts off this guise and becomes a young Javanese living in colonial society who lays accusations against Dutch colonial rule.

Nevertheless, the governor-general's impression of the article as a "lampoon" seems to indicate that a Dutchman seeing the title of the article would gain the overriding impression that he was being ridiculed. And the statement to the Council of the Indies by the adviser Rinkes, that the first article "had virtually no impact on the natives," suggests rather that it had a profound impact on the Dutch.

The government made not the least attempt to analyze this predominantly psychological shock: they did nothing to deal emotionally with the hatred this first article had stirred up among them. Rather, Governor-General Idenburg and the high officials of the colony adhered to the *zakelijkheid* approach, concentrating on being efficient lawyers in the practical application of the provisions of the law.[46] Not once did they address themselves to Soewardi's logic or attempt to present any counterargument.

The government of the Indies thus functioned solely as a group of colonial bureaucrats who were devoted first and foremost to zakelijkheid, and in this they typified the mode of Dutch colonial rule. Such a scheme had no major part for ideologues (or demagogues) to proclaim the justness of colonial rule. What was needed were outstanding "technocrats," not outstanding statesmen, for it was a feature of Dutch rule in the Indies, shown strikingly in this case, that the colony was deemed to be administrable within the limits of authority of such "technocrats."

When Soewardi thus raised doubts about the justness of colonial rule, the government from the governor-general down responded not as "colonialists" but as "technocrats." The right or wrong of Soewardi's ideas were not their prime concern, but the effects these ideas would bring. Nor were they concerned with refuting Soewardi's ideas or pressing for his "conversion."[47] Their concern was focused on eliminating the immediate "danger," and to this end they concentrated on removing him from colonial society.

While suppressing to the utmost their emotional response to Soewardi and Tjipto, Idenburg and his colleagues vented their hatred on their fellow Dutchman Dekker, whom they called "liar" and "totally untrustworthy." Dekker was seen as "the most dangerous," and should this "dangerous character" propagate his ideas to native society through his "intermediaries," Tjipto and Soewardi, the danger would grow immeasurably. To this group of "technocrats," Dekker was a danger because he was an alien element who denied their zakelijkheid. Underlying their hatred for him was the fear that his ideas and actions might lift the lid of the "Pandora's box" of native society.

Native society was to the colonial government uncanny and unaccountable, being, as Rinkes put it, "full of the mystery of the wayang." The mode of rule which stamped native society as "incomprehensible" and dealt with concrete problems arising therein by means of zakelijkheid, had been greatly strengthened through the period of the Ethical policy, one of the primary objectives of which had been to create from native society new intellectuals who would be comprehensible to the Dutch (and who were primarily expected to become "professionals"—*vakman*).

The fear that Dekker would open Pandora's Box was counterpart to the idea that native society was expecting the arrival of "good tidings" from outside, that is, the "good tidings of the West" introduced through the Ethical policy. It was the fear that, together with "good tidings," the "devil's temptation" could also only come from outside. The Native Committee incident was thus the other side of the Ethical policy medal to the example of R. A. Kartini (1879–1904), who was considered to have introduced to native society the "good tidings" of Holland as the "intermediary" of J. H. Abendanon, onetime director of the education department in the colonial government.[48] In the Native Committee incident Dekker was regarded as an "evangelist of heresy," Tjipto and Soewardi as his apostles.

But could "Pandora's box" only be opened from the outside? Wasn't Soewardi in fact pushing against the lid from the inside? This point will be examined in the light of Soewardi's article.

THE MODE OF RESISTANCE

Why Soewardi wrote the article in question and why he gave it the title he did are, as mentioned, questions the colonial government never raised, either in interrogating Soewardi or in their own council. They attributed his motivation entirely to Dekker's demagogy, and with Soewardi went no further than to confirm that he was really the author. At one time they apparently believed that he had simply lent his name to the true author (probably Tjipto): they could not imagine that the outwardly gentle Soewardi could have written such a "treasonable" article.[49] Soewardi himself, moreover, did not elaborate on his motives.

In the Indonesian and Javanese languages, the use of the subjunctive mood to denote a hypothetical proposition, as "If I were . . . ," is far from uncommon (*sekiranya saya* or *seandainya saya* in Indonesian, *saupama aku* in Javanese). Its usage, however, is normally limited to feasible actions or realizable situations, unlike the Dutch "*als ik was*," which can equally well be used to entertain impossible hypotheses.

Because Soewardi was actually a Javanese and could never be a Dutchman, his choice of the title *Als ik eens Nederlander was* indicates that he was sensitive to this difference between Dutch and Javanese (and Indonesian) and tried to make use of it. In creating this title, therefore, he demonstrated not only his proficiency in Dutch but also the ability to manipulate the language and make it a weapon.

To contemporary Dutchmen the proposition "If I were a Dutchman" was both shocking and inflammatory.[50] They must have found it inadmissible that a young Javanese should, by his own efforts, have mastered the means of criticizing them by placing himself in their shoes, and moreover, have written his criticisms in their language. This reaction stood in stark contrast to their almost unconditional acceptance and praise of Kartini's *Door Duisternis tot Licht* (Through darkness into light), a collection of her letters singing the praises of the "good tidings" of the Ethical policy, which would bestow the light of the West to dispel the darkness of native Asian society.

As for Soewardi, this article launched him upon a course that would firmly establish his authority among later nationalists, who also regarded the article as authoritative. This was due, above all, to the fact that, with Tjipto, he was exiled for this article, martyred into making an austere "pilgrimage" (*samadi*), and thus became associated with the image of the Javanese ascetic. But about the article itself, two points can be made.

Soewardi's was the first article ever in which a Javanese used the Dutch language to assert his views on colonial rule. Such political self-assertion by a native (*inlander*) on an equal linguistic footing with the Dutch was readily associated in the Javanese mind with the image of the wayang character Prince Wrekudara Bima, the only man who could converse with the gods in *ngoko*.[51] Soewardi's proficiency and manipulative skills allowed him to use Dutch in exactly the same way that ngoko was used in Javanese society, namely, as a language spoken among equals and by superiors to inferiors. Soewardi was almost certainly the first Javanese to use Dutch in this way.

Second, the article revealed Soewardi's outstanding ability to invent and manipulate language. Later nationalists revered his talent for writing. Certain words and phrases of his creation were frequently used symbolically to express the essence of a certain situation or action. Sometimes people studied his writings as if expecting an oracle.

In this sphere, Soewardi was among the most successful of the nationalists. One fundamental feature of Indonesian nationalism that merits further discussion elsewhere is the nature of leadership, which depends primarily on the creation of a symbolism and style that are linked to the traditional cultural system, and on the manipulation of that symbolism and style; and in *If I were a Dutchman*, Soewardi displayed a unique talent, particularly in the originality of the title, for symbolizing and stylizing Javanese values.

The Javanese values that are stylized in this article can be summed up in the terms "masquerade" and "satire." Soewardi develops his argument from the hypothesis that he was a Dutchman; and thereby it assumes a certain burlesque quality. The article censures the Dutch by repeated use of irony and ridicule, climaxing in a passage on the collection of donations from natives to finance the Dutch independence celebrations. "Dutchmen sensitive to reckoning of accounts" ensure themselves a healthy profit; but from the same standpoint, the balance sheet for native society shows not a penny of profit. Using a completely different "standard of reckoning," the article next demonstrates that the Dutch scheme also makes not a penny of profit for the Dutch. This standard, however, was totally incompatible with the zakelijkheid that formed the basis of colonial rule. It was this that Soewardi tried to explain to the Dutch by masquerading as a Dutchman; and it was thus natural that any Dutchman reading the article would feel "ridiculed."

How "satire" and "masquerade" function in the Javanese cultural tradition can perhaps best be illustrated in the context of the wayang, which can be considered to represent the soul of Javanese culture.[52]

There appears in the wayang a group of clowns called *punakawan*. *Punakawan* originally meant "attendants," and in the wayang they appear as clowns who attend the heroes. By their curious appearance and behavior they provide farce and comedy that provokes the audience's laughter. Being of common birth, rather than noble warriors of the satria class like the heroes, they are not bound by the laws or moral code of the satria, whose values at times they cuttingly criticize. This criticism is always satirical, taking the form of irony and ridicule, and the "satire" is accompanied by laughter.

There also appear characters who are sometimes messengers, sometimes incarnations of gods. Whether masquerading as aristocrats or commoners, they enter into human society always with the ultimate objective of realizing the will of the gods. Typically, they appear as counselors of kings and royalty or teachers of princes, and when the hero encounters difficulty they suggest to him the means to surmount it. Called pandita, adjar, or guru, these characters function as prophets who enter suddenly at front of stage in a moment of crisis.

The framework of every wayang scene (*lakon*) can be said to be built of these two disparate groups of characters, the jesters and the incarnations of gods. Many scenes are woven of a woof of laughter, confusion, and satire provided by the jesters on a weft of realization of the will of the gods through their incarnation.

There are, in addition, several wayang characters who combine these two elements: clowns who are at the same time incarnations of deity. A typical example is Semar, a character thought to be purely of Javanese origin. He is a god who comes to earth to nurture the princes of the kingdom of Pendawa. Masquerading as a clown, one moreover who is unnaturally ugly, he maintains a stream of cheerful banter and antics in keeping with his role.[53] On occasion, this becomes a scathing satire of the entire value system of the satria. At the same time, Semar is endowed with great wisdom; and when he is moved, by anger or grief, to shed his disguise, no one on earth can resist him. Of all wayang characters, Semar is the closest to the hearts of the Javanese people.

The "masquerade" and "satire" of the wayang, which are crystallized in the distinctive personality of Semar, can also be said to figure in Soewardi's article. Throughout his life Soewardi admired Semar as an ideal and a model.[54] And while it is not clear whether the young Soewardi had Semar consciously in mind when he wrote his article, he nevertheless skillfully displayed the two Javanese values of "masquerade" and "satire" that are symbolized in Semar. This he achieved through stylization of these values in the light of and by adapting to the situation of his own times.

Viewed in this way, Soewardi was not Dekker's "intermediary"as the government feared; rather he acted as the "intermediary" of Javanese society. And through the process of the Native Committee incident, Soewardi Soerjaningrat emerged among the earliest members of the "nationalist intelligentsia."

JAVANESE INTELLECTUALS' PERCEPTIONS OF THE WEST (1913–1922)

Having examined the course of events by which Soewardi and Tjipto were exiled from Java, we turn now to trace Soewardi's tracks between the time of his exile in 1913 and the founding of the Taman Siswa school in 1922, several years after his return to Java. This period saw the emergence of a group of Javanese intellectuals around Soewardi, who, in what might be called a "rebirth of Javanism," embraced some remarkable ideas that set the ideological background for the founding of Taman Siswa. We shall examine the substance and characteristics of these ideas while charting Soewardi's ideological course.

Soewardi's Perception of Holland

SOEWARDIS WRITINGS

Accompanied by his wife, Soewardi set sail for Holland from Batavia on 6 September 1913. On 13 September, in the Bay of Bengal, he wrote a piece summarizing his activities on the Native Committee, which was published in Holland by the committee later in the year.

The arrival of the three leaders of the Indische Partij in Holland provided fresh impetus to the Indonesian students residing there. They joined the Indische Vereeniging (Indies Association), which the students had established in 1908. Soon thereafter, Tjipto began publishing *De Indiërs* (The Indians) and with Dekker launched a vigorous campaign of words, while at the same time pursuing contacts with members of the Dutch Social Democratic Party.

Soewardi, however, retreated a pace from Tjipto and gradually turned to activities of a different kind. While it is not totally clear what Soewardi did between 1913 and 1915, according to Le Febre he settled in The Hague, where he studied for a teaching qualification, and in 1915 joined the board of Holland's first Montessori school when it opened that year. Also in The Hague he cooperated with Jan Ligthart, "teacher of love."[55] In August 1917 his banishment was lifted, but the war in Europe delayed his return to Java for another two years.

During his six-year stay in Holland, between the ages of twenty-four and thirty, Soewardi wrote thirty articles.[56] Of these, he wrote four in 1913, four in 1914, none in 1915, eleven in 1916, six in 1917, and five in 1918, thus being most productive in 1916 and 1917. Following his arrival in Holland he published seven articles in *De Indiërs*, while another fifteen appeared in *Hindia Poetra*, of which he was editor-in-chief in 1916 and 1917.

Hindia Poetra was first published in March 1916, and under Soewardi it ran until April 1917. A second series followed from August 1918 to August 1923 under Jonkman, published as the organ of the Indonesisch Verbond van Studeerenden (Indonesian Alliance of Students), which was led by enlightened, pro-Indonesian Dutchmen. The principles for which this group stood, together with the freshness of the name of the alliance (supposedly the first time the term "Indonesia" was used in the title of a society), attracted Indonesian students then in Holland.[57] To this second series, however, Soewardi contributed little.

Soewardi's articles can be grouped by content roughly as follows.

(a) Those concerned with the centenary of Dutch liberation. These were written in 1913 and early 1914.

(b) Obituaries and personal commentaries. These were mainly written between 1916 and 1918.

(c) Reports and commentaries on the state of the nationalist movement in the colony. These articles were the most numerous and spanned the whole of Soewardi's period in Holland. They included an article protesting the arrest and detention of the militant journalist Mas Marco on a charge of publishing articles disruptive of "peace and order." An advocate of populist-socialist ideals, Mas Marco had as his motto *"sama rasa sama rata"* (sharing equally, feeling at one), which had immediately captured Soewardi's imagination. Soewardi's exile had also resulted from governmental suppression of free speech, and his writing on this incident was particularly vehement.[58]

(d) Articles on the problems of language education in the colony and the broad relationships between language and nation.

(e) Discussions from an editor's standpoint of such matters as editorial policy and writing.

As a leader of the Indische Partij, which, since its formation, had continued to advocate independence for the Netherlands Indies,

Soewardi upheld this political stance in these writings; and at the same time, he began to assert himself in the cultural sphere, on which his writings evinced an even greater passion. While only the two articles making up the above category (d) have a direct bearing on this sphre, these are the longest and the most accomplished of his writings of this period. The specific aspects of culture they dealt with were language and education.

In a different way, the articles classified under (b) express in a unique and original form Soewardi's interest in culure. In the obituaries of Noto Dirodjo and Wahidin Soedirohoesodo, in particular, he traces the lives of these two pioneer nationalists and describes now their lives were themselves embodiments par excellence of Javanese culture.

That Soewardi should have praised these men for having so remarkably embodied Javanese culture is itself noteworthy; but it is also noteworthy that in so doing he originated the custom of writing this style of obituary to contemporary nationalists. Later, in different times and different circumstances, many such obituaries would appear to furnish the rising generation with an important legacy (*warisan*) of the ideas of departed nationalists.[59] By recording the lives and ideas of Wahidin and Dirodjo while he was exiled in Holland in the mid-1910s, Soewardi became the first person in the nationalist movement to create a legacy of the generation that created Budi Utomo.

SOEWARDI AND *HINDIA POETRA*

Almost half of Soewardi's articles were written in 1916 and 1917, and most of them appeared in the first series of *Hindia Poetra* (March 1916– April 1917), which Soewardi himself published.

Several interesting indications of the significance Soewardi attached to his activities at this time are contained in a retrospective article he wrote in 1952, "On the Indonesian Press Bureau in The Hague."[60] The Indonesian Press Bureau (Indonesische Persbureau) was, according to Soewardi, founded by him in The Hague in 1913 for the purpose of collecting and disseminating information about the Indonesian nationalist movement, and was the first institution formally to use the term "Indonesia" in its title.[61] Its head office was his home, into which poured a steady stream of newspapers and magazines from various parts of Indonesia.

Besides reporting news of Indonesia in Holland, the bureau aimed in various ways to introduce to the Dutch the traditional performing arts of Indonesia. These two goals mirrored the two facets of the contemporary situation in Holland that caused Soewardi greatest despair.

The first of these was the treatment accorded colonial affairs in the

Dutch legislature. Rarely did they become the subject of serious and careful debate, the normal procedure being for the leader of the house to read cursorily through a motion and then to rap the table with his gavel to confirm its approval by the majority of members: colonial affairs were dealt with almost exclusively as "gavel matters." To counter this situation, the bureau sent members of the Second Chamber Dutch translations of articles advancing Indonesians' own views. As a result, the bureau was able to influence considerably the activities in the chamber of the progressive faction (Social Democratic Labor Party) on such questions as the constitution of the Volksraad and the treatment of overseas students.[62]

The second problem was more basic, relating to the superficiality of the average Dutchman's view of Indonesia. On one hand it was said that "Indonesia is a cork upon which Holland floats;"[63] that "disaster would befall Holland overnight should Indonesia be lost;" and that "Indonesia is an emerald necklace." In this much the Dutch loved Indonesia, though ultimately it was the colony's fertile lands and rich produce they loved. On the other hand, of Indonesia's history and culture, they believed that neither civilization nor culture existed in this backward and barbaric land. It was to change such perceptions that the bureau staged various exhibitions and performances in Holland's cities. These attempted to demonstrate that Indonesia actually had a far longer history than Holland, during the course of which a rich and unique culture had been built. To the same end, Soewardi himself gave lectures at Leiden, Utrecht, and other Dutch universities.

From 1916, the bureau's activities were expanded and invigorated by the monthly publication of *Hindia Poetra*. In 1918, the bureau took charge of publications to mark the tenth anniversary of the founding of Budi Utomo and published *Soembansih*. And in cooperation with Adi Poestaka, a publishing company in The Hague run by Noto Soeroto, the bureau published biographies of nationalist pioneers written by Soewardi.[64]

Soewardi's retrospective article on the Indonesische Persbureau, summarized above, raises several notable points, the first of which concerns the very existence of such a "bureau." In view of the absence of any other sources which refer to it, it seems probable that the bureau was invented by Soewardi in later years in giving a name to his activities of this period.[65] The fact that his article ignores Jonkman's Indonesisch Verbond van Studeerenden, of which he knew, and that he ascribes the founding of the bureau to 1913 also suggests Soewardi's intent to claim precedence in use of the term "Indonesia" (not only does this article completely ignore the students' alliance, it refers to the period from 1918, when the alliance was formed and the second series of *Hindia Poetra* was published, in terms of the publication of Budi Utomo's *Soembansih* and the cooperative activities with Noto Soeroto).

The second point of interest is that Soewardi claims to have concentrated his energies on enlightening the Dutch (and in this at least his aims agreed with Jonkman's) by propagating the culture of his homeland. This was a reversal of the Ethical policy, for now it was the turn of the Dutch and of Dutch society to be enlightened. The ignorance to be dispelled was, according to Soewardi, twofold: the perception of colonial problems exclusively in terms of the concept of zakelijkheid (in Soewardi's words, "colonial affairs are dealt with as 'gavel matters'"); and the situation in Dutch society that automatically stifled interest in the colony's history and culture.

Such a perception of Holland can readily be understood as providing the background for Soewardi's switch from politics to culture. And in the same context, Soewardi, as a native of the colony, was incomparably better placed to give enlightenment than any Dutchman (even Jonkman), while no Dutchman (even Jonkman) could be regarded as more than an outstanding pupil.

If such perceptions, together with Soewardi's confidence and enthusiasm, were the basis for publication of *Hindia Poetra*, his articles in that publication can be said to have served his purpose remarkably well. And while his sights were set on cultural problems, it was specifically on the question of language that he made his views known.

LANGUAGE AND NATION

Soewardi became involved in this question through his nomination to participate in the First Colonial Education Congress (*Eerste Koloniaal Onderwijscongres*), which was convened in The Hague in late August 1916 to consider the improvement of primary education in the colony.[66] As a scheduled speaker on the second theme of the congress, "What language should be used in native schools?" he not only prepared a report to the congress but also recorded his views in a separate article.

Soewardi's contentions on the language question can be summarized as follows.

(1) Language and nation are one; to deny a language is both unnatural and dangerous. To advocate doing so is corrupt.

(2) If a common language was deemed necessary for the Indies, this should not be Dutch but Malay, which was already effectively becoming the lingua franca.

(3) While Dutch was necessary as the key to acquisition of Western science and technology, it was necessary only as the means to educate intellectuals who could translate the fruits of that science and technology.

The first of these points was at the same time a criticism of Tjipto's advocacy of the abolition of the Javanese language. His second point was that the adoption of a single common language in the native schools in all regions of the Indies would be an effective means of integrating these regions more firmly in the future, and in that event Malay was the only language that would meet the requirements. And thirdly he contended that the role of Dutch should properly be limited.

Soewardi thus, on one hand, called for a shift in the political stance of the Indische Partij towards the systematic introduction of the Malay (Indonesian) language as a means to unite the community of the Indies (Indonesia); and on the other, as a Javanese intellectual, he expounded the inseparability of culture (in this case Javanese culture) and language in terms of the unity of language and nation, and extolled the beauty of the Javanese language itself.

As Soewardi himself noted, the specific question of what language should be used in native schools developed into a debate on the more abstract level of language and nation, and in particular, Javanese language and Javanese society. And the difference of opinion between Soewardi and Tjipto on the Javanese language mirrored the disparate ideals held by contemporary Javanese intellectuals of what Javanese society and Javanese culture should be. These two modes of thought, which can for the moment be labeled "Westernized" and "native," shaped the subsequent history of political thinking in Indonesia. How they developed in the late 1910s and early 1920s we shall see in the next section.

The Cultural Debate Among Javanese Intellectuals

THE DISPUTE BETWEEN TJIPTO AND SOEWARDI

(A) On nationalism: While Soewardi, Noto Soeroto, and Soerjopoetro were pleading the cause of Javanese culture in Holland, in Java a kinsman of theirs of the House of Paku Alam, Soetatmo Soeriokoesoemo, was also advocating Javanese nationalism. Formerly associated with the Native Committee for the Commemoration of One Hundred Years of Dutch Liberty, Soetatmo had become active in the Volksraad as a leading member of Budi Utomo and had formed The Committee for Javanese Nationalism (Het Comité voor het Javaansch Nationalisme). From 1918 to 1923, in Weltevreden (now central Jakarta) and Yogyakarta, Soetatmo published as the organ of this committee the Dutch-language magazine *Wederopbouw*.

In 1918, a dispute arose between Soetatmo and Tjipto which showed on a wider scale and more fundamentally the differences between Soewardi and Tjipto that were referred to earlier. Their views are contained in *Javaansch of Indisch Nationalisme?* (Javanese or Indies Nationalism?).[67]

Soetatmo's argument for Javanese nationalism ran broadly as follows.[68] To the thirty million Javanese the words "nation" (*natie*) and "nationalism" were unfamiliar. The Javanese people possessed their own culture. Whether or not individual Javanese were aware of the fact, they formed a single people by virtue of having their own language and culture and of being brought up to perform the duties that were theirs as a result of being born into that culture.

The raison d'être of Budi Utomo was to ask afresh, "Why, for what purpose, were we born Javanese?", thereby sustaining the unity of the Javanese people and also contributng to their development. This endeavor could be carried out only by members of the culture: outsiders could not help. The criticism that Budi Utomo was factionalist was therefore totally unfounded. Its intention rather was to sow the seeds of a future nationalism by uniting the bearers of this unitary culture in a search for self-identity.

There was on the other hand no such thing as a united people of the Indies. What unity existed was no more than the product of Dutch rule. The Indies nationalism of the Indische Partij and the Islamism of Sarekat Islam were at best a reaction to Dutch rule. Budi Utomo, on the other hand, advocated Javanese nationalism as the means of self-expression for the Javanese. In the present period of cultural struggle, it was vital, therefore, to understand Budi Utomo's standpoint—that the Javanese should continue to fulfill the duties defined by the fact that they were born and raised in Java.

In response, Tjipto argued that Soetatmo totally lacked an understanding of history, particularly the currents of world history. One look at the present world situation showed clearly that Europe was more developed than Asia. The path to development should therefore be sought in the study of European history. Undeniably, the Indies contained a diversity of cultures and peoples; but Dutch history, for example, showed that Holland had developed from a collection of principalities in medieval times into a unified nation.

As far as ethnic and cultural differences went, the Javanese were closer to the Malays than the Dutch were to the Frisians of Friesland in northern Holland. Even better examples of diverse peoples forming unified nations could be found in the histories of Austria (the Hungarian empire), Switzerland, and Belgium. It was natural, therefore, to aim to fuse the Javanese people into an Indies nation, and when that time came, the Javanese people should if necessary sacrifice their ethnic individuality. The Javanese did not yet have their own nation but were merely a component part of the Indies nation or, more precisely, the Indies colony. The Indies was their homeland, and it was their duty to strive toward the formation of an Indies nation.[69]

The passion Tjipto displayed for a unified Indies nation lay in the same orbit as his harsh self-perception, voiced in 1916, that "just as the *adat* of Java is the product of conditions of slavery in the middle ages, so Javanese is the language of slaves."[70] Soewardi, however, rejected the call for the extinction of Javanese as decadent, arguing that the language could never die out so long as Javanese culture persisted. These differences between Tjipto on the one hand and Soewardi and Soetatmo on the other also persisted, providing the molds for two important trains of thought that ran through the later history of the nationalist movement.

(B) On kerakjatan: A more pressing question on which Tjipto and Soetatmo again clashed was what direction the burgeoning People's Movement (*Pergerakan Rakjat*) of the late 1910s should take. From 1918 into the early 1920s, a dispute arose between them over what *kerakjatan* meant; and examination of this dispute in the light of a meticulous and incisive analysis by Takashi Shiraishi will bring into relief the ideological structure of Taman Siswa, which Soetatmo founded with Soewardi in 1923.[71]

The views of Tjipto and Soetatmo emerged at the Congress for Javanese Cultural Development (Congres voor het Javaansche Cultuurontwikkeling) held at Surakarta in Central Java from 5–7 July 1918. In addressing the central themes of the direction and the means of the future development of Javanese culture, both men focused on the concept of *opvoeding* (education).

Soetatmo's argument, according to Shiraishi, was that the development of Javanese culture should allow the essence of "beauty" (*schoonheid*) to be realized through the opvoeding (moral upbringing) that was a principle of Javanese culture. Such opvoeding should be the task of panditas who transcended all political parties and religions, men who had achieved complete self-control through a life of asceticism and meditation removed from society, and had thereby acquired a knowledge of the nature and laws of the higher order that ruled all men. In ancient Java the education of boys had been exclusively in the hands of such panditas. The boys lodged with them and received instruction from them, striving for perfection for themselves and their descendants. Now, however, such panditas no longer existed; only the wayang was managing barely to perform this educational function.[72]

Tjipto's response was that the Javanese cultural tradition was Hinduism (the coexistence of the Javanese and the gods, and the "caste system" governing language and status), which was now fettering the progress of the Javanese. Soetatmo's view of opvoeding ignored the major task of progress, which was to improve the people's welfare through acquisition of Western science and technology. It was, moreover, a delusion, for in fact men had taken up the life of abstinence and asceticism for the specific purpose of securing a future for their descendants, who might as a result ascend the throne of Java. Soetatmo's opvoeding, therefore, would merely revive Hinduism and stifle progress. For the Javanese to make progress, Java's *adat*, particularly the "caste system," should be destroyed.[73]

This dispute between Soetatmo and Tjipto over opvoeding related directly to their dispute over kerakjatan.

Soetatmo saw the age of the People's Movement and kerakjatan as an "age of madness" (*djaman édan*). In 1920 he published a pamphlet entitled *Sabdo-Panditto-Ratoe*, which was followed by an article published in the July issue of the monthly *Theosofische Maandblad*, entitled "Democratie en Wijsheid" (Democracy and wisdom).[74] In the former, he portrays the age as one in which "the Indies are experiencing chaos, a hell," where "struggle breaks out everywhere: nobility against nonnobility, kromo against ngoko, capital against labor, rulers against ruled, government against the people; the society is upside down and is totally out of joint."[75] In the latter, he likens his own position to engaging in "the desperate sport of rowing a boat against the current at the moment of spate [*op het oogenblik van bandjir*], at the instant the river overflows its banks."[76]

The "spate" (*bandjir*) that was causing such "chaos" was democracy (*democratie*). To bring order to this chaos, namely, to give direction to kerakjatan, would bring liberation from the "age of madness," and Soetatmo intended to accomplish this through the ideological feat of "rebuilding" Javanese culture. Th ideology that Soetatmo proposed for the core of this "rebuilding" was none other than the old formula of Manunggal Kawula lan Gusti (unification of master and servant).

Tjipto on the other hand believed that colonial rule had produced the "age of madness." According to Shiraishi, Tjipto saw it as an "age of decay."[77] "Decay" meant that authoritarian rule and capitalist exploitation by the Dutch had stifled the people's courage and creativity, and as a result the Javanese had lost their spirit of independence. The path out of this situation was for every Javanese to inherit "the will of Dipanegara as a fighter against moral decay."

> In Tjipto's view, the pergerakan signaled the awakening and moral revival of the people, producing satria, morally upright and politically inde-

pendent subjects of the time. Thus it offered the possibility of the golden age being realized through the transformation of the Javanese into satria, whom Tjipto called the "Indiers."[78]

Dipanegara was thus presented not as a pandita but as a model satria. At the core of Tjipto's understanding of kerakjatan lay the view that

> those fighting against Dutch colonial domination and the "feudal" prijaji order were in effect undergoing trials from which they would emerge as the reincarnation of satria. He called those who went through these trials the "Indiers."[79]

In sum, then, Tjipto's idea was to mold Indies nationalism by giving force to the People's Movement through the rebirth of satria; and Soetatmo's was to rebuild Javanese nationalism by giving order to the People's Movement through the rebirth of pandita. Soetatmo's thinking was developed in detail in *Wederopbouw* (Reconstruction), the Dutch-language monthly publication he ran.

SOETATMO AND WEDEROPBOUW

Besides proclaiming itself "the publication of the Committee for Javanese Nationalism," *Wederopbouw* carried the subtitle "the monthly magazine on the Javanese youth movement and the spiritual life of the Javanese." The members of the editorial committee were named as Soetatmo, Abdul Rachman, and R. H. Soemadiparadja, followed by Noto Soeroto and Soerjopoetro as members resident in Holland, and Roedjito and Prawirowiworo as office managers. The cover of each edition carried the formula mentioned in chapter 1: "Beauty, which controls Power. Power, which possesses Beauty. Wisdom, which brings Justice."

The aim of *Wederopbouw* was expressed in its title. "Reconstruction" meant the restoration and rebuilding of the Javanese ideals of social structure, social morals, and social dignity, which had been lost as a result of foreign rule. These ideals were conceived of as order, tranquility, prosperity, and good fortune in society, and the unity of kawula and gusti in human relations. "Reconstruction" also implied that while these ideals had undoubtedly been realized in the unified states of Madjapahit and Mataram, Dutch colonial rule had sapped from the four descendant principalities of the Mataram kingdom, including Yogyakarta and Surakarta, the vitality to reconstruct themselves. Reconstruction could now only be accomplished by those among Javanese youth who took to heart the moral norms and spiritual lifestyle of Javanese society. Specifically, this meant the young people

involved in Budi Utomo, who were mostly the sons of lower-class nobility.

Seen in the light of the history of political thought in Java, these features of *Wederopbouw* reveal the latent strength of Javanese culture in the way that Budi Utomo—the human relations formed within the organization and the spiritual climate that caused their formation and defined their substance, rather than the organization itself—sought to give direction not just to Javanese nationalism but to a wider, Indonesian nationalism, and to provide an ideological foundation for that nationalism.

Wederopbouw also showed a remarkable ability to "translocate" history and culture (not just those of Java but of other parts of the Indies and of the West), which stemmed from the act of expressing Javanese culture in the Dutch language. This act meant that a wider readership than just Javanese was assumed, and it resulted in Javanese concepts being expressed in terms of more "universal" concepts (for example, those of Theosophy) that had already been expressed in another language (especially Dutch). At the same time, the more important Dutch concepts of the time (for example, *democratie, ontwikkeling,* God) were explained and associated with Javanese concepts.

As a result of this, Javanese culture itself came under scrutiny and was laid before the Javanese with its outlines sharpened by purification or endowed with new meaning. That Javanese culture should come under scrutiny in the Dutch language (subsequently the Indonesian language would take over a similar role) was prerequisite for the development and burgeoning of the "Javanese cultural debate" between Soetatmo and Tjipto. Through this debate, Javanese culture came to be revived according to the respective understandings of Tjipto and Soetatmo, and the situations they confronted came to be repositioned in the revived context.

The context Soetatmo envisaged was, firstly, one of Javanese society characterized by the unity of kawula and gusti; and the major prerequisite for the establishment of that unity was "wisdom" (this he expressed by the Dutch *wijsheid*).[80] Secondly, he believed that "democracy without wisdom is a catastrophe for us all" (*Demokratie zonder wijsheid is een ramp voor ons allen*).[81] "Wisdom" was the keyword of *Sabdo-Panditto-Ratoe,* written in 1919, in which he linked together *witjaksana* (*wijsheid*) and democracy. It was Soetatmo's intention to implant democracy, the pervading spirit of the time, into the conceptual context of Javanese culture, the essence of which he identified as "kawula-gusti." This meant, moreover, that he defined himself as a pandita.

Having examined the substance of the cultural activities of

Soewardi, Tjipto, Soetatmo, and others, we shall look finally at why they evinced such passion over cultural problems and what the basis was for the sense of mission and the self-confidence that they displayed.

JAVANESE INTELLECTUALS' PERCEPTIONS OF THE WEST

The forerunner of Taman Siswa was the Selasa Kliwon society, formed late in 1921 for the purpose of spiritual training by nine Javanese, many of whom would become the leaders of Taman Siswa. Among them were Soewardi and Soetatmo, whose respective writings in *Hindia Poetra* and *Wederopbouw* we have just examined; Soerjopoetro, who formed a link between Soewardi and Soetatmo (as did Noto Soeroto, who, while not a member of Selasa Kliwon, belonged like the other three to the House of Paku Alam); and Ki Ageng Soerjomentaram, the chairman of Selasa Kliwon and a remarkable man, who was born a prince of the Yogyakarta sultanate but—in a manner reminiscent of the wayang character Semar, the god who appeared in the world as a clown—renounced his court rank, left public office, and lived out his life as a peasant.[82]

There was in the background of the activities of these young Javanese intellectuals who returned from *Hindia Poetra* and *Wederopbouw* to Selasa Kliwon and Taman Siswa, a common spirit of the age, a spirit in which they had found meaning in both Europe and the colony and which had given them self-confidence to champion the revival of Javanese culture. It was a complex of ideological currents flowing in Europe that expressed doubt and criticism of the European perception of modern man.

The Dutch society that Soewardi saw was basically the modern face of Europe, a vast soil of zakelijkheid, the rationalistic ethos that supported colonial administration. But at the same time he understood that criticism of that modern society was in the process of being born there. His interest was particularly drawn by the contemporary "rediscovery" of the Orient, which set against the European view of modern man the philosophy of the East, especially India, and the oriental image of mankind, and therein sought man's salvation in the modern age.

Soewardi was most influenced by the ideas of Tagore, winner of a Nobel prize in 1913, the year Soewardi landed in Holland, and especially his educational theories, which were bearing fruit at his ashram. On Tagore's death in 1914, Soewardi published an obituary in *Pusara*, in which he recounts at length how profoundly Tagore had influenced both himself and Taman Siswa. Tagore's appearance, Soewardi states, had given new impetus to Europe and left an even deeper impression on Soewardi himself.[83] That impression, we can infer, continued to inspire in Soewardi pride and confidence that it was the Javanese who could truly understand Tagore.

The first of the Javanese intellectuals to take notice of Tagore and endeavor to spread his ideas was Noto Soeroto. In an article in *Wederopbouw*, he introduces Tagore's ideas in reliving the sweet memories of his childhood in Java at a time before he knew Europe.[84] Both he and Soewardi found in Tagore's educational ideas the "ideal type" of education for Java.

In Holland, Soewardi found himself in sympathy with the ideas not just of Tagore, but of Montessori, and of Rudolf Steiner, who had founded the Society of Anthroposophy in 1913.[85] These ideas inspired Soewardi with the enthusiasm to identify himself afresh with his own culture and to attempt to "rebuild" that culture. Above all else it was undoubtedly the self-pride and self-confidence he gained through contact with these ideas that supported his activities at the Indonesian Press Bureau.

Similar circumstances also existed in Java, where Theosophy had influenced Javanese intellectuals since the time of the Ethical policy. Theosophy emphasized the mystical elements common to all religions and advocated that, because God is immanent in man, man can know God by truly knowing himself. Its doctrines were syncretistic and its aim was to serve the universal brotherhood of man.[86] Its core, nevertheless, was Indian mysticism and Indian wisdom: the *Bhagavad-Gita* was adopted as a scripture, for example, and emphasis was given to the ideas of Rama Krishna (1634–1668) and to yoga. Following the founding of the Theosophical Society in 1875, the influence of Theosophy spread worldwide: to Amsterdam, where a branch of the society was established in 1897, and from there to the colony.

The situation in the Indies is recounted in *Theosofisch Maandblad*, the publication which carried Soetatmo's "Democracy and Wisdom." Officially entitled *Theosofisch Maandblad van Nederlandsch-Indië*, this was the organ of the Netherlands Indies Theosophical Society (Nederlandsch-Indische Theosofische Vereeniging) and was published monthly, beginning in July 1901, originally from Semarang, and later from Weltevreden.

The inaugural issue states that the decision to publish was taken by the Semarang Central Indies Lodge of the Theosophical Society on 12 July 1901, before which, on 5 January 1901 seven persons had met to discuss the founding of the Semarang "Branche der Theosofische Vereeniging." It also states that the Semarang Freemasons' Lodge played a major part in preparing for the founding.[87] The first president of the Semarang Theosophical Society lodge was one D. G. van Niewenhoven Helbach, but by the time the first issue of *Theosofisch Maandblad* was published, he had handed it over to P. A. V. Asperen v. d. Velde and was himself engaged in establishing similar lodges in Batavia and Bandung.[88] In 1902, the first lodge to be established by Javanese was formed in Yogyakarta, with R. M. P. Djajeng Irawan as president, Mrs. C. Voorneman as secretary and treasurer, and a membership roll including Radhén Toemenggoong Sosronegoro (this unusual spelling appears to be based on the Dutch pronunciation), Radhén Toemenggoong Poerwokoesoemo, Radhén Soerah Mangkoedhimedjo, and Radhén Mas Nottosebrotto.[89]

Exactly when *Theosofisch Maandblad* transferred its editorial office to Weltevreden is uncertain, although it is known that volume 11 was published there in 1912 under the editorship of D. van Hinloopen Labberton. In view of the fact that the Nederlandsch-Indische Theosofiche Vereeniging was recognized as a juristic person with headquarters in Batavia in a declaration issued by Governor-General Idenburg on 2 November 1912, it is conceivable that Labberton transferred the publication of *Theosofisch Maandblad* to Weltevreden, central Batavia, at about the same time.[90]

This first issue from Batavia names the society's leadership in 1912 as Labberton, president; W. Karssen, vice-president (resident in Jakarta); and Mr. A. G. Vreede, secretary (resident in Bogor). It also lists branches in the main Javanese cities of Jakarta, Bogor, Bandung, Semarang, Yogyakarta, Klaten, Surakarta, Surabaya, Malang, and Medan, each of which had a president, secretary, and treasurer. The secretary of the Surakarta branch was Raden Mas Ngabei Mangoendipoera, while the secretariat was attached to the House of Mangkoenegara, indicating a strong involvement of this princely house with the Theosophical Society.[91]

Most prominent among the society's officers in the years that followed was Labberton, who was also closely connected with the movements of the Javanese nobility, particularly Budi Utomo.[92] Labberton served continuously as president until his return to Holland in April 1923, when he was replaced by J. Kruisheer.[93] Under Labberton, inasmuch as it sought "the harmony of East and West" through the understanding of Eastern "mysticism," the Theosophical Society was sympathetic to Javanese intellectuals; and at the same time, its aim agreed with that of the Ethical policy, which advocated the spiritual union of the two peoples. Just how profoundly Theosophy influenced *Wederopbouw* is indicated by the fact that the formula cited earlier from *Wederopbouw* relating Beauty, Power, and Justice itself derives from the

Wisdom-Tradition with which Theosophy is concerned ("Wisdom, supported by strength and made manifest in beauty, rules in a true brotherhood").[94]

To the young Javanese intellectuals who saw Theosophy as something born to overcome the spiritual crisis of the West, it represented, like Tagore's thinking, the ideological vanguard of the age. In their view, the path to follow was definitely not, as Tjipto advocated, the West, but rather, the Indian world, the womb of Javanese culture, as advocated by Tagore and Theosophy. Adhering to Javanese culture and rebuilding its ideal type would not be escapism or regression; it would be to place themselves in the vanguard of the age.

To this end, their major task was to position Sarekat Islam, Sarekat Rakjat, the PKI, and the other burgeoning nationalist groups firmly within the context of Javanese culture. This meant fixing within the framework of their ideal of Javanese society, a society of order and tranquility, the spirit of the times that was the essence of the nationalist movement, namely, the growing orientation toward "the People," "*demokratie*," and "the Indies" (Indonesia). Their solution was to bind this orientation firmly to Javanese culture through the notion that the "reconstruction" of Java would be impossible without the spirit of the age and that without Javanese culture this spirit could only bring catastrophe. Fundamental to their success would be the acceptance of Soetatmo's concept of wisdom, particularly his thesis that "democracy without wisdom is a catastrophe."

The young Javanese intellectuals' perceptions of the West in the period from the mid-1910s to the mid-1920s thus generated two antithetical modes of thought on the relationship of Javanese culture to nationalist ideology.

One of these, typified by Tjipto's thinking, focused through the lens of Western modernity on the hopelessness in Java's situation. In the extreme, it found expression in the contention that only "the destruction of Javanese culture" would prepare for the "rebirth of Indonesia." Its aim of dispelling the darkness of Java with the light of Europe was identical to that of the Ethical policy. And a decade later, in the early 1930s, this same view of enlightenment—which was based on Tjipto's impassioned pursuit of the creation of "politically independent subjects"—was adopted unchanged by Sjahrir and Hatta.[95]

The second mode of thought, which owed much to Soetatmo, was oriented toward what might be called the "conquest of modernity." It saw Java's situation as being far from hopeless. Rather, it recognized a cultural resonance between traditional Javanese ideals and the ideas of the European vanguard against the crisis of the modern age, and it saw in traditional Javanese culture the potential to overcome this crisis.

During the process of establishment of the Selasa Kliwon society and eventually Taman Siswa, Soetatmo's thinking remained fundamental. Soewardi, on the other hand, though he had moved closer towards Soetatmo's ideas since his stay in Holland, firmly maintained the qualities of an anticolonialist fighter that he had displayed in the days of the Native Committee, the qualities that Tjipto associated with the satria. There was in Soewardi something of both the pandita and the satria; and in the course of its development, Taman Siswa was to display these same qualities.

Mochamad Tauchid, one of the post-Independence leaders of Taman Siswa, has explained Soewardi's change of name to Ki Hadjar Dewantara in 1928, in anticipation of his fortieth birthday, as signifying that he had changed from a *satrio-pinandito* (a satria with the spirit of a pandita) to a *pandito-sinatrio* (a pandita or guru prepared to take up arms to protect the nation and the people).[96] Such a change of character clearly took place not in 1928, however, but in 1922 when Taman Siswa was formed. In the following chapters we shall see how Taman Siswa displayed the combined qualities of the pandito-sinatrio in the course of its development.

NOTES

1. Details of Dekker's life are skillfully brought together in the following work, upon which the description herein is based: P. W. van der Veur, "E. F. E. Douwes Dekker, Evangelist for Indonesian Political Nationalism," *The Journal of Asian Studies* 17 (1958): 551–556.

2. Interest in Multatuli (Douwes Dekker) remains strong in Holland even today. A brief account of his life and critique of his work appears in G. Termorshuizen, "Pendahuluan," an introduction to the Indonesian version of Multatuli, *Max Havelaar*, translated by H. B. Jassin (Jakarta, 1973), pp. vii–xviii.

3. A detailed account of the contemporary situation can be found in two works by Akira Nagazumi: Akira Nagazumi, *Tōnan Ajia no kachitaikei 2, Indoneshia* [Value systems of Southeast Asia 2: Indonesia] (Tokyo: Gendai Ajia Shuppankai, 1970), pp. 81–147; idem, *The Dawn of Indonesian Nationalism: The Early Years of the Budi Utomo, 1908–1918* (Tokyo: The Institute of Developing Economies, 1972), pp. 26–50. On Soetomo and his ideas, listed are his autobiography, a biography, and an excellent comparative study of Soetomo, Tjipto, and Soewardi by Scherer: R. Soetomo, *Kenang-kenangan* (Surabaya, 1934(?)); Imam Supardi, *Riwayat Hidup dan Perdjuangannja* (Jakarta, 1951); Savitri Prastiti Scherer, "Harmony and Dissonance: Early Nationalist Thought in Java" (M.A. thesis, Cornell University, 1975).

4. Akira Nagazumi, "Budi Utomo no seiritsu to hatten (1)" [The founding and de-

velopment of Budi Utomo (1)], *Shigaku zasshi* [Historical Journal] 76, no. 2 (1967): 9.

5. Soetomo, *Kenang-kenangan*, p. 86. This passage is in part translated into English in Nagazumi, *The Dawn of Indonesian Nationalism*, p. 35.

6. The way in which Wahidin personified Javanese culture is described vividly by Akira Nagazumi in the works just cited, particularly *Tōnan Ajia no kachi taikei*, pp. 99–113. Also pertinent is Benedict O'G. Anderson, "A Time of Darkness and a Time of Light: Transposition in Early Indonesian Nationalist Thought," Paper for the Congress of Human Science at Mexico City, 1976. This outstanding article uses Soetomo's autobiography, Nagazumi's study of Budi Utomo, and the results of Scherer's research to consider the encounter between Wahidin and Soetomo, and through this to show why nationalism was an "awakening" for nationalists of the early twentieth century.

7. In addition to Van der Veur, *Douwes Dekker*, the situation at the time of the founding of the Indische Partij, the party's program, and the government's reaction are dealt with in detail with meticulous use of sources in Abdurrachman Surjomihardjo, "An Analysis of Suwardi Surjaningrat's Ideals and National-Revolutionary Actions [1913–1922]," *Madjalah Ilmu-ilmu Sastra Indonesia* 2, no. 3 (1964): 317–406.

8. Biographical sketches of Tjipto may be found in Scherer, "Harmony and Dissonance," and in M. Balfas, *Dr. Tjipto Mangoenkoesoemo Demokrat Sedjati* (Jakarta and Amsterdam: Djambatan, 1952).

9. Scherer, "Harmony and Dissonance," p. 102.

10. Soetomo, *Kenang-kenangan*, pp. 82–85. In his reminiscences, Soetomo recounts how, in 1929, when he was overcome with grief at the death of his friend Goenawan, Tjipto had remarked: "It is exactly as if the wayang puppet had outlived the puppeteer" (ibid., p. 95). Though in retrospect Soetomo admits that the simile was "admirably put," it is clear that he was deeply hurt by the implied criticism.

11. These events are all detailed in the works by Nagazumi cited in notes 3 and 4 above.

12. This bibliographical sketch of Soewardi is based on Scherer, "Harmony and Dissonance," pp. 60–64.

13. The foregoing is based on Pranata Ssp., *Ki Hadjar Dewantara, Perintis Perdjuangan Kemerdekaan Indonesia* (Yogyakarta, 1958), pp. 32–36. It was only natural that the wayang should frequently appear in Soewardi's speeches and writings, and that on 6 September 1913, the eve of his banishment to Holland, he bade a sad farewell to the wayang. The theme (*lakon*) of the performance he watched was associated with King Yudhistiro. Sajoga, "Riwajat Perdjuangan Taman-Siswa, 1922–1952," *Taman Siswa 30 Tahun* (Yogyakarta, 1952), p. 197.

   Yudhistiro was the foremost of the five princes of the kingdom of Pendawa, the elder brother of Bima and Ardjuna. To the Javanese he represents the ideal of kingly virtue. The blood coursing his veins is white. He never angers, never argues, never refuses a request, and is frugal. He spends his time in meditation and accumulating wisdom. His mysticality lies not in a magical weapon but in his custody of the holy book, *Kalimasada*, which records the secrets of religion and the universe. He is the epitome of gentleness, mercy, self-reflection, and refinement of bearing— the complete control of passion—and represents the highest state of the Javanese spiritual world.

   A cousin of the five princes of Pendawa was Kresna, an incarnation of the omnipotent god Visnu. He was an outstanding politician, diplomat, and military strategist. In the final battle between the kingdoms of Pendawa and Kurawa, known as Bratayudha Jayabinangun, in which Pendawa regained the throne that was usurped, it was not the wise men of Pendawa who secured the victory but Kresna. (The long feud between these two royal houses, which originated from a common line, is unfolded in the *Mahābhārata*.) Kresna would not hesitate to tell artless lies or to break rules if necessary. Although a *satria* (warrior-noble), he would lightly disregard the petty virtues of his class. The long struggle between the

Pendawa and the Kurawa saw continual scheming and treachery in both camps; but only in Kresna was it acceptable, for his ultimate purpose was that of the gods, to overthrow the Kurawa kingdom, and in his veins flowed the blood of the gods.

14. This outline of the incident is based on official communications to the governor-general from the resident and assistant resident of Priangan, the public prosecutor of Bandung, and the adviser on native affairs, and on dispatches from the governor-general to Holland. These official communications are called "mailrapport," which are indexed by a serial number and the year of writing. All mailrapport on the same topic are gathered into a dossier called a "verbaal," on which the date of filling is recorded. Mailrapport are cited herein as "Mailr.," followed by the number and year; and where they are included in a verbaal, its date and number are also given.

15. Mailr. 1695/1913 (Verbaal 25 September 1913, no. 56).

Committee member Soejatiman Soeriokoesoemo is said to have been the then superintendent (*opzichter*) of the government department of works (Burgerlijke Openbare Werken; B.O.W.). Elsewhere, however, this post is recorded as being held by one Soetatmo Soeriokoesoemo. R. C. Kwantes, ed., *De Ontwikkeling van de Nationalistische Beweging In Nederlandsche-Indië* (Groningen: H. D. Tjeenk Willink, 1975), p. 662. From this, as will be described later in this chapter, it is clear that this Soejatiman is one and the same person as Soetatmo Soeriokoesomo (1888–1924).

Soetatmo, like Soewardi, was of the House of Paku Alam. From 1919 he ran the Dutch-language magazine *Wederopbouw* (Reconstruction); in the early 1920s he helped found the Selasa Kliwon society in Yogyakarta; and from 1923 he was chairman of Taman Siswa. In this way Soetatmo traveled with Soewardi for the greater part of his life, and it is interesting that as early as 1913 he was involved in the Native Committee.

The committee treasurer, Wignjadisastra, worked at the time as managing editor of the newspaper *Kaoem Moeda*. He was also a teacher and, until 1919, a member of the central committee of Sarekat Islam.

Of the other committee members, nothing is known about Mrs. Soeradja, while Roem was a native doctor. Abdul Muis (1890–1959) was a native of West Sumatra, who worked at the time both as editor of the *Hindia Sarekat* magazine and secretary to the Bandung branch of Sarekat Islam, of which he was an active and influential member. His talents found fullest expression in his writings, however, of which *Salah Asuhan* (Wrong Education), published in 1926, won him acclaim as a pioneer of modern Indonesian literature.

16. Mailr. 1596/1913 (Verbaal 25 September 1913, no. 56).

Article 111 of the Constitutional Ordinance reads as follows:

Section 1. Natives shall have the rights of association and assembly.

Section 2. For the sake of public order, natives shall be supervised or restricted by regulation in the pursuance of these rights.

W. A. Engelbrecht, ed., *De Wetboeken, Wetten en Verordeningen Benevens de Voorlopige Grondwet van de Republiek Indonesië* (Leiden: A. W. Sijthoff's Vitgeversmij, 1956), p. 216.

17. Mailr. 1596/1913 (Verbaal 25 September 1913, no. 56).

18. When first asked to translate Soewardi's manuscript from the Dutch, Abdul Muis is said to have refused for fear of the consequences of its radical content; but Tjipto persuaded him to take the plunge by saying, "Don't worry. I'll take all responsibility." M. Balfas, *Dr. Tjipto Mangoenkoesoemo*, p. 18. When the article was published, moreover, the committee announced that for "unavoidable reasons" the four members other than Tjipto, Soewardi, and Muis had resigned [Mailr. 1695/1913 (Verbaal 25 September 1913, no. 56)]. With his arrest in late July, Muis also made clear his intention to resign when he wrote to Tjipto and Soewardi, "I can no longer follow your present way of doing things." He entreated Soewardi to convey his feelings to Tjipto and reproached Tjipto for his strong emotionality [Mailr. 1618/1913 (Verbaal 25 September 1913, no. 56)]. These circumstances tell how

radical Tjipto and Soewardi appeared even to the progressive youth of the time.

19. Mailr. 1596/1913 (Verbaal 25 September 1913, no. 56).
20. Mailr. 1695/1913 (Verbaal 25 September 1913, no. 56).
21. A translation of this article into Indonesian appears in M. Balfas, *Dr. Tjipto Mangoenkoesoemo*, pp. 22–24.
22. Abdul Muis was arrested because of his membership in the Native Committee. Wignjadisastra was arrested because his newspaper, *Kaoem Moeda*, had published an article on the Native Committee.
23. Mailr. 1596/1913 (Verbaal 25 September 1913, no. 56).
24. Mailr. 1618/1913 (Verbaal 25 September 1913, no. 56).
      On August 2 Tjipto's younger brother Goenawan sent him a telegram from his workplace in Bengkulu: "The activities of the Native Committee are right. The people long for the success of your activities" [Mailr. 1618/1913 (Verbaal 25 September 1913, no. 56)]. Tjipto also sent a telegram, to his father in Semarang: "My life's work has just begun. Farewell." (M. Balfas, *Dr. Tjipto Mangoenkoesoemo*, p. 1.) Pangeran Soerjodiningrat on August 2 and Soewardi's wife on August 3 each sent a telegram to the governor-general pleading for leniency toward Soewardi [Mailr. 1694/1913 (Verbaal 25 September 1913, no. 56)].
25. Mailr. 1694/1913 (Verbaal 25 September 1913, no. 56).
26. This article comprised five sections, the essence of which was that the governor-general could at his own discretion direct someone to live in a specific area or ban someone from living in a specific area (Engelbrecht, ed., *De Wetboeken*, p. 193).
27. The Council of the Indies was an advisory body to the governor-general, established to deliberate the major problems of the colony. Details may be found in G. Stibbe, ed., *Encyclopaedia van Nederland-Indië*, vol. 3 (The Hague and Leiden: Martinus Nijhoff and E. J. Brill, 1919), pp. 523–526.
28. S. L. van der Wal, ed., *De Opkomst van de Nationalistiche Beweging in Nederlands-Indië, Een Bronpublicate* (Groningen: E. J. Brill, 1967), pp. 326–329.
29. That the government made this exception can be thought due to the considerations that Dekker was legally Dutch, that Tjipto had on one occasion worked to eradicate the plague, and that Soewardi was an aristocrat of the House of Paku Alam. A petition to the governor-general to pardon Soewardi came from the leaders of the Budi Utomo. The petition, together with the telegrams from the Paku Alam family, indicates a strong disposition on the Javanese side to dissociate Soewardi from Dekker and Tjipto (Scherer, "Harmony and Dissonance," pp. 75–76). Tjipto on the other hand seems to have had a number of friends and admirers among the Dutch, while his reputation among leading Javanese, particularly the prijaji of Yogyakarta, was reportedly poor (van der Wal, ed., *De Opkomst*, pp. 336, 339–340). This is interesting in view of the fact that later, while Soewardi was stressing a "return" to Java, Tjipto continued to incline toward a Dutch way of thinking.
30. Mailr. 1695/1913 (Verbaal 25 September 1913, no. 56).
31. At first, the public prosecutor of Bandung confiscated Soewardi's article on the grounds that it contravened Article 26 of the Publications Ordinance, which forbade "the belittling of Dutch authority and the instigation of hostility among the peoples of the Indies." Offenders were liable to imprisonment for one to three months and a fine of 10 to 500 guilders. Mailr. 1695/1913 (Verbaal 25 September 1913, no. 56).
32. M. Balfas, *Dr. Tjipto Mangoenkoesoemo*, p. 56.
33. Soewardi Soerjaningrat, "Vrijheidsherdenking en Vrijheidsberooving," in Douwes Dekker, Tjipto Mangoenkoesoemo, and Soewardi Soerjaningrat, *Mijmeringen van Indiers over Hollands Feestvierderij in de Kolonie* (Schiedam: De Toekomst, 1913), p. 8.
34. Van der Wal, *De Opkomst*, p. 311.
35. Ibid., p. 326.
36. The contemporary Dutch view of Dekker is reflected directly in Van Niel's critique of the man as temperamental, egotistical, and possessed of an inferiority complex about Multatuli. Robert van Niel, *The Emergence of the Modern Indonesian Elite* (The Hague, 1960), pp. 62–63.

37. Van der Wal, *De Opkomst*, pp. 355–357

38. Ibid., p. 340.

39. Mailr. 1596/1913 (Verbaal 25 September 1913, no. 56).

40. Mailr. 1618/1913 (Verbaal 25 September 1913, no. 56).

41. Mailr. 1695/1913 (Verbaal 25 September 1913, no. 56).

42. The two phrases in question were "*rawé rawé rantas, malang malang putung*" and a reference to the *Kalimasada*. The former is a proverb, "All difficulties will surely be overcome;" the latter, the sacred book owned by Yudhistiro, the holiest of all the wayang characters. It is believed that no one has ever yet opened this book. When Islam began to spread through Java in the sixteenth century its propagandists reportedly found it effective to identify the *Koran* with the *Kalimasada*.

43. Governor Janssen reported that "Dekker is the most dangerous person." Mailr. 1618/1913 (Verbaal 25 September 1913, no. 56).

44. This can also be inferred in the switch in the law invoked against them, from Article 26 of the Publications Ordinance to Article 47 of the Constitutional Ordinance. Van der Wal, *De Opkomst*, p. 321.

45. Mailr. 1695/1913 (Verbaal 25 September 1913, no. 56).

46. *Zakelijkheid* in one sense comes close in meaning to the "rationality" that Max Weber cited as characteristic of a modern bureaucracy, indicating a mode of action or thinking that accords with the business (*zaak*) at hand. It has a wider meaning, however, and is frequently cited by the Dutch in reference to their national character. Benedict Anderson notes: "*Zakelijkheid* is a virtually untranslatable Dutch word roughly covering the idea of efficiency, competence, businesslike practicality, and unsentimental precision." Benedict R. O'G. Anderson, "Japan, the Light of Asia," in *Southeast Asia in World War II: Four Essays*, ed. Josef Silverstein, Southeast Asia Studies, Monograph Series, No. 7 (New Haven, Conn.: Yale University, 1966), p. 36, n. 23.

47. The interrogation of Soewardi did not touch upon the substance of his article.

48. Daughter of the *bupati* (regent) of Jepara, Central Java, Kartini had learnt Dutch from early childhood and attracted the attention of the Dutch by her intelligence and love of learning. As was then customary for the daughters of Javanese aristocracy, however, she was obliged to forsake a higher education. Instead she entered into frequent correspondence with Dutch intellectuals and friends, ardently setting forth her observations and feelings on Javanese nature and society and her opinions on the situation of Javanese women. Written from 1899 until just before her death in September 1904, these letters were compiled and published in 1911 by Abendanon, the director of education in the colony at the time they were written. The title he chose for this collection, *Door Duisternis tot Licht* (Through darkness into light), shows the dichotomous conception of the Ethical policy of Javanese society as backward and "dark" and modern Western society as "light." By 1923 the book was in its fourth edition, and Abendanon, in the introduction, expressed his pleasure that the decade or so since the first edition had seen no fewer than three different Malay translations of the work published. He also noted that the book had attracted attention in America and various European countries. Here Kartini was seen not only as the "intermediary" bearing the "good tidings" of the Ethical policy to native society, she was being publicized as the flower of Holland's "evangelical spirit." Raden Adjeng Kartini, *Door Duissternis tot Licht* (1923), pp. viii–x.

49. M. Balfas, *Dr. Tjipto Mangoenkoesoemo*, pp. 1–24.

50. In presenting criticisms and recommendations concerning Indonesian activities under the cultural agreement between Holland and Indonesia, the Dutchman Renes states that Soewardi had given him the right to speak to independent Indonesia from the standpoint of "if I were an Indonesian." This example shows not only that Soewardi's title remains registered in the memory of the Dutch, but also how it is remembered. Bernard Renes, "Het Hoger Onderwijs Indonesie: Mogelijkheden en Beperkingen," *Overzicht* 5, no. 9 (1976): 32–39.

51. Bima is the second of the five princes of Pendawa. He has long, pointed fingernails.

He can cross a thousand miles of mountains and rivers in an instant without any vehicle. He has massive muscles, wiry hair, bulging eyes, and a voice like a cracked bell. His bravery is without equal; he crushes foes without mercy. Though far from pleasant to behold, he is honest, loyal, and warm-hearted. Nevertheless, he bows to no man; and even the gods, he, and he alone, addresses in *ngoko*. (In Javanese society ngoko is spoken between equals and by superiors in speaking to inferiors; *kromo* is the language used by inferiors to address superiors). In short, he speaks to the gods as an equal.

52. My discussion of the wayang draws heavily on the following works: Benedict R. O'G. Anderson, *Mythology and Tolerance of the Javanese*, Modern Indonesia Project, Cornell Monograph Series (Ithaca, N.Y.: Cornell University, 1965); idem, "The Idea of Power;" and Pak Hardjowirogo, *Sedjarah Wajang Purawa* (Jakarta, 1968).

53. Semar is fat, with exceptionally large chest and buttocks. He wears men's clothing but women's makeup. His face could be a man's or a woman's.

54. A picture of Semar hung on the wall behind the desk at which he worked in the Taman Siswa headquarters in Yogyakarta.

55. W. Le Febre, "Taman Siswa," *Orientatie*, no. 43 (1951): 358.

56. The thirty articles are as follows:
(i) "Vrijheidsherdenking en Vrijheidsberooving"/"Memodji Kemerdikaan Merampas Kemerdikaan," in Douwes Dekker, Tjipto Mangoenkoesoemo, and Soewardi Soerjaningrat, *Mijmeringen van Indiers over Hollands Feestvierderij in de Kolonie* (Schiedam: De Toekomst, 1913), pp. 7–10; "Memoedji Kemerdikaan dan Merampas Kemerdikaan," ibid., pp. 35–38.
(ii) "Een Schets van de Vereening 'Sarekat Islam,'" *De Indiers* 1, no. 3 (6 Nov. 1913): 26–27. (Hereafter cited as *DI*.)
(iii) "Dr. Radjiman en de Beweging," *DI* 1, no. 7 (4 Dec. 1913): 33.
(iv) "De Onafhankelijkheidsfeesten en de Stovianen," *DI* 1, no. 7 (4 Dec. 1913): 33.
(v) "Rectificatie," *DI* 1, no. 13 (13 Jan. 1914): 155–156.
(vi) "Javaansche Intellectueelen en de Onafhankelijkheidsfeesten en de Stovianen," *DI* 1, no. 14 (19 Jan. 1914): 175–176.
(vii) "Javanen in Europeesche Kleeding," *DI* 1, no. 16 (5 Feb. 1914): 191–192.
(viii) "Onze National Kleeding"/"Pakaian Nasional Kita," *DI* 1, no. 37 (2 July 1914): 134–138. [Reproduced in *Karja K. H. Dewantara, Bagian Ke-IIA: Kebudajaan* (Yogyakarta: Madjelis Luhur Persatuan Taman Siswa, 1967), pp. 264–279.]
(ix) "Ter Inleiding," *Hindia Poetra* 1 (1916–1917): 1–3. (Hereafter cited as *HP*.)
(x) "Ter Gedachtenis," (coauthored with Mr. C. Th. Deventer and R. Basoeki) *HP* 1: 6–7.
(xi) "Een Moderne Javaansche Vorst"/"Seoroang Radja Djawa Jang Modern," *HP* 1: 25–27. [*Karja K. H. Dewantara: Kebudajaan*, pp. 332–335.]
(xii) "Het Oordeel over Hindia Poetra," *HP* 1: 33–36.
(xiii) "Taal en Volk"/"Bahasa dan Bangsa," *HP* 1: 74–76. [*Karja K. H. Dewantara: Kebudajaan*, pp. 106–108.]
(xiv) "Welke Plaats behooren bij het Onderwijs in te nemen, Eensdeels de Inheemsche Talen (ook het Chineesch en Arabisch), Anderheels het Nederlandsch?"/"Bagaimanakah Kedudukan Bahasa-bahasa Pribumi (djuga Bahasa Tionghoa dan Arab) disatu Pihak dan Bahasa Belanda dilain Pihak dalam Pengadjaran?" *Verslag van het Eerste Koloniaal Onderwijs Congress*, Aug. 1916, The Hague. [*Karja K. H. Dewantara: Kebudajaan*, pp. 110–186.]
(xv) "Wahidin Soedirohoesdo in Memoriam," *HP* 1: 113–115. "Wahidin Soedirohoesodo," *Nederlandsch-Indië Oud en Niew*, 1 (1916–1917): 265–270. (Hereafter cited as *NION*.)
(xvi) "De Opstand in Djambi," *HP* 1: 155–158.
(xvii) "Indië Weerbaar," *HP* 1: 145–153, 177–181, 211–214.
(xviii) "De Medezeginsrecht," *HP* 1: 192–198.
(xix) "Wederzijdsch Wantrouwen," *HP* 1: 203–208.
(xx) "Van de Redaktie van Hindia Poetra," *HP* 1: 209–211.

(xxi) "Pangeran Ario Noto Dirodjo, in Memoriam," *HP* 1: 215–216. "Pangeran Ario Noto Dirodjo (Oud-voorzitter van 'Boedi-Oetomo,' overleden 22 Mei 1917) en zijn Aandeel in de Opleiding van het Javaansche Volk"/"Pangeran Ario Noto Dirodjo dan Sumbangannja dalam Kebangkitan kembali Bangsa Djawa," *NION* 2 (1917–1918): 95–101. [*Karja K. H. Dewantara: Kebudajaan,* pp. 335–353.]

(xxii) "Arrestatie en Veroodeeling van Mas Marco," *HP* 1: 261–263.

(xxiii) "Nieuwe Persorganen: 'De Indiëer,' 'Shung Hwa Hui Tsa Chih' en 'Onze Koloniale Politiek,'" *HP* 1: 265–271.

(xxiv) "Stroomingen en Partijen in Oost Indië," *Nieuwe Amsterdammer,* 2 June 1917.

(xxv) "Terug naar het Front," *De Groene Amsterdammer,* 15 September 1917.

(xxvi) "De Opleiding voor Indië in Holland," *Indië in de Nederlandsche Studentenwereld* (1918), pp. 20–22.

(xxvii) "Het Javaansch Nationalisme in de Indische Beweging," *Soembangsih: Gedenkboek Boedi-Oetomo: 1908, 20 Mei 1918* (Amsterdam, 1918), pp. 27–48.

(xxviii) *Het Indisch Nationaal Streven, Interview met den Heer Kol,* (The Hague: I. P. Bureau, 1918).

(xxxix) "Van de Indonesische Redactietafel," *HP* 2 (1918): 2–3.

(xxx) "Het Herdenkingsfeest van het 10-jarig bestaan der Vereeniging 'Boedi Oetomo,' 1908—20 Mei—1918," *NION* 3 (1918–1919): 98–104.

57. Under the influence of Van Vollenhoven, Snouck Hurgronje, and others of the Leiden school who were interested in the customary law and religion of the colony, Jonkman developed an interest in the society and culture of the Indies. From 1917, as leader of procolonial students, he rallied together groups of Indonesian, Chinese, and Dutch students in Holland (mainly at Leiden and Utrecht universities), and in November that year amalgamated them into the Indonesisch Verbond van Studeerenden, of which he became chairman. The objectives of this alliance were threefold: to seek greater cooperation between members by expanding their knowledge of the Indies; to arouse wider awareness of the need for research into the Indies; and to spur Dutch youth to inquire whether Dutch activities in the colony were fair and impartial. To this end the association sponsored seminars in Wageningen, The Hague, and elsewhere, and publicized its activities in *Hindia Poetra.* Its ideal was to bring about the "harmony of East and West," and for Holland and Indonesia together to revive their respective golden ages, thereby overcoming all difficulties and establishing between the two nations (the Indonesian nation included the Indonesian Chinese) an everlasting relationship of trust—expressed by the word *volkenbond.* J. A. Jonkman, *Het Oude Nederlands Indië, memories Mr. J. A. Jonkman,* (Assen: Van Gorum, 1971), pp. 19–45.

58. In his later years, Soewardi speaks highly of Mas Marco as ranking with Soetatmo Soeriokoesoemo among the pioneers who influenced him most. Ki Hadjar Dewantara, *Demokrasi dan Leiderschap* (Yogyakarta: Majelis Luhur Taman Siswa, 1959), pp. 5–8. "*Sama rasa sama rata*" derived from the title of a poem Mas Marco wrote in 1918. Mas Marco, "Sama rasa dan sama rata," *Sair Rempah-rempah,* vol. 1 (Semarang: Druk N.V., Sinar Djawa, 1918).

59. The nature of nationalist bequests and the mode of inheritance is considered in terms of the relationship between Wahidin (predecessor) and Soetatmo (successor) in Benedict O'G. Anderson, "A Time of Darkness."

60. Ki Hadjar Dewantara, "Tentang Indonesische Persbureau di Den Haag," *Dari Kebangunan Nasional Sampai Proklamasi,* (Jakarta: Endang, 1952), pp. 97–104.

61. Ibid., p. 97.

62. Ibid., p. 101.

63. Ibid., pp. 101–102. This analogy was subsequently used by Sukarno to emphasize Holland's weakness. Kenji Tsuchiya, "Sukaruno to Hatta no ronsō" [The dispute between Sukarno and Hatta], *Tōnan Ajia Kenkyū* [Southeast Asian Studies] 9, no. 1 (1976): 78.

64. Dewantara, "Tentang Indonesische Persbureau," pp. 103–104.

65. I have found only one brief reference to the press bureau, which states that it over-

saw publications marking the tenth anniversary of Budi Utomo: Team Studie Taman Siswa, *Laporan Studi Sejarah Pendidikan Swasta Taman Siswa* (Yogyakarta: Team Studie Taman Siswa, 1974), pp. 150–151. This, however, could well be based on Soewardi's memoirs.

66. *Erste Koloniaal Onderwijscongres: Stenografisch Verslag* (The Hague, 1916), pp. 62–67. This record is a considerably condensed version of Soewardi's article cited in note 55 (xiv) above.

67. R. M. S. Soeriokoesoemo, A. Muhlenfeld, Tjipto Mangoenkoesoemo, and J. B. Wens, *Javaansch of Indisch Nationalism?* (Semarang: H. A. Benjamins, 1919).

68. Ibid., pp. 1–7.

69. Ibid., pp. 15–34, 61–64.

70. Soewardi Soerjaningrat, "Taal en Volk," *Hindia Poetra* 1 (1916–1917):74–76.

71. Takashi Shiraishi, "'Jinminshūgi' o megutte: Chiputo Mangunkusomo vs. Sutattomo Suriyokusumo" [On 'Kerakjatan': Soetatmo Soeriokoesomo vs. Tjipto Mangoenkoesoemo] *Tōnan Ajia Kenkyū* 17, no. 4 (1980): 741–755. *Translator's note.* A slightly modified version of the above article has subsequently appeared in English: Takashi Shiraishi, "The disputes between Tjipto Mangoenkoesoemo and Soetatmo Soeriokoesoemo: Satria vs. Pandita," *Indonesia* no. 32 (October 1981): 93–108. This discusses the debates in terms of "the pergerakan" rather than the "kerakjatan" (jinminshūgi) of the Japanese article and Prof. Tsuchiya's work. On the term "kerakjatan," Benedict Anderson notes that it is "almost impossible to translate, except by some neologism like 'people-ness.' *Rakjat*, technically meaning 'the people,' always has the sense of 'common people'" (Benedict R. O'G. Anderson, *Java in a Time of Revolution: Occupation and Resistance, 1944–1946* (Ithaca, N.Y. and London: Cornell University Press, 1972), p. 211, n. 17); Ruth McVey renders the term "People-mindedness" (Ruth T. McVey, "Taman Siswa and the Indonesian National Awakening," *Indonesia* no. 4 (October 1967): 140).

72. Shiraishi, "'Jinminshūgi' o megutte," pp. 745–747.

73. Ibid., pp. 747–748.

74. Soetatmo Soeriokoesoemo, *Sabdo-Panditto-Ratoe: Het Recht is van den Wijze* (Weltevreden, 1920); idem, "Democratie en Wijsheid," *Theosofisch Maandblad voor Nederlandsch-Indië* 19 (1920): 308–314.

75. S. Soeriokoesoemo, *Sabdo-Panditto-Ratoe*, p. 5. See also Shiraishi, "'Jinminshūgi' o megutte," p. 747. The English translation is from Shiraishi, "The disputes," p. 101.

76. S. Soeriokoesoemo, "Democratie en Wijsheid," p. 308.

77. Shiraishi, "'Jinminshūgi' o megutte," p. 752.

78. Ibid. The English translation is from Shiraishi, "The disputes," p. 195.

79. Ibid., p. 754. The English translation is from Shiraishi, "The disputes," p. 108.

80. As discussed in chapter 1, *wijsheid* corresponds to the Javanese *witjaksana* or *witjaksuh* and the Indonesian *bidjaksana*. As also mentioned in chapter 1, Soewardi (Dewantara) translated it by the term *kebidjaksanaan*.

81. Abdoel Rachman, "Democratie en Wijsheid," *Wederopbouw* no. 10–12 (1920): 192–199. Soetatmo used this claim directly as a banner for his "Sabdo-Panditto-Ratoe" when it appeared in *Wederopbouw*.

82. On the life and deeds of Soerjomentaram, see Marcel Bonneff, "Ki Ageng Surjomentaram, Prince et Philosophe Javanais (1892–1962)," mimeographed (Paris, 1977); Grangsang Surjomentaram, "Riwayat Hidup Singkat Ki Ageng Surjomentaram," *Berita Buana*, 24 July 1975.

83. Ki Hadjar Dewantara, "Hubungan Kita dengan Rabindranath Tagore,"*Pusara* 11. no. 8 (1941) [*Karja K. H. Dewantara: Kebudajaan*, pp. 357–360].

84. Noto Soeroto, "Rabindranath Tagore's Opvoedingsidealen," *Wederopbouw* 4 (May 1921): 75–84.

85. The suggestion that Soewardi was somehow influenced by Rudolf Steiner (1861–1925) and anthroposophy was made to me by Professor Kraak of Utrecht University. Although the nature of the relationship is not clear, the educational ideas of Jan

Ligthart, with whom Soewardi had some connection during his stay in The Hague, were also said to be held in high regard by those involved in the Rudolf Steiner Schools, where education was based on anthroposophy (interview with Mr. P. C. Veltman, principal of the Steiner School, Leiden, February 1979).

Javaansch of Indisch Nationalism?, cited in note 67 above, carries an advertisement by the publisher, H. A. Benjamins of Semarang, which lists among the company's publications a translation into Dutch of one of Steiner's works: *Hoe verkrijgt men bewustzijn op hoogere gebieden?* (translated by J. v. W. K.). From this it can be assumed that Steiner's work was being read in Java in 1918, when the advertisement appeared.

For more information on Rudolf Steiner, see the series of publications by the Rudolf Steiner Kenkyūkai edited by Professor Yoshiyuki Nitta of Tokyo University.

86. *Encyclopaedia of Religion and Ethics*, s.v. "Theosophical Society."
87. "Centraal-Indische Loge Semarang der Theosofische Vereeniging," *Theosofisch Maandblad van Nederlandsch-Indië*, vol. 1 (1901–1902): 2–3.

This suggests a connection between the Freemasons and the Theosophical Society in Indonesia. A Masonic lodge (named La Constante et Fidele) was established in Semarang in 1798. According to Paul W. van der Veur, "Freemasonry in Indonesia from Radermacher to Soekanto, 1762–1961," Ohio University Papers in International Studies, Southeast Asia Series, no. 40 (1976), pp. 2–8, 33–37, Freemasonry in the Indies flourished in and around Batavia from the 1780s among high officials of the Dutch East Indies Company. The first lodge established in Batavia, La Choisie, disappeared in around 1767, but later the same year and in the following year two new lodges were formed in the city. In 1798, a lodge was set up in Semarang, at that time an administrative and military center, at the initiative of a high company official. Subsequently, in 1809, under the governor-generalship of Daendels (1808–1811), himself thought to be a Freemason, a lodge was established in Surabaya, the center of East Java. This was followed by lodges in Pondok Gede on the outskirts of Bogor (1813) and Batavia (1837, named *De Ster in het Oosten*). Masonic activities saw a resurgence in the latter part of the nineteenth century, from the 1870s, with lodges being formed in various parts of Java. Also, in 1895, *Indisch Maconniek Tijdschrift* began publication in Semarang.

Freemasons in the colony were overwhelmingly Dutch (statistics for 1940 put the membership at 1,262 Dutchmen, 50 Indonesians, and 14 Chinese), but in addition there were some Javanese nobles. Pangeran Ario Noto Dirodjo, the son of Paku Alam V and onetime president of Budi Utomo, heads a list that includes many bupati and *wedana* (district heads).

88. "Centraal-Indische Loge Semarang," p. 7, and "De Theosofische Beweging, Nederlandsche Afdeeling," ibid., p. 4.
89. "De Javaansche Theosofische Loge te Djokjakarta," *Theosofische Maandblad van Nederlandsch-Indië* 3 (1903–1904): 145–146.
90. Mailr. 1978/1912. Labberton was then living in Buitenzorg (Bogor) and teaching Javanese at the Gymnasium Willem III.
91. *Theosofisch Maandblad voor Nederlandsch-Indië* 11 (1912).

Volume 13, issued in 1914, was published by Indonesische Drukkerij. While it is unclear whether this name was used before 1914, this nevertheless appears to be the earliest usage of the term "Indonesia" by a commercial printing company.

92. Akira Nagazumi, *The Dawn of Indonesian Nationalism*, pp. 71–73, 110.
93. *Theosofisch Maandblad voor Nederlandsch-Indië* 22 (May 1923): 231–232.
94. *Encyclopaedia of Religion and Ethics*, s.v. "Theosophical Society." The influence of theosophy early this century also reached the Minangkabau. The center of the Theosophical Society in West Sumatra was the teacher-training school in Bukittinggi. Taufik Abdullah, "Modernization in the Minangkabau World," in *Culture and Politics in Indonesia*, ed. Claire Holt, Benedict R. O'G. Anderson, and James Siegel (Ithaca, N.Y.: Cornell University Press, 1972), p. 233 n.

95. On Hatta and Sjahrir, see Kenji Tsuchiya, "Sukaruno to Hatta," pp. 61–88. An English translation of this article appears as "The Dispute between Hatta and Sukarno in the early 1930s," in *Southeast Asia: Nature, Society and Development*, ed. Shinichi Ichimura (Honolulu, Hawaii: University Press of Hawaii, 1977), pp. 211–243.

96. M. Tauchid, *Ki Hadjar Dewantara, Pahlawan dan Pelopor Pendidikan Nasional* (Yogyakarta: Madjelis Luhur Taman Siswa, 1968), p. 19.

3

THE FOUNDING AND
EXPANSION OF TAMAN SISWA,
1922–1930

This chapter examines the founding and expansion of Taman Siswa in the period 1922–1930, the situation in Taman Siswa schools across the country, the educational ideas advanced by Taman Siswa, and its background in relation to the contemporary nationalist movement.

THE FIRST WINDU

Founders and Principles

The first Taman Siswa school was opened in Yogyakarta on 3 July 1922 under the name Nationaal Onderwijs Instituut Taman Siswa (Taman Siswa National Educational Institute), offering a kindergarten (*kindertuin*) and a teachers' course (*kursus guru*). For about a year before this, Soewardi had taught at the private Adhi Dharma school run by his elder brother, Raden Mas Soerjopranoto.[1] And during this time, preparations for the new school were being made by the Selasa Kliwon society.

According to Pronowidigdo, one of its members, this "club" was formed in late 1921 at the initiative of Soetatmo Soeriokoesoemo and Ki Ageng Soerjomentaram, who rallied together a group of young Javanese of "revolutionary spirit." It met on four occasions, the meetings being held once every thirty-five days (on Kliwon Tuesdays) at the home of Soerjomentaram.[2] Its nine members included, in addition to Ki Ageng Soerjomentaram and Soetatmo Soeriokoesoemo, Pronowidigdo, Prawirowiwaro, R. M. Gondoatmodjo, B. R. M. Soebono, Soerjopoetro, Soerjoadipoetro, R. Soetopo Wonobojo, Soerjodirdjo, and Soewardi Soerjaningrat.[3] Of these, Soerjopoetro and Soerjoadipoetro were Soewardi's uncle and youngest brother, respectively. Gondoatmodjo was a leader of Budi Utomo who had served on the committee of the Dharma Wara scholarship society[4] and had represented Paku Alam on a national committee which was formed to prepare the elections for the newly created Volksraad. Soetatmo Soeriokoesoemo had similarly represented Paku Alam on this committee. Prawirowiworo had connections with both *Wederopbouw* and Dharma Wara, and Soetopo Wonobojo was also an active member of Budi Utomo. Although little is known about the remaining three, it is clear that the membership of Selasa Kliwon had, in addition to blood ties with the house of Paku Alam, strong connections with Budi Utomo.[5]

The meetings of Selasa Kliwon resulted in a decision to institute educational facilities for the younger generation and offer educational activities for adults, the former in Soewardi's charge, the latter in Soerjomentaram's, in order to foster a spirit of independence through education. An article in the 8 February issue of *De Expres* states that Soewardi was preparing to institute a teacher-training school, indicating that Selasa Kliwon must have reached its decision at about that time.[6] On 3 July, on the veranda (*pendopo*) in front of the Adhi Dharma school, Soewardi summarized in seven points his purpose in setting up the Taman Siswa school.[7] In the subsequent history of Taman Siswa these points came to be formulated as "unalterable principles," which were revered and upheld as the founding spirit of the organization. They may be summarized as follows.

(1) Education (*pendidikan dan pengadjaran*) in any nation should aim to nurture the seeds passed down from earlier generations so that the nation could grow both spiritually and physically. Just as the individual should develop the spirit (*jiwa*) and the body (*badan*), so the nation should aim to develop its culture and society. The means used to this end must be based on the customs (*adat-istiadat*) of the people. In this way the people could develop rapidly and smoothly in accordance with natural law (*kodrat alam*).

(2) The education Indonesians had so far received from the West was far from immune from the influences of colonial policy. It was, in short, education for the benefit of the other side (*sana*); and it had maintained this character since the times of the Dutch East Indies Company, remaining essentially unchanged even under the Ethical policy. Strangely, however, such education was gladly accepted by the bourgeoisie (the prijaji and the middle classes), who sent their children to schools where education was not conducive to the development of mind and body but merely provided a graduation certificate and allowed them to become laborers.

(3) Education in the colonial spirit had prevented the establishment of a social community and resulted in a life of dependence on Western nations. This situation was unlikely to be resolved solely through external confrontation by the political movements but required the seeds of an independent lifestyle to be implanted within the people through a national education system.

(4) A new educational system should be established that would benefit native society rather than the colonists, and that was based on the people's own culture. In earlier times, as an independent people, Indonesians had maintained their own educational system in the asrama, pondok, and pesantren.

(5) It was also notable that a new current of educational ideas was emerging in Europe and America. Grounded in "Independence" (*kemerdekaan*) and "idealism," these ideas were a reaction to educational methods grounded in "compulsion," which regarded human beings as machine components and which attached importance to an "intellectualism" that promoted only worldliness and "materialism." These ideas, expounded by Montessori and Tagore, for example, had gradually come to be regarded as suitable for a national education system; and these ideas also corresponded to the traditional Javanese notion of *among*, the idea of leading children rather than giving them orders, so that they would grow up sound in mind and body.

(6) Implementation of such a national education system required the greatest possible degree of independence. No assistance should therefore be accepted from anyone if it also meant accepting internal or external restraints. To be able to stand alone, Taman Siswa had to establish a self-supporting system (*zelfbedruipingssysteem*) that was built upon "thrift."

(7) Education should be for all, not just the upper stratum of society. If only the upper classes were educated the nation would not grow strong. Education must begin with the lower classes, where its spread was most needed, in order to bring them greater order and greater strength.

In this speech, then, Soewardi rejected the education implemented in the colony as being merely diploma-oriented and serving ultimately the interests of the colonial administration. As an alternative, he cited the latest European educational ideas and in this context advocated the revival of the traditional Javanese schools, the asrama, pondok, and pesantren. In other words, he advocated the building of the ideal type of educational system from his own cultural tradition in order to avert from Indonesia the crisis of modern Europe. Such was to remain Taman Siswa's standpoint over the following years.

Early Developments

Reactions to the newly formed Taman Siswa were diverse. Some people were supportive and joined the educational movement; some (mainly teachers at schools run by the colonial government) opposed it on the grounds that it would lower educational standards; and others (mainly government officials) denounced it as a Communist school. Taman Siswa's policy, laid down by Soewardi, was to remain silent, accepting those who supported its objectives and letting the critics and denigrators say what they would: "For the first *windu* [eight years], say nothing."[8]

Before the Yogyakarta school was six months old, requests had been received from several areas for similar schools to be set up, and on 31 December 1922, Soewardi conferred with Soetatmo Soeriokoesoemo to determine the future character and activities of Taman Siswa. On 6 January of the following year, Soetatmo invited Taman Siswa leaders to his home to inform them of his discussions with Soewardi. At this time a Central Committee (*Instituutraad*) was formed, with Soetatmo as first chairman, Soerjopoetro as second chairman, Soewardi as secretary, and five other members: R. Roedjito, Soebono, M. Ng. Wirjodihardjo, Pronowidigdo, and Soetopo Wonobojo. Of the Central Committee members, no fewer than six had been members of Selasa Kliwon (Soewardi, Soetatmo, Soerjopoetro, Soebono, Pronowigdo, and Soetopo Wonobojo); Soewardi, Soetatmo, and Soerjopoetro were all of the House of Paku Alam; and Soetatmo, Pronowidigdo, and Soetopo Wonobojo were all central figures in Budi Utomo.[9]

At the same meeting, Taman Siswa was defined as a school for the education of the people. No stipulations were made for an overall organization, it being decided that schools in the provinces should have autonomy over their activities; but to maintain general order (*ketertiban*) Soewardi was given "dictatorial rights" (*hak diktator*). This meant that, within less than a year of its founding, there were established in the nucleus of Taman Siswa the two fundamental principles of "democracy" (*kerakjatan*) and "leadership" that were to permeate the movement in later years.

With this, branches of Taman Siswa began to be set up in various regions. Notodipoetro provided the driving force in Surabaya; Panoedjo Darmobroto was active in Tegal; and in Cirebon a preparatory committee (Komite Taman Siswa) began work. Applicants to teach at Taman Siswa schools also began to emerge, the earliest among them being Soedyono Djojopraitno, who was appointed to the Wonokromo branch on the outskirts of Surabaya, and Moerana, who was appointed to the Cirebon branch. By early March 1923, Taman Siswa schools had been established in the four towns of Tegal, Cirebon, Surabaya, and Wonokromo. In addition, Poeger transferred the private school he was running in Malang to Taman Siswa. Many more requests for Taman Siswa schools were reportedly received by the Central Committee in Yogyakarta, but these had to be deferred for lack of suitable teachers.

In response to the support for Taman Siswa's objectives and the requests for schools that emerged across Java, the first Taman Siswa congress (Konperensi Besar) was held in Yogyakarta from 20–23 October 1923. At the conference, Taman Siswa's founding principles were expressly stated for the first time, and a curriculum was decided. The Central Committee that had been formed in January the same year was expanded and reorganized as the Supreme Council (Hoofdraad; it was subsequently renamed Madjelis Luhur, the Indonesian title which it still retains). This was further divided into the Central Committee of the Supreme Council (Badan Pengurus) and the Regional Representatives Committee (Gedelegeerden); and appointments were made to both committees. Organizational regulations were still not made, however; emphasis was laid instead on the upholding of Taman Siswa's principles and comradeship under Soewardi's "leadership."

The appointments to the Supreme Council made at the congress were as follows.

Central Committee
    First Chairman   Soetatmo Soeriokoesoemo
    Second Chairman   Soerjopoetro
    Secretary   Soewardi Soerjaningrat
    Members   Pronowidigdo
                    Wirjodihardjo
                    Roedjito
                    Soejoedi
                    Soerjoadipoetro
    Adviser   Prawirowiworo
Regional Committee
    1 Soetopo Wonobojo (Bogor)
    2 Sukarno (Bandung)
    3 Panoedjo Darmobroto (Tegal)
    4 Besar (Tegal)
    5 Tjokrodirdjo (Semarang)
    6 Hardjosusastro (Semarang)
    7 Soetedjo Brodjonagoro (Surakarta)
    8 Soedyono Djojopraitno (Wonokromo)
    9 Notodipoetro (Surabaya)
  10 Soewarno (Surabaya)
  11 Ali Sastroamidjojo (Surabaya)
  12 Poeger (Malang)
  13 Gondokusumo (Pasuruan)

Of the members of the original Central Committee, Soetopo Wonobojo had become the Bogor representative on the regional committee, while Soebono's name now appeared on neither committee.

Their place on the Central Committee was taken by Soejoedi and Soer-joadipoetro, together with Prawirowiworo as adviser. Soerjoadipoetro (Soewardi's younger brother) and Prawirowiworo had both been members of Selasa Kliwon. Prawirowiworo was an executive officer of the Yogyakarta branch of Budi Utomo, and since April 1922 had been on the editorial staff of *Wederopbouw*. Increasingly, the nucleus of Taman Siswa was being consolidated by people linked through the House of Paku Alam, Budi Utomo, and Selasa Kliwon.

On the regional committee, in addition to Tjokrodirdjo, Soedyono, Poeger, Notodipoetro, Panoedjo, and other nationalists, the names of Sukarno and Ali Sastroamidjojo appear. The latter, then a young lawyer freshly returned from his studies at Leiden University, was impressed by Soeward's educational ideas in a meeting with him and volunteered his services to Taman Siswa.[10]

In these early years, Taman Siswa gradually gathered support across Java, and schools were opened in a number of towns and cities. An overall organization was not at this time deemed necessary: rather, the network of schools centered on Yogyakarta was held together under Soewardi's leadership by the comradeship of the former members of Selasa Kliwon, who, together with several new leaders who joined the fringe of their group, constituted the central leadership of Taman Siswa.

Ideological Development

One feature of Soewardi's speech given at the opening ceremony of Taman Siswa on 3 July 1922 was his criticism of "obeisance to Western civilization." This attitude was to become firmly entrenched within Taman Siswa, finding its strongest expression a decade later in an article by Soedyono, which is discussed in chapter 5. Soewardi himself also resumed this theme in an article entitled "Associatie antara Timur dan Barat" (Association between East and West),[11] published in *Wasita*, the organ of Taman Siswa.

Soewardi's article argued that despite claims that "the present age [was] one of association of Eastern culture and Western culture, association of East and West," what had really happened in the colony of the Indies was that "after the decline of the Mataram kingdom in the nineteenth century, [Indonesians] lost [their] free national spirit (*roch kebangsaan merdeka*) and [their] own ideas died." Now they were living "as if lodging in someone else's hotel" and, being content to "eat good food and sleep" all they would, they gave no thought whatsoever to putting their own house in order. They had been poisoned by the West's materialism and hedonism, tainted to the marrow of their bones by the idea that their ultimate goal should be to live like the white man. While this situation persisted, they could not hope to foster a national spirit in their children. While they distanced themselves from the culture, language, and arts of the people and copied the lifestyle of the Dutch, they could not secure national independence. He concluded:

> If we wish to lead a national lifestyle, we should choose only those Western ways of life that are truly beneficial to us. At that time we shall have escaped from the situation in which "love is blind," and shall be able to choose calmly and with clear thoughts and feelings. Only then will association and evolution (*associatie dan evolutie*) be possible.

In this article Soewardi encapsulated the ideology of the Ethical policy in the phrase *associatie dan evolutie*; and at the same time he asserted that "association and evolution" could not take place without the national culture first being revived. Copying Western civilization was the lifestyle of the bourgeoisie (*hidupnja orang bourgeois*) and was no more than the semblance of "association." This remark appears to have been directed against the Javanese colonial officials who began to emerge following the decline of Mataram in the nineteenth century as the result of colonial policies that culminated in the Ethical policy. Western civilization, moreover, was perceived as rapacious and corrupt, the antithesis of the pure, sacred, national culture.

The view that "obeisance to Western civilization has locked this land in darkness" was diametrically opposed to the ideology of the Ethical policy, that the "light" of the West would illuminate the "darkness" of the Indies (this is captured in the title of Kartini's collected letters, *Door Duisternis tot Licht*). And those who could escape such obeisance were regarded as "free men."

These "free men" aspired to create a society in which "order and tranquility" were maintained, and at the same time they intended to bring about that order and tranquility by themselves. Their model of order and tranquility, moreover, was to be found neither in Western culture nor in the empty shell of prijaji culture, but rather, in the traditional Javanese culture.

In July 1922, Soewardi had cited the asrama, pondok, pesantren, and other traditional schools as providing models for a national educational system. As discussed in chapter 1, these were religious communities located in outlying areas that were "independent" of the temporal ruler. Here, through a variety of ascetic practices, people would acquire the wisdom to perceive the will of Sang Hyang Tunggal. As soon as the ruler began to lose hold on the kasektèn that maintained order and tranquility, they would appear at the seat of power and play a decisive part in the collapse of society's order or in the establishment of a new order. This image of an independent intelligentsia was reproduced in the emphasis Taman Siswa's placed on independence, the refusal of monetary grants, and simplicity of lifestyle.

In 1928, Soewardi contributed two articles to the inaugural edition of *Wasita*. Entitled "It is the pondok and asrama system that is the national system" and "The merits of the pondok system," he detailed therein the system operated in the pondok, asrama, and pesantren and argued forcibly that this should be the basis for a national education system. The first article ran as follows.[12]

> From ancient times to the present day, our people have had places of education. Today they are called pondok and pesantren, formerly they were called pawijatan and asrama. They were characterized by the fact that the home of the teacher (*ki adjar*) was the place where the pupils (*santri* and *tjantrik*) lodged and at the same time was used as the place for education. There, because teacher and pupil lived together day and night, moral education (*pengadjaran*) and intellectual training (*pendidikan*) were naturally combined into one. Today the pondok are used exclusively for religious education; but in the days when they were called asrama, not only was religious instruction given at the teachers' homes which were the asrama, various sciences (*ilmu*) were also taught. As well as religion, in other words, earth sciences, astronomy, jurisprudence, language, the fine arts, and military arts, all knowledge that the teacher had acquired through study was passed on. . . .
>
> In addition, in this educational system, pupils were ordered according to their stage of development. . . .
>
> From this we can draw the following conclusions about the traditional educational system of our people.
>
> (a) We have had an educational system since antiquity.
>
> (b) This system combined religions instruction and general education.
>
> (c) In one pawijatan the various stages were ordered from the lowest to the highest.[13]
>
> (d) In the pawijatan and asrama, the highest ranking teachers (pandita) lived under the same roof as other teachers and pupils.
>
> (e) Pupils at an advanced stage were also the teachers of pupils at a lower stage.
>
> (f) There were both men and women teachers and pupils.
>
> All those who desire to know the framework of our Taman Siswa should become well acquainted with the composition of the pawijatan, for it is this very composition, brought into accord with the modern age, that serves as the basic principle for our organization.

In the second article, after the preliminary remark that "we are ill-equipped for politics and will leave such matters to our colleagues in the political forum, ourselves concentrating on education," Soewardi states that the system of the pondok and pawijatan offered two great benefits in establishing a national education system. First, expenses would be minimal. Not only would the teachers' residences double as schools, but both teachers and pupils would have sworn themselves to a life of abstinence. Second, by virtue of the fact that teachers and pupils lived together, education would cover all facets of human character. Youth would be exposed personally to the lifestyle and ideas of their elders, would undergo moral as well as intellectual education, and would also receive a broad social training.[14]

The high regard in which Soewardi held the traditional Javanese educational system contrasted sharply with the views of the Indonesian nationalist movement, typified by Budi Utomo, which looked solely to Western culture and Western education as a means to reach its goal of raising the living standards of the people. Having experienced personally the Western educational system, Soewardi was the first to attempt to find a model in traditional education.

Besides criticizing the colonial education system and proposing a way to overcome its shortcomings—by combining the latest Western educational ideas with the traditional Javanese school system, and thereby creating a new image of free and independent man—the principles of Taman Siswa also showed a "popular orientation" in the proposal to "broaden the scope of education." In the course of its development, Taman Siswa's kerakjatan, of which this was one manifestation, grew increasingly stronger and attracted many nationalists to the movement.

Ki Hadjar Dewantara

On the occasion of his fortieth birthday, 2 May 1928, Soewardi abandoned the noble title of Raden Mas and took a new name: Ki Hadjar Dewantara. "Ki" was understood as equivalent to "Kijai," as indicated by the existence of several contemporary instances in which the name is spelled Kjahi Hadjar Dewantara,[15] and Soewardi's own definition of "Ki" as meaning "Kijai."[16] As well as being a term of respect for elderly Javanese men, "Kijai" was a title for those who had won respect by discovering the arcana of mankind and religion and in many cases for village religious leaders and the heads of pesantren. Following Soeward's example, other leaders of Taman Siswa used simply the title "Ki" rather than academic or noble titles (for example, Ki Soedyono, Ki Poeger, and others), while women were entitled simply "Nyi."

The ideal kijai in Javanese culture is probably the wayang character Semar, who was discussed in the previous chapter, and of whom Soewardi was particularly fond. Semar was a god incarnated as a commoner, who, by using humor and irony to expose human folly and by mediating between the gods and men, was able to realize the will of the gods on earth.

Before Soewardi, Ki Ageng Soerjomentaram, the leader of the Selasa Kliwon society, had assumed the title "Ki". Born a prince of Yogyakarta (his father was Hamangku Buwono VII), Soerjomentaram had renounced his court rank and left the palace for the country to live as a farmer. He had also founded Selasa Kliwon with Soewardi and others. What he advocated was the wisdom to stand aloof from egotism and selfishness in order to find the path to a state of tranquility.

"Hadjar," the second element of Soewardi's new name, was equivalent to adjar, a teacher of an asrama or pondok.

"Dewantara" meant literally "mediator of *dewa*." Contained in the word "dewa" (god) is probably the implication of the one God who stands above all heroes, all other gods, and all raksasa, and who defines their roles and destinies. Known as Sang Hyang Tunggal or Sang Hyang Wenang, he is lord of the universe, the ultimate source of power, ruler of time and space.

In sum, the name Ki Hadjar Dewantara, by which I shall hereafter refer to Soewardi, shows how he defined himself: as a kijai and an adjar who, like Semar, would strive to convey God's will to men. And in calling himself "teacher who mediates for God," Dewantara was styling himself a true pandita. This was reflected too in the title of *Wasita*, the monthly publication from Taman Siswa headquarters under Dewantara's chief-editorship, which he founded in October 1928, the year he took his new name. This title was explained as meaning *sabda pandita*, "word of the pandita."[17] This self-definition again demonstrates that the founding of Taman Siswa was prompted by the recognition of the age as one "bereft of a true *pandita*."[18]

At the same time, as we saw in the previous chapter, Mochamad Tauchid viewed Dewantara's new name as signifying his conversion from "a satria with the spirit of a pandita" to "a pandita prepared to take up arms to protect the nation and the people." Through his new name, Dewantara's "fight" was linked to "God's will."[19]

THE EXPANSION OF TAMAN SISWA

After the congress of October 1923, a succession of established private schools, like Poeger's school in Malang, joined the Taman Siswa movement as branch schools. In Bandung, the administration of a school affiliated with the Sarekat Rakjat (People's Association) was entrusted to Sukarno, then a student at Bandung. Thereafter, the school was headed by R. M. Sosrokartono, the elder brother of Kartini.[20]

In Jakarta, Medan, and elsewhere on the east coast of Sumatra, schools were similarly transferred to Taman Siswa by Budi Utomo. Around Medan in particular, Budi Utomo one by one transferred schools it was running to Taman Siswa, with the result that between 1925 and 1929 Taman Siswa schools were established in Medan, Tebingtinggi (Deli), and Galang. The Galang school, established in 1925, represented Taman Siswa's first expansion out of Java. Contemporary circumstances indicate, however, that it did no more than take over the activities of Budi Utomo among Javanese migrants; it was not until the 1930s that Taman Siswa extended beyond Javanese society in Sumatra.

In Pacarkeling, East Java, another private school was transferred to Taman Siswa by Sadikin, an influential leader of the movement in this area. And in Yogyakarta, Soerjowidjajan entrusted a private school known as Ati to the movement.

At the same time, a combined junior high school and teacher-training school (Mulo-Kweekschool) had been opened in Yogyakarta in July 1924, and preparations were made to dispatch native-born teachers to the new schools in the various regions.

From around 1926, Taman Siswa's activities began to attract more widespread interest, and articles on the movement began to appear in newspapers and magazines published in Central Java. In October 1926, for example, an article appeared in *Sediyo Tomo* comparing the Taman Siswa schools with the Santiniketan school that Tagore had opened in Bulpur, Bengal.[21] And following a visit by Tagore in August 1927 to the Taman Siswa headquarters, relations were established between the schools in Bengal and Yogyakarta involving the exchange of students.[22]

From 1928, following the publication of *Wasita*, more and more branches of Taman Siswa were set up across the country, while the established schools continued to round out their programs. In the following sections we shall examine the situation, looking first at the Taman Siswa school in Yogyakarta, then, based on accounts in *Wasita*, at the branches in East Java, Central Java, West Java, and Sumatra. It should be noted that the order in which the schools are described in each of these areas is not necessarily that in which they were established.

Yogyakarta

In 1923 the Taman Siswa school in Yogyakarta became the subject of a detailed report prepared by the colonial government. It included a report by Soewardi covering such matters as Taman Siswa's aims, current situation, teachers, and curriculum. The following is an overview based on Soewardi's report.[23]

The administrative committee in Yogyakarta consisted of eight members: Soetatmo Soeriokoesoemo, chairman (a Volksraad deputy); Soerjopoetro, vice-chairman (self-employed); Soebono, treasurer (self-employed); Roedjito, first secretary (proprietor of Mardimulya publishing company); R. Sabitah, second secretary (architect); Soetopo, adviser (editor-in-chief of *Budi Utomo* magazine); Pronowidigdo (former teacher from Yogyakarta); and Soewardi, director of teaching staff.[24]

The teaching staff were twelve in number: Soewardi, Soerjopoetro (a former student of Delft Technical College), R. M. Soewandhi (a STOVIA dropout),[25] R. Koento Sarojo (a Mulo graduate), Miss R. Soerjatie, Miss R. Soerjatien, Mrs. Soewardi Soerjaningrat (a former employee of a Fröbel school in The Hague), Mr. Hardjodiningrat (a former employee of the Catholic Fröbel school in Yogyakarta), Miss Francina (a teacher for three years at the Adhi Dharma school), and Miss Djoemilah, Rum Muryadi, and Siti Amini (all employees of Taman Siswa since graduation from primary school).

As of October 1923, these twelve teachers were in charge of a total of 213 students in eleven classes, ranging in age from four to seventeen years: 39 kindergartners, 42 first-graders (15 in class A, 27 in class B), 47 second-graders (19 in class A, 28 in class B), 21 third-graders, 9 fourth-graders, 9 fifth-graders, 14 sixth-graders, 8 seventh-graders, and 24 in the college-preparatory class (*schakelschool*).

A range of subjects was taught commensurate with the ages of the various classes. These included languages (Javanese, Malay, English, and Dutch, the latter broken down into reading, speaking, writing, composition, and grammer), arithmetic, science, history (including Javanese history, history of the Indies, Dutch history, "chronicles," and field trips to historical sites), singing of Javanese songs, general knowledge (current colonial affairs and general religious study), sports (gymnastics and Boy Scout-type group training), handicrafts, and dancing.

Lessons were conducted in five 90-minute sessions of two lessons each between the hours of 7:30 A.M. and 8:00 P.M. The school week ran from Monday to Saturday. Depending on their grade, pupils studied between ten and twenty subjects. In all grades emphasis was placed on language study: in grades six and seven in particular almost half of all classroom hours were devoted to Dutch (see Table 1). From this it can be inferred that the Taman Siswa curriculum laid heavy stress on practical education. That Taman Siswa offered the opportunity for such practical education cannot be overlooked as one of the reasons for its spread through the country.

TABLE 1. CURRICULUM OF THE TAMAN SISWA SCHOOL, YOGYAKARTA, 1923

SUBJECT	NUMBER OF LESSONS PER WEEK								
	KINDER-GARTEN	FIRST GRADE	SECOND GRADE	THIRD GRADE	FOURTH GRADE	FIFTH GRADE	SIXTH GRADE	SEVENTH GRADE	PRE-COLLEGE
Javanese	2	4	2	2	3	3	2		2
Dutch									
Speaking	3 ⎫7	3 ⎫	4 ⎫	4 ⎫	3 ⎫	3 ⎫	4 ⎫	4 ⎫	3 ⎫
Reading	4 ⎭	5 ⎪	5 ⎪	4 ⎪	3 ⎪	3 ⎪	4 ⎪	4 ⎪	3 ⎪
Sentence patterns		2 ⎬12	4 ⎬15	4 ⎬16	4 ⎬13	4 ⎬13	11 ⎬22	8 ⎬19	6 ⎬17
Composition		⎪	⎪	2 ⎪	2 ⎪	2 ⎪	2 ⎪	2 ⎪	4 ⎪
Dictation		2 ⎭	2 ⎭	2 ⎭	1 ⎭	1 ⎭	1 ⎭	1 ⎭	1 ⎭
Verbal arithmetic	2	2	2	2	2	2	3	2	2
Written arithmetic	1	3	3	2	3	2	3	1	1
Mental arithmetic		1	1	1	1	1	1	1	
Commerce	2	2	2	2					
Composition	3	3	2	1	1	1			2
Singing (music)	2	2	2	2	2	2	2	2	2
Sports	4	2	2	2	2	2	2	2	2
Domestic science (handicrafts)			2	2	2	2	(1)	(1)	
Geography				2	2	2	2	2	1
Nature study					2	2	2	2	2
History						2	2	2	2
Malay					1	2	2	2	
Civics							2	2	2
English								3	
Algebra & geometry								4	
Bookkeeping								(2)	
Drawing	2	2	2	2	2	2	2	2	2

Source: Mailrapport 84 × /1924, p. 6.
One lesson lasted 45 minutes.

On 3 July 1924, the teacher-training school was opened at the Taman Siswa school in Yogyakarta, bringing a further expansion of the teaching staff and curriculum. This was an attempt to create a system to supply teachers to the branch schools from within Taman Siswa.

Initially the school had a staff of five: Soerjopoetro, Soewardi, and Soewandhi, together with M. Ng. Wirjodihardjo (a former teacher at a government elementary school, now pensioned), and Soerjoadipoetro (a graduate of a Yogyakarta technical school). Their students numbered sixty, of whom fourteen were graduates of the Taman Siswa school and sixteen were graduates of the Yogyakarta HIS (Hollandsch-Inlandsche Scholen), while the remainder came from outside Yogyakarta, including some from parts of Sumatra and from Bali.

In the following years the student population grew and the staff changed. In 1925, M. Ng. Sastroprawiro was appointed to the staff, and the next year he was joined by Pronowidigdo, Sarmidi Mangoensarkoro, Soekarso (a former student of the NIAS medical school), and Soekemi, an HKS graduate and former headmaster of the Muhammadijah elementary school in Solo, who replaced Soerjopoetro when the latter transferred to Bandung.[26] Also appointed to the staff in 1926 were Oesman Sastroamidjojo (a former student of RHS[27]), Soewirjo (a former STOVIA student), and Miss R. A. Loorni (a graduate of the A.M.S. high school in Yogyakarta).

Notable among the staff appointed in 1926 are Soekemi and Sarmidi. In the 1930s Soekemi gained substantial influence in Central Java as an activist in the PNI-Baru (Indonesia National Education party) led by Sjahrir; and Sarmidi became a leader of the PNI (National Party of Indonesia). Thus, several years before they became politically active, and before their respective parties came into conflict, Soekemi and Sarmidi were both associated with Taman Siswa.

No staff changes were recorded in 1927, but in 1928 Sarmidi left for a teaching appointment in Jakarta, at the Ardjuna school run by the Theosophical Society.[28]

The subjects taught by these teachers were as follows. Soewandi: Dutch, general history, Dutch history, and geography; Pronowidigdo (principal): Javanese, Javanese culture, and Javanese history; Sastroprawiro (secretary): Malay; Soekarso: mathematics, geology, botany, and zoology; Dewantara (Soewardi Soerjaningrat): Dutch, educational theory, and gamelan music (*gending*); Loorni: English, Dutch, and algebra; Sarmidi: Dutch, geography, and biology; Soewirjo: English, Dutch, and chemistry; Soekemi: educational theory, bookkeeping, drawing, and geography.

By 1927, of the 60 students who entered the Taman Siswa Mulo-

Kweekschool in 1924, 18 had completed the second year of the Mulo course and advanced to the Kweekschool; 13 had advanced to the third year of Mulo; and the remainder had dropped out.

In 1928, two of the eighteen Kweekschool students, Moenar and Sadono, became teachers at Budi Utomo schools (which were subsequently transferred to Taman Siswa) at Tebingtinggi (in the Medan area) and at Weleri (near Kendal, west of Semarang), respectively. Two others transferred to different schools, one as a student, one as a teacher. And the remaining fourteen were appointed as teachers at Taman Siswa schools across the country: Soewardjo, Soekardjiman, and Soenarto in Yogyakarta; Rr. Isti Kartini in Bandung; Oejik in Malang; Soemadi in Mojokerto; Iskaq in Plosso; Soeroso in Genteng; Achmad in Porong; Rr. Achadiah and Soetrisno in Tanggul; Soegining and Soeparto in Slawi; and Toemar in Tegal.

In the same year that this first group of graduates took up appointments across the country, enrollment in the teacher-training school rose to 160. In the following year, 1929, six more graduates took up appointments at Taman Siswa schools, two in Medan, one in Tegal, and three in Yogyakarta.

Besides the regular teacher-training course, a system had been adopted whereby graduates of general courses at other schools who particularly wished to become Taman Siswa teachers were given training in educational theory and methodology. On completion of the course, these students, called *tjantrik*, received a license from Taman Siswa headquarters.

In the autumn of 1928, nine such graduates were assigned to Taman Siswa schools around the country: R. Moerana and R. Soetedjo to Cirebon; Soerjoadipoetro, R. Ngoesmanadji, and R. Sardjono to Bandung; R. Moerma to Pemalang; R. Soedarmo to Malang; R. R. Moerdijah and R. A. Mangoenatmodjo to Tanggul.[29] Two others, R. Prasondjo and R. Soeroso (also known as Wijono), took up appointments at the Kartijoso school in Semarang and the Setia Hati school in Bali, respectively. Numerous other graduates stayed in Yogyakarta to teach at the Taman Siswa school there.[30]

East Java and Madura

(1) SURABAYA

The Surabaya school was established on 12 November 1922.[31] The school board (*instituutraad*) was chaired by Notodipoetro, with A. Soeroto as secretary, R. Martohardjono as treasurer, Bintarti, Brotoadiwidjojo, and Wardojo as members, and Dr. G. Soewarno and Dr. Moh. Salih as advisers.[32] Initially there were 11 students, but by 1928,

346 boys and girls were enrolled. Wardojo was headmaster, and there were seven other teachers.[33] On 1 July 1927, six students entered the newly instituted sixth-grade class, but in December the same year, all of them having passed the colonial government's examination for petty officials (*kleinambtenaarsexamen*), most left for higher government-run schools.

(2) WONOKROMO

The Wonokromo school in the suburbs of Surabaya was opened on 1 July 1923 as a subschool of the Surabaya branch, with an initial enrollment of seven pupils.[34] Closely involved in the opening were Notodipoetro (the head of the Surabaya branch), Tirtoatmodjo, Sosrosepoetro, Hardjosoemarto, Djojosoedarmo, and Samsoe. The headmaster was Soedyono. By 1928, there were four teachers and 110 pupils.[35] In 1923 the school broke away from Surabaya, and from 1924 it was run by Soedyono.

(3) MOJOKERTO

This school was established in May 1925 by Srihadi, Notoatmodjo, R. Moh. Slamet, Sadikin, and others. Chairman of the school board was Srihadi (and from 1926, Notoatmodjo), and Sadikin was headmaster.[36] The initial enrollment of 44 pupils had by 1928 swelled to 180, while the teaching staff numbered four.[37] One of the teachers, Iskaq, worked exclusively as headmaster of a subschool set up in Plosso in October 1927.

(4) MOJOAGUNG

This school was launched on 8 June 1924 with one teacher (R. M. Djoeber), twelve pupils, and a school board consisting of Srihadi, Moh. Marzoeki, Arip, and Kardjidin.[38] In 1929, however, the board was dissolved and the teacher assumed responsibility, consulting with his pupils' parents when important decisions were to be made. Enrollment at this branch rose to seventy by late 1926, but fell back to forty by late 1928, the reasons being that parents had moved away because of employment and that few children in the Mojoagung area attended school. From 1925 the uniform tuition fee (elsewhere this was 3.5 guilders monthly) was abandoned in favor of a fee of 1.75 to 3.5 guilders, determined by parental income.

(5) KENCONG

The Kencong school opened on 1 September 1928, established by R. Soeharto, R. Soewito, R. Margi, R. Slamet, M. Soeradi, and R.

Aditomo.[39] Forty-seven pupils enrolled (by early 1929 the number had risen to sixty-seven), and Soekadhi Mertoredjo was appointed head-master. This school emphasized "self-reliance," following its own curriculum that included dry-field farming and vegetable gardening, and made a point of showing pupils their results only if they transferred to another school.

(6) KRAKSAAN

This school was opened on 1 August 1928 through the efforts of R. Abdoelalim, R. Moh Soekri Hadikoesoemo, R. Soenarjo, and M. Kasiadi, with the guidance of Soedyono (Wonokromo) and Sadikin (Mojokerto).[40] The eight pupils initially enrolled were taught by Sadikin, who subsequently moved to Mojokerto and handed over his responsibilities to Soeroso. In July 1929, when Soemardi came from Klaten to assist Soeroso, the school had fifty-three students in six grades, and the setting of the curriculum was entrusted to the teachers. Evening classes for laborers were also instituted. Monthly tuition fees were set at 1.5, 2, or 2.5 guilders according to parental income, and an entrance fee of 2.5 guilders was also charged.

(7) TANGGUL

This school had a staff of four headed by Soemadi Mangoenatmodjo, and 153 pupils on its register in 1928.[41] The curriculum included courses in Javanese dance, Swedish exercise, and hand-to-hand fighting, as well as conventional courses.

(8) CILURING

The school opened on 1 July 1929 with fifty pupils. The teacher was R. Ngoesmanadji.[42]

(9) JEMBER

From 1 July 1929, the school offered an expanded range of courses and facilities: evening classes in Dutch for laborers (3 guilders per month); private classes for laborers (8 guilders per hour; 20 guilders per 8 hours); a supplementary course (supplementary lessons for poor students at 4 guilders per hour or 10 guilders per 8 hours); private instruction for schoolchildren and adults (at the same rates as the supplementary course or private classes for laborers, halved for groups of two or more); a three-month literacy course covering the three R's (this was open to all races for a monthly fee of 2 guilders, which could be waived for poor Indonesians); dormitory facilities (20 guilders monthly for board and lodging, with ten percent discount for Taman

Siswa and HIS pupils); cheap rental of textbooks and supplementary readers.[43]

At the same time, daytime courses were expanded with the addition of elementary and *schakelschool* courses to the existing Fröbel school. Four- to six-year-olds could enter the Fröbel school, six- to eight-year-olds the elementary school, and middle-school graduates with good results the teacher-training course. The monthly tuition fees, payable in advance, were set respectively at 3.5, 2.5, and 2 guilders.

The school board at the time of this expansion consisted of R. Notojoedo as chairman, A. Koesoema as secretary and treasurer, Mrs. Akoep Goelangge, Astrodjojo, and R. Safioedin Soerjopoetro. In the 1930s Safioedin Soerjopoetro would distinguish himself not just as head of the Jember branch but as leader of all Taman Siswa schools in the eastern tip of Java (the so-called Oost Hoek, or "East Hook," to the east of Surabaya).

(10) JOMBANG

This school opened on 1 July 1929 with twenty-eight pupils and one teacher, Achmad 'nDaroe, a graduate from the Taman Siswa school at Plosso.[44] Reflecting the influence of the Mojokerto and Plosso branches in Jombang, its opening ceremony was attended by Pamoedjihardjo, Sadikin, Soedyono, and Jacob from the former, and Iskaq and Sardjono from the latter.

(11) MADURA

On 1 September 1929 a school was opened at Bangkalan.[45] It had forty pupils, eleven of them girls. The school board consisted of R. Adi Notowidjojo as chairman, R. P. Wirodiningrat as secretary, Moch. Sam as treasurer, R. A. Djojoadikoesoemo, H. Moch. Ramli, M. Wirokoesoemo, and H. Banadji.

Central Java

(1) SLAWI

The school opened on 18 May 1924 with fifty-five pupils.[46] Soon enrollment had risen to one hundred, but fell back to twenty-eight as the result of internal discord, the details of which are not clear. By early 1929 numbers had risen gradually to forty pupils and two teachers, Parto Hadisoetjipto and Soegining Tjokromihardja. However, in the school's first five years no fewer than seventeen teachers had left.

Conditions in the school finally settled down in 1929. In mid-

January the pupils published a school newspaper and formed a pupils' association. Educational methods generally followed those of the head school in Yogyakarta, but in the sixth grade the Dalton system was adopted. The school board at this time consisted of nine members: Soeroso, Joesoef, Boenawan Roesmipoetro, Padmowisastro, Soetidjab, Wirjosoedarmo, Parto Hadisoetjipto (who was also headmaster), R. P. R. Darmobroto, and Dr. Mr. R. Gondokusumo.

(2) TEGAL

The school was founded on 5 August 1923 by Roewijodarmobroto.[47] The initial roll of 60 pupils had by 1929 lengthened to 198. These included four Chinese and one Arab. Students were divided into grades one through eight, and the curriculum was based on that of the HIS, the Dutch primary schools. Among the pupils were a number who had dropped out of HIS and re-enrolled with Taman Siswa. The board was made up of Mr. Besar as chairman, Panoedjo Darmobroto as secretary, Mr. Sastromoeljono as adviser, and Hr. Sagir, a teacher at the Tegal HIS.[48] The curriculum included Javanese dance, Swedish exercise, and group training. Many of the pupils joined the Boy Scouts. The headmaster was Tjitrosatomoko, and there were seven other teachers.[49]

(3) SOLO

As of July 1927 a committee had been formed to prepare for the opening, which was scheduled for shortly thereafter.[50]

(4) KROYA

A local founding committee and headquarters in Yogyakarta were recruiting teachers and making other arrangements for the opening, which was scheduled for January 1930s.[51]

West Java

(1) BANDUNG

The school opened on 1 September 1926 with 60 pupils and six teachers.[52] By 1928 there were 400 pupils in the kindergarten, middle school, handicraft school, and other sections. Of these, 40 percent were boys and 60 percent girls; and 80 percent were Sundanese and 20 percent Javanese. The chairman of the board and headmaster was Soerjoadipoetro, and there were eleven teachers, including R. Ngoesmanadji.[53]

(2) CIANJUR

The school was opened on 3 November 1928.[54] The founding committee that made the arrangements for the opening consisted of Moch. Jakin as chairman, Iman Soewardi as secretary, Semeroe, Soekardi, Harsojo, Koerdi, Abdoel Salam, Hadji Abdoel Halim, and Hadji Djoedi. There were also two advisers, Wirasendjaja and Winatapoera.

The occupations of the Taman Siswa staff in Cianjur are also recorded. Jakin was self-employed, Iman a builder's assistant, Semeroe a forest warden, Soekardi an agricultural improvement officer's assistant, Harsojo a lawyer, Koerdi a clerk in the regency offices, Abdul Salam a clerk to the assistant resident, Abdoel Halim a man of religion, Djoedi a farmer and merchant, while the advisers were both HIS teachers. From this it appears that this branch of Taman Siswa was organized mainly by petty government officials, including school teachers.

At the opening ceremony, Soerjoadipoetro, the chairman of the Bandung school board (and also of the Cianjur board), delivered a congratulatory address in which he spoke on Taman Siswa's principles. In March 1929 Soerjoadipoetro transferred to Yogyakarta to teach at the Mulo. He was replaced as headmaster of the Bandung school by M. Soekemi, who was sent from Yogyakarta, while Sukarno took over as chairman of the board at Bandung.

(3) CIREBON

The school opened on 6 July 1923. In April 1929 it purchased a school building for Taman Siswa's exclusive use for a sum of 6,500 guilders.[55]

(4) JAKARTA

In February 1929 a founding committee was inaugurated in Jakarta.[56] In addition to the chairman, Moestadjab, and the secretary, Abdul Rachman, it had six members: Mrs. Martedjo Bendahari, Angronsoedirdjo, Basiroen, Sadiman, Soegardo, and Tahir. Shortly thereafter, the Jakarta chapter of Budi Utomo offered to transfer to the committee the running of its school (equivalent to an HIS) in the Jatibaru district of the city. As a result, the school building, pupils, equipment, and facilities were transferred to Taman Siswa. With the 55 pupils who had already applied for admission to the committee, a school of 130 pupils in seven grades came into Taman Siswa's hands.

The founding committee also carried through its plans to establish a school in the district of Kemayoran. Inaugural ceremonies for the schools at Kemayoran and Jatibaru (Tanah Abang) were held on the same day, 14 July 1929, and on the following day lessons began.

The school board for the Jakarta area consisted of M. H. Thamrin as chairman, Sarmidi Mangoensarkoro as secretary, Mr. Sartono, and Tondjokoesoemo.[57] Sarmidi Mangoensarkoro was appointed head-master of both schools, together with full-time teachers including Mrs. Sarmidi (formerly Rr. Sri Soelandari) and three part-time teachers.

In both its administration and its curriculum the Jakarta branch was well-organized. At Kemayoran, early mornings were set aside for a kindergarten (under Mrs. Sarmidi), while in the evenings language courses (Indonesian, Dutch, English, and German), a three-times-weekly writing class (for adults and children), and a teacher-training course (Indonesian history and educational theory taught by Sarmidi, national government science and national cultural theory taught by Joesoepadi Danoe Hadiningrat) were started. In addition the library was opened to the public, and a boarding school (20 to 30 guilders monthly) was operated under Mr. Sarmidi's supervision.

As the foregoing suggests, the running of the Jakarta branch of Taman Siswa came to rest squarely on the shoulders of Sarmidi, who served as secretary of the board and as headmaster, and who as head of the boarding school ate and lodged with his students. Later, in fact he came not only to represent Jakarta as the *pemimpin umum* (general leader) of the Jakarta branch, but also to play a leading role in the Taman Siswa movement.[58]

Sumatra

(1) NORTH SUMATRA (MEDAN AREA)

In December 1928 the Medan chapter of Budi Utomo set up a founding committee called Ngoedi Tomo, and on January 6 of the following year a school of the same name opened in the Budi Utomo offices.[59] Twelve children who had dropped out of HIS enrolled. Their teacher was Moenar, who transferred from the school Budi Utomo had run in Galang since 1925. In the summer of 1929, the Budi Utomo general conference resolved to open no more schools of its own and to throw its full support behind the educational activities of Taman Siswa, following the line on national education set forth at the 1928 and 1929 assemblies of the PPPKI (Permufakatan Perhimpunan-perhimpunan Politik Kebangsaan Indonesia; Association of Indonesian People's Political Organizations).[60] Consequently, the Medan school (apparently together with the Galang school) was transferred to Taman Siswa's control.

(2) TEBINGTINGGI (DELI)

In April 1929 a Taman Siswa founding committee was set up consisting of R. Soedjono as chairman, Noer Hasim gelar Soetan Perlaoengan as secretary and treasurer, and R. Rachmad; through their efforts, a

Taman Siswa school opened its doors in Tebingtinggi on 1 July 1929.[61]

The name Noer Hasim suggests that he was probably a Minang-kabau, and as such he would have been among the first of his people to be drawn into Taman Siswa. Nevertheless, as stated earlier, the Taman Siswa schools in Sumatra, where Javanese migrants were concentrated around Medan, were essentially set up through the mediacy of the Javanese organization Budi Utomo.

At the inaugural ceremony, which was conducted by Soedjono and attended by Rachmad, H. Ibrahim, Dt. Boengsu, and members of the local chapter of Budi Utomo, two important announcements were made: that from July 1929 the Budi Utomo school at Tebingtinggi would not accept any subsidies from the local government; and that thenceforth the Budi Utomo school would be transferred to Taman Siswa.

At the same time, the school board was approved. It consisted of Soedjono as chairman, Soetan Perlaoengan (Noer Hasim) as secretary and treasurer, Ibrahim, Dt. Boengsu, and Rachmad. Resolutions were passed to take over the facilities of the Budi Utomo school, to solicit the services of Iwa Kusuma Sumantri as adviser, and to recruit further teachers immediately.[62]

Distribution of Schools

The foregoing details of Taman Siswa headquarters in Yogyakarta and the regional branches derive from reports on individual schools that appeared in *Wasita* in 1928 and 1929. In November 1928, *Wasita* reported that the number of schools in Java had reached twenty. Although this figure and the names of the schools do not fully agree with the foregoing, these twenty schools were, in order of establish-ment, as follows:[63] (1) Yogyakarta (Central Java), (2) Surabaya (East Java), (3) Wonokromo (East Java), (4) Tegal (Central Java), (5) Cire-bon (West Java), (6) Mojokerto (East Java), (7) Slawi (Central Java), (8) Pemalang (Central Java), (9) Malang (East Java), (10) Mojokerto (East Java), (11) Bandung (West Java), (12) Tanggul (East Java), (13) Porong (East Java), (14) Plosso (East Java), (15) Ambulu (East Java), (16) Kencong (East Java), (17) Kraksaan (East Java), (18) Genteng (East Java), (19) Jember (East Java), and (20) Cianjur (West Java). In addition, preparatory committees had at this time been set up in the towns of Bojonegoro and Bondowoso in East Java.

These twenty schools were distributed predominantly in East Java, where thirteen of them lay; of the remainder, four were in Central Java, and three in West Java. A closer look at the distribution shows three schools in Central Java on the Java Sea coast around Tegal, together with the main school in Yogyakarta; and in West Java, two schools in the Bandung area and one at Cirebon on the north coast. East Java, on the other hand, evinced a far more positive response to Taman Siswa, with one group of schools being established along the Brantas river around the twin centers of Surabaya and Mojokerto, and several more schools centered on Jember in the East Hook.

In the next six months or so, four more schools were opened: (21) Medan (east coast Sumatra), (22) Jakarta (West Java), and (23) Galang and (24) Tebingtinggi (both east coast Sumatra).[64] Between July and September 1929 four more followed: (25) Ciluring (East Java), (26) Jombang (East Java), (27) Madiun (East Java), and (28) Bangkalan (Madura). At the same time preparatory committees were set up in Surakarta and Kroya (both Central Java).

The period between November 1928 and September 1929 thus saw the number of Taman Siswa schools grow from twenty to twenty-eight, with three new schools opened in the Medan area of Sumatra, one in West Java, three in East Java, and one in Madura. It was notable not only that schools had been opened in Medan and Jakarta, but that Taman Siswa became established in the important strongholds of the orthodox Muslim association, Nahdatul Ulama, in Jombang and Madura.[65]

The number of Taman Siswa schools continued to grow apace, and by July 1930 (the month before Taman Siswa's first national congress) there were fifty-two schools across Indonesia. Twenty-four new schools had been opened since the previous autumn. Listed by area, the fifty-two schools were as follows.[66]

> Sumatra (3 schools): Medan, Tebingtinggi, Galang.
> Kalimantan (3 schools): Banjarmasin, Marabahan, Kualakapuas.
> West Java (9 schools): Kemayoran (Jakarta), Jatibaru (Jakarta), Kebunjeruk (Jakarta), Bogor, Cirebon, Citepus (Bandung), Lengkong (Bandung), Ciguriang, Cianjur.
> Central Java (9 schools): Tegal, Pemalang, Slawi, Kroya, Magelang, Kota (Yogyakarta), Godean (Yogyakarta), Pedan, Solo.
> East Java (27 schools): Madiun, Ngawi, Ngambré, Bojonegoro (scheduled), Mojokerto, Mojoagung, Jombang, Cukir, Plosso, Kraksaan, Kota (Malang), Turen (Malang), Porong, Kranggan (Surabaya), Temanggungan (Surabaya), Pacarkeling (Surabaya), Wonokromo, Tanggul, Jember, Ambulu, Kencong, Lumajang, Talun, Kalisetail, Ciluring, Probolinggo, Kertosono.
> Madura (1 school): Bangkalan.

It was, then, in East Java that Taman Siswa expanded most vigorously. Throughout the period from late 1928 to mid-1930, almost 60 percent of Taman Siswa's schools were concentrated there. In particular, many new schools were opened in the area between Surabaya and Jombang and in the East Hook around Jember. Through the steady growth of new schools in the surrounding areas, the Surabaya and Wonokromo branches became centers of a network of schools. Subsequently, a similar network grew up around Malang and Jember.

In West Java and Sumatra, Taman Siswa schools were concentrated in the large cities, particularly the centers of the colonial administration. These were Medan in Sumatra, and Jakarta and Banding in West Java.

In Central Java, apart from a cluster around Tegal, schools were concentrated in Yogyakarta. And in its scale and substance Yogyakarta dominated the others, forming the major center of Taman Siswa's activities.

In sum, then, Taman Siswa schools of this period, while centered in Yogyakarta, expanded remarkably around multiple subcenters in East Java; and at the same time branches were established in Medan, Jakarta, Bandung, and elsewhere.[67]

The Founding Process of Branch Schools

While the "eight years of silence" prescribed by Dewantara meant that Taman Siswa would refrain from actively publicizing its educational ideals and educational system, it also meant that the Supreme Council would not actively enforce its control over the founding of branch schools.[68] Nevertheless, the founding of the branch schools almost invariably followed a set pattern. A local committee would first be formed by people wishing to found a school in the Taman Siswa spirit. This committee would secure and equip a schoolroom, provide educational materials, recruit pupils, and hire suitable teachers. In East Java in particular, certain individuals were active in the organization and administration of several schools, including Notodipoetro in Surabaya, Soedyono in Wonokromo, and Sadikin in Mojokerto. In Jakarta, Sarmidi was involved both in the takeover of the Budi Utomo school and in setting up a new Taman Siswa school.

Once opened, schools would be run by a school board and a teacher's group, in most cases with the founding committee taking over as the board. When, as sometimes happened, the headmaster was also a board member, his influence would be particularly strong. Typical of such leaders were Sarmidi in Jakarta, Soedyono in Wonokromo, Sadikin in Mojokerto, and Safioedin Soerjopoetro in Jember.

Apart from the new schools, Taman Siswa also took over the administration of existing schools. Most notable were the Budi Utomo schools, three of them in the Medan area and one in Jakarta; but there were also the SI school in Bandung and three privately run schools in Malang, Pacarkeling, and Yogyakarta.

In recruiting teachers, school boards would either themselves find teachers who supported Taman Siswa's educational policy and were prepared to follow it in their own teaching, or they would request that the Supreme Council dispatch a teacher from Yogyakarta. Of the schools opened before 1928, most chose the former option, though sometimes appointees were sent to Yogyakarta for a period of training. Among them were teachers at Surabaya, Wonokromo, Mojokerto, Tegal, and Cirebon. At Bandung, on the other hand, Soerjoadipoetro, a member of the Supreme Council, personally took charge of administration and teaching.

From 1928 the situation changed, when graduates of the Taman Siswa teacher-training school in Yogyakarta began taking up appointments around the country. The rapid expansion of Taman Siswa schools from this year was supported by the functioning of this new system of supply.

SOCIAL BACKGROUNDS AND THE NATIONALIST MOVEMENT

We turn finally to the social backgrounds of the people responsible for the founding, running, and support of Taman Siswa and its schools, and to Taman Siswa's relation to the nationalist movement.

Social Backgrounds

Those involved with Taman Siswa in the 1920s can broadly be divided into four groups. First, there were the founders of the original Taman Siswa school who subsequently became the main members of the Supreme Council and who occupied central positions in Taman Siswa's activities. Second, there were those who responded to events in Yogyakarta by founding and running the regional schools. Third, there were people who, while not directly involved in Taman Siswa's activities, provided active support with various forms of assistance. And fourth, there were the parents who sent their children to the Taman Siswa schools. Here we shall concern ourselves with the first three of these groups.

THE FIRST GROUP

This group was mostly composed of former members of Selasa Kliwon, and can thus be called the Selasa Kliwon group. Being either aristocrats of the house of Paku Alam (Soerjopoetro and Dewantara), leaders of Budi Utomo (Soetopo Wonobojo and Pronowidigdo), or both (Soetatmo), its members were closely united. Two of them died early, Soetatmo in October 1924 and Soerjopoetro in November 1927. But together with Soetatmo's close friend Tjokrodirdjo (a government official from Semarang and regular contributor to *Wederopbouw* from the late 1910s, who, though not a member of Selasa Kliwon, joined Taman Siswa immediately after its formation), Dewantara and Pronowidigdo remained active in Taman Siswa and became the senior elders of its first generation of leaders.

The Selasa Kliwon group remained "peripheral" as far as both the colonial bureaucracy and Javanese nobility were concerned, yet at the same time their attention was focused on these institutions. In this sense, the Selasa Kliwon society can be said to have been a "study club;" and, indeed, in the early 1930s, Taman Siswa did define it as a "religious study club."[69]

As a study club, like the Indonesia Study Club that Soetomo set up in Surabaya in 1924 and the General Study Club that Sukarno set up in Bandung, Selasa Kliwon provided a forum where members of the "nationalist intelligentsia" born of the twentieth century could consider the direction and substance of the nationalist movement. And whereas Soetomo's study club gave birth to the Indonesian People's Party, and Sukarno's to the Indonesian National Party, the Selasa Kliwon society attached cultural meaning to the nationalist movement, thereby giving birth, through Soetatmo and Dewantara, to Taman Siswa. Such was the background of those who formulated Taman Siswa's founding principles, which contained a clear statement of their intention to revive Javanese culture as a means to overcome the crisis of the times.

THE SECOND GROUP

This group was made up of people who responded directly to the Selasa Kliwon group by participating in Taman Siswa's activities. They can broadly be divided further into those recruited directly by the Selasa Kliwon group in Yogyakarta, and those who undertook to set up and run Taman Siswa schools across the country. The former included Soewandhi, Sarmidi, and Soekemi (and later Sajoga, Sudarminta, and Mochamad Tauchid[70]); the latter Soedyono, Notodipoetro, Poeger, Sadikin, and Safioedin Soerjopoetro. These subgroups were far less homogeneous than the Selasa Kliwon group, but together represented the second generation of Taman Siswa leadership. The former were in many cases nobility from Yogyakarta and Surakarta; the latter were the heads of Taman Siswa schools in East Java. Thus they can be termed respectively the Central Java group and the East Java group.

Soewandhi was a high-ranking noble from Yogyakarta. As an early contributor to *Wederopbouw* and in other ways, he was close to the Selasa Kilwon group. On the other hand, he joined the newly formed PNI, of which he was an active member until 1930. Sarmidi, as already noted, was a noble from Surakarta who grew up under the influence of Theosophy. Also a member of PNI, his politics were radical nationalist. Soekemi, though a native of East Java, studied in Yogyakarta where he became a Taman Siswa teacher. He was also a leading light of the PNI in Java, and was later active in founding the PNI-Baru. Sajoga and Mochamad Tauchid were likewise members of the PNI-Baru, Tauchid later distinguishing himself as a leader of Sjahrir's Indonesian Socialist Party.[71]

The backgrounds of members of the East Java group are less well documented. In Surabaya the Taman Siswa founding committee was composed of doctors and other intellectuals, while in Kraksaan, Kencong, Mojoagung, and other branches in East Java, lesser nobility bearing the title "Raden" were active participants in Taman Siswa. In Tegal, two members of the founding committee held law degrees (indicated by the title Mr.).

Others who at one time were involved to some degree in Taman Siswa's activities included Sukarno, Ali Sastroamidjojo, Sartono, Sunario, and other members of the intellectual elite who had gained law degrees in Holland or engineering degrees (indicated by the title Ir.) in the colony. They were all leaders of the PNI at the time of its establishment in 1927.

Soedyono and several other Taman Siswa teachers had previously taught at various types of school run by the colonial government. And, as at Cianjur, petty officials in the colonial government were also involved in Taman Siswa.

THE THIRD GROUP

This group comprised Taman Siswa sympathizers who provided material support. Most notable among them were the members of Budi Utomo who, as noted, not only presented their own schools to Taman Siswa in Jakarta and Medan, but at their convention in the summer of 1929 resolved to give their full support in educational matters to Taman Siswa. Given that the spread of education had been one of Budi Utomo's highest priorities when it was established as a movement by lesser nobility, this represented a remarkable contraction of its sphere of activity. In the early 1920s, however, Budi Utomo had shunned involvement in the burgeoning People's Movement and remained doggedly "Javanist" (*kejawaen*). Those who became involved in the People's Movement, like Dewantara and Soerjopranoto, left Budi Utomo. Eventually, however, Budi Utomo came to regard the Selasa Kliwon group and Taman Siswa as the only remaining channel, and an excellent one at that, through which they could take part in the People's Movement; and this they did by supporting Taman Siswa totally.

Taman Siswa and the Nationalist Movement

Taman Siswa can thus be said to have absorbed the Javanist element of Budi Utomo and at the same time to have structured through a definite channel the energy of the People's Movement, particularly the Sarekat Rakjat. The transfer to Taman Siswa of the Budi Utomo school in Jakarta and the Sarekat Rakjat's school in Bandung shows clearly this dualism in Taman Siswa.

Although naturally there were differences from place to place, those involved in the establishment of Taman Siwa across Java were generally enlightened intellectuals, low-grade officials, and lesser nobility. They were the social classes that the newly formed Budi Utomo had aimed to mobilize. Now Taman Siswa presented them with a new forum in which to act. It offered them simultaneously a revival of Javanese culture and the spirit of nationalism. From the late 1920s, moreover, nationalists associated with Taman Siswa, including Sukarno, began to emerge in the van of the nationalist movement.

Corresponding to Budi Utomo's own move to unite with the People's Movement through Taman Siswa, the social classes that it had sought to mobilize became simultaneously involved both in Taman Siswa and in the political movement of the nationalists, namely, Sukarno's PNI, Sartono and Sukarno's Partindo (Partai Indonesia or Indonesian Party), and Hatta's and Sjahrir's PNI-Baru. In other words, Taman Siswa took over the role of cultural movement to which Budi Utomo had aspired, at the same time functioning as a link between the social classes that had supported Budi Utomo and the nationalist movement. The nationalist movement had as its stated aims the destruction of the *Beamtenstaat*, the administrative state controlled by Dutch officialdom, and the formation of a new state: the overthrow of colonial rule and the attainment of national independence. And Taman Siswa had developed hand in hand with this movement.

NOTES

1. As vice-chairman of the central committee of Sarekat Islam from 1919 and the leader of Personnel Fabriek Bond, a sugar workers' union in Central Java, Soerjopranoto came to wield tremendous influence in the People's Movement. He

was also a central figure in the Yogyakarta faction of SI, which opposed the left-wing faction centered in Semarang (later to become the core of the Communist Party). His activities in SI are documented in Ruth McVey, *The Rise of Indonesian Communism* (Ithaca, N.Y.: Cornell University Press, 1965), chapters 3 and 4; and Robert van Niel, *The Emergence of the Modern Indonesian Elite* (The Hague: van Hoeve, 1960), chapter 3. On the Adhi Dharma school, I have no information.

2. Ki Pronowidigdo, "Lahirnja Taman Siswa," *Pendidikan dan Pembangunan Taman Siswa* (Yogyakarta: Madjelis Luhur Taman Siswa, 1976), pp. 305–308.

3. Information on these members is based on the following: Suratman, "Masalah Kelahiran Taman Siswa," *Pusara* 25, no. 1–2 (1964): 37–38; and M. Tauchid, *Ki Hadjar Dewantara, Pahlawan dan Pelopor Pendidikan Nasional* (Yogyakarta: Madjelis Luhur Persatuan Taman Siswa, 1968), p. 18.

4. Darma Wara was a scholarship foundation set up in late 1913, during Noto Dirodjo's presidency of Budi Utomo, to expand educational opportunities for Javanese youth. Due to lack of funds, however, it achieved little, and eventually the organization itself disappeared. Its members were: Raden Ario Soeriadiningrat as president, Raden Rijo Nitidhipoero as vice-president, Raden Ardiwinata as secretary, Raden Mas Prawirowiworo as treasurer, Raden Mas Pandji Gondoatmodjo, Pangeran Ario Tedjokoesoemo, and Mas Ngabehi Dwidjosewojo. Many of them were related to the house of Paku Alam. See Nagazumi Akira, *The Dawn of Indonesian Nationalism* (Tokyo: Institute of Developing Economies, 1972), pp. 91, 198.

5. The preceding is based on: Nagazumi, *Dawn of Indonesian Nationalism*, pp. 98, 206; Suratman, "Masalah Kelahiran Taman Siswa," p. 37; and Tauchid, *Ki Hadjar Dewantara*, p. 18.

6. Mailr. 421/I, Geheim (Verbaal 12 March 1923, No. 45). [S. L. van der Wal, ed., *Het Onderwijsbeleid in Nederlands-Indië, 1900–1940*, (Groningen: J. B. Wolters, 1963), p. 365.]

7. Sajoga, "Riwajat Perdjuangan Taman Siswa, 1922–1952," *Taman Siswa 30 Tahun* (Yogyakarta: Madjelis Luhur Taman Siswa, 1952), pp. 203–204.

8. On the "eight years of silence," Dewantara is reported to have said that "the time will not have come for us to show ourselves in public" until eight full years have passed and results have been achieved. Ki Djoe Nitik, "Sedikit Riwajat tentang berdirinja Taman Siswa," *Wasita* first ser. 1, no. 8 (May 1929): 264. This attitude suggests that Dewantara was strongly aware of the ideal roles of the pesantren and pondok, such as were discussed in chapter 1 herein.
    The following summary of Taman Siswa's history is based on the following sources: Pronowidigdo, "Lahirnja Taman Siswa;" Sajoga, "Riwajat Perjungan Taman Siswa;" "Peringatan 10 tahun Taman Siswa," *Pusara* 2, no. 5–6 (May 1932): 37–40, and no. 7–8 (June 1932): 54–57. Where different terms are used in these sources in reference to the same event, I have adopted the term used in the earliest account (*Pusara*, 1932). These accounts have been checked against those published in *Wasita* between 1928 and 1930, and in some cases I have followed the *Wasita* accounts.

9. Pronowidigdo, "Lahirnja Taman Siswa," p. 30.

10. Ali Sastsroamidjojo's support for Taman Siswa is detailed in his autobiography. On returning from Holland, Ali visited Soewardi at his home in Yogyakarta, where he was impressed by both Soewardi's personality and his educational ideas, and resolved to send his own children to the Taman Siswa school. He also undertook to teach a class in ancient history and contributed several articles to *Wasita* on customary law. Ali remarks that the Taman Siswa teachers ran the schools with dedication, regardless of their meager salaries and the fact that payment tended to be late. Ali Sastroamidjojo, *Tonggak-tonggak di Perjalananku* (Jakarta: P. T. Kinta, 1974), pp. 73–80.

11. Ki Hadjar Dewantara, "Associatie antara Timur dan Barat," *Wasita* first ser. 1, no. 11–12 (August–September 1929): 321–324.

12. Ki Hadjar Dewantara, "Systeem Pondok dan Asrama itulah systeem Nasional,"

Wasita first ser. 1, no. 2 (November 1928): 39–41.

13. Soewardi lists the following thirteen ranks from the lowest pupil to the highest teacher (the corresponding titles for females are given in parentheses): (1) indung-indung (indung-indung), (2) ulu guntung (ubon-ubon), (3) tjèkèl (dedunjik), (4) tjantrik (mentrik), (5) manguju (sontrang), (6) djedjanggan (bidang), (7) putut (endang), (8) wewasi (dahjang), (9) adjar (pandita perempuan), (10) pandita dwidjawara (as 9)—this term is explained as meaning *pengadjar*, "one who teaches," (11) pandita wiku (as 9)—this is explained simply as *semèdi*, "pilgrimage," presumably meaning one who has completed a pilgrimage, (12) pandita begawan (as 9)—this is explained as meaning *bekas radja*, "one who was formerly a king," (13) pandita resi (as 9)—this is explained as meaning *asal dari asing*, "one come from overseas."

In 1933, Soewardi applied this ranking system to the Taman Siswa grades from pupil to teacher. Taman Anak, kindergartners, corresponded to indung-indung; Taman Muda, primary school pupils, to ulu guntung and ubon-ubon; Taman Dewasa, middle school pupils, to tjèkèl and dedunjik; and Taman Guru, students of the teacher-training course, as well as those who had studied elsewhere and were being retrained as Taman Siswa teachers, to tjantrik and mentrik. Soewardi points out that this usage of the term tjantrik was already established within Taman Siswa.

Young teachers corresponded to manguju and sontrang; older teachers in charge of an entire school corresponded to djedjanggan and bidang. Those who taught for many years without acquiring assets for themselves or their families would gain the title of adjar (the ninth rank) or higher. The seventh and eighth ranks, namely putu (endang) and wewasi (dahjang), had originally been titles accorded those who returned to "worldly society" (*dunia masjarakat*) after a period of retreat at a school, and accordingly these titles were applied to adult students.

From this, it is clear that to be worthy of the title adjar, a Taman Siswa teacher was expected to present all of his assets to Taman Siswa and to open his own house as a school. Needless to say, Soewardi set the example.

This application of nomenclature is cited from Ki Hadjar Dewantara, "Nomenclatuur dalam Pendidikan Kebangsaan, Susunan Nama Nama Kesiswaan," *Pusara* 4, no. 3 (December 1933): 37–38.

14. Ki Hadjar Dewantara, "Faidahnya Systeem Pondok," *Pusara* 1, no. 2 (November 1928): 41–43.

15. See, for example, the review of *Darma Kondo* contained in "Darmo Kondo, 20–25 February 1928," *Overzicht van de Inlandsche en Maleisch-Chineesche Pers*, or *Inlandsche Pers Overzicht* (hereafter cited as *I.P.O.*), 1928, p. 30.

16. Dewantara, "Systeem Pondok dan Asrama," p. 39. Here, the term Ki adjar is used in explanation of Kjai guru.

17. This definition appeared in the preface to the inaugural edition of the second series of *Wasita*, published from 1935. *Wasita* second ser. 1, no. 1 (March 1935): 1.

Although announced as "a magazine for parents and teachers," a general publication for those interested in education, *Wasita* was essentially the organ of Taman Siswa, and from the April 1929 issue (volume 1, number 7), it was in fact explicitly stated to include this function. Publication continued for a year, with volume 1, number 12 appearing in September 1929 (numbers 9 and 10, and 11 and 12 were combined issues), and was then suspended for a year, resuming with volume 2, number 1 in July 1930. Following the issue of volume 2, number 2 in August 1930, publication was again suspended for a year, resuming with the combined issue of numbers 3–6 in August 1913, only to cease again immediately. The reasons cited in that issue for the year's interruption were, firstly, a shortage of manpower and other problems in Yogyakarta and, secondly, that the growth of Taman Siswa had created the need for an official organ. It was also announced that, accordingly, publication of *Wasita* would be transferred to the Malang branch. Nothing, however, materialized from Malang.

Not until March 1935 did publication resume under this title, with volume 1, number 1 of the second series. The new *Wasita* was devoted to educational matters, proclaiming itself "a general educational journal for all teachers and educators (*pemimpin anak-anak*)." The editorial offices at 26 Jalan Stasion, Yogyakarta, were staffed by Dewantara, Soewandhi, and Ngoesmanadji, under Dewantara's chief-editorship. This move allowed *Pusara* to function solely as Taman Siswa's official organ, while *Wasita* covered educational ideas and doctrines, Javanese culture, and broader issues in the field of national education.

18. Soetatmo Soeriokoesoemo, see chapter 3.
19. This definition by Tauchid appears in his biography of Dewantara written in 1968, and as such was interpretative of Dewantara's life and Taman Siswa's history. This linkage of Dewantara's "fight" to "God's will" is discussed in the following chapters in connection with the subsequent activities of Dewantara and Taman Siswa.
20. *I.P.O.*, 1926, p. 40; Van der Wal, *Het Onderwijsbeleid*, p. 425.
21. *I.P.O.*, 1926, pp. 261–262.
22. On Tagore's visit to Taman Siswa and the subsequent exchange between the two schools, see Ki Hadjar Dewantara, "Hubungan Kita dengan Rabindranath Tagore," *Pusara* 11, no. 8 (August 1941): 131–134 (reproduced in idem, *Karja K. H. Dewantara, II A: Kebudajaan* [Yogyakarta: Madjelis Luhur Persatuan Taman Siswa, 1967], pp. 357–360).
23. Mailr. 84x/1924.
24. Except for Sabitah, all were either associated with Selasa Kliwon or early members of Taman Siswa's Supreme Council.
25. In the 1930s, Soewandhi rose to prominence in the leadership of Taman Siswa. Besides being an editor of the second series of *Wasita*, he was a member of the Supreme Council.
26. Soekemi's association with the Muhammadijah school before becoming a Taman Siswa teacher is of great interest. Also, HKS is thought to be the abbreviation of *Hogere Kweekschool voor Inlandsche Onderwijzers* (higher training school for native teachers).
27. RHS is thought to be the abbreviation of *Rechtshogeschool* (high school of law).
28. The foregoing account of conditions in Yogyakarta from 1924 is based on "Mulo dan Kweekschool Nasional," *Wasita* first ser. 1, no. 1 (October 1928): 22–26. Another Ardjuna school, founded in Banjarnegara in July 1913, is mentioned in a government document, which described its facilities and curriculum as being "extremely crude." Nevertheless, it does indicate that an Ardjuna school had been established elsewhere in the colony besides Jakarta. Mailr. 1098/1692 (Verbaal 16 January 1933–S).
29. Ngoesmanadji subsequently became an editor of the second series of *Wasita*. Sardjono became an influential leader of Taman Siswa schools in West Java in the early 1930s (see chapter 6).
30. The foregoing is based on "Mulo-Kweekschool Taman Siswa di Yogyakarta," *Wasita* first ser. 1, no. 9–10 (June–July 1929): 303–304.
31. "Taman Siswo Surabaja," *Wasita* first ser. 1, no. 2 (November 1928): 61.
32. Notodipoetro, like Soedyono and Poeger, was among the first to set up and run a Taman Siswa school in East Java. Later he played an important role as leader of the Surabaya branch. He died on 23 June 1937. *Pusara* 7, no. 9–10 (July–August 1937): 150. Wardojo remained active in Taman Siswa and was elected chairman of the Supreme Council for the period 1966–1970 at the Supreme Council congress held on 10 December in Yogyakarta. *Pusara* 28, no. 1–2 (January–February 1967): 7.
33. The seven teachers were: Seti Rahajoe, Darsini, Dwitosewojo, Soekowidjojo, Abdul Gani, Dalmo, and Soekirno.
34. "Taman Siswo Wonokromo," *Wasita* first ser. 1, no 1 (November 1928): 61–62.
35. The four teachers were: Soenargo, Soeheji, Roeslan, and Hardjo.

36. "Taman Siswo di Modjokerto," *Wasita* first ser. 1, no. 1 (November 1928): 62–64.
37. The three other teachers were Sardjono, Pamoedjihardjo, and Iskaq.
38. "Taman Siswo Modjoagung," *Wasita* first ser. 1, no. 5 (February 1929): 166.
39. "Taman Siswo Kentjong," *Wasita* first ser. 1, no. 5 (February 1929): 166–167.
40. "Taman Siswo Kraksaan," *Wasita* first ser. 1, no. 11–12 (August–September 1929): 363.
41. "Taman Siswo di Tanggul," *Wasita* first ser. 1, no. 4 (January 1929): 120–131. The other three teachers were R. R. Moerjidah, Soetrisno Tjiptosentoso, and Soemadi Tjokromanggolo.
42. "Taman Siswo di Tjluring," *Wasita* first ser. 1, no. 9–10 (June–July 1929):306.
43. "Taman Siswo Djember," *Wasita* first ser. 1, no. 9–10 (June–July 1929): 304–306.
44. "Taman Siswo Djombang," *Wasita* first ser. 1, no. 11–12 (August–September 1929): 361.
45. "Taman Siswo di Madura," *Wasita* first ser. 1, no. 11–12 (August–September 1929): 361–362.
46. "Taman Siswo Slawi," *Wasita* first ser. 1, no. 6 (March 1929): 196–197.
47. H. D. S. "Taman Siswo Tegal," *Wasita* first ser. 1, no. 5 (February 1929): 165–166.
48. Sastromoeljono is thought to have been Sukarno's lawyer at his trial in 1930.
49. The seven teachers were: Oentoeng, Darman, Wirjoadmodjo, Asjiah, Soemirah, Soelatin, and Toemar Handokosoero.
50. "Taman Siswo di Solo," *Wasita* first ser. 1, no. 11–12 (August–September 1929): 363.
51. "Taman Siswo di Kroja," *Wasita* first ser. 1, no. 11–12 (August–September 1929): 364.
52. "Taman Siswo Bandung," *Wasita* first ser. 1, no. 3 (December 1928): 128–130.
53. The remaining ten teachers were: Soerjoadipoetro, Sastrawinata, Soepijah (female), Soekarmi (female), Isti Kartini (female), Soedinah (female), Sardjono, Djoeman, R. Soemitro, and R. M. Sapari.
54. "Taman Siswo di Tjiandjur Chabar Taman Siswo," *Wasita* first ser. 1, no. 6 (March 1929): 198–199, 204.
55. "Taman Siswo Cheribon," *Wasita* first ser. 1, no. 7 (April 1929): 227. The date of opening is that given in the table at the end of *Taman Siswa 30 Tahun.*
56. "Bukaan Taman Siswa di Betawi," *Wasita* first ser. 1, no. 8 (May 1929): 265; S. Mangoensarkoro, "Taman siswa Djakarta," *Wasita* first ser. 1, no. 11–12 (August–September 1929): 357–360.
57. Thamrin was an influential nationalist leader in the 1930s, and in 1939 was appointed president of Gapi (Gabungan Politik Indonesia), an association of Indonesian nationalist organizations. Sartono, on returning to Indonesia after graduating from Leiden University's law faculty, joined the PNI and became Sukarno's right-hand man. In 1913 he established the Partindo (Partai Indonesia), which was subsequently opposed by Hatta and Sjahrir's PNI-Baru.
58. This was the earliest use of the term *pemimpin umum* (general leader). Sarmidi Mangoensarkoro was born on 23 May 1904, the son of an official of the Surakarta royal household. He attended a technical institute in Yogyakarta and after graduating became president of the Yogyakarta branch of the youth organization Jong Java. Later, influenced by the Ardjuna school in Jakarta, he joined the Jong Theosofen Organisatie. In 1928 he joined the PNI, and in October of that year he attended the Second Youth Congress, at which the "Youth Pledge" was adopted. Abdurrachman Surjomihardjo, "Ke Sarmidi Mangunsarkoro (23 Mei 1904–8 Djuni 1957)," *Pusara* 27, no. 7 (July 1957): 22–23.
59. Indonesisch-Nationale School di Medan," *Wasita* first ser. 1, no. 4 (January 1929): 128; "Taman Siswo di Sumatra Oostkust," *Wasita* first ser. 1, no. 7 (April 1929): 227–228; "Hoofdbestuur B. O. dan Taman Siswo," *Wasita* first ser. 1, no. 11–12 (August–September 1929): 342.
60. See chapter 4.

61. Wg. St. Perlaoengan, "Taman Siswo Tebing-Tinggi," *Wasita* first ser. 1, no. 11–12 (August–September 1929): 362.

62. Iwa Kusuma Sumantri graduated from Leiden University's law faculty in 1925, and in February 1928 he set up practice in Medan. At the same time he was a leader of the labor movement. Kenichi Goto, trans, *Indoneshia minzokushūgi no genryū: Iwa Kusuma Sumantori jiden* [The source of Indonesian nationalism: The autobiography of Iwa Kusuma Sumantri] (Tokyo: Waseda University, 1975: 1–78.)

63. "Persatuan Taman Siswo," *Wasita* first ser. 1, no. 2 (November 1928): 64.

64. "Persatuan Taman Siswo," *Wasita* first ser. 1, no. 7 (April 1929): 226.

65. Throughout the colonial period, Taman Siswa tended to have the greatest number of schools and to be most active in East Java. There were three reasons for this.

First was the presence of Nahdatul Ulama. Formed in 1926 to counter the Islamic reform movement, particularly Muhammadijah, which was based in Central Java, Nahdatul Ulama expanded from the pesantren of East Java. As a nationalist education movement ranking with Taman Siswa, Muhammadijah gained strength in the towns and cities of Central Java and in West Sumatra but was totally unable to establish branches or open schools in East Java due to the resistance of Nahdatul Ulama. Taman Siswa thus gained the opportunity to expand into that region; and it appears to have enhanced its chances by proclaiming the pondok, pesantren, and other religious schools then being run in East Java by the kijai of Nahdatul Ulama to be the "ideal type" of nationalist education.

On the process of development of Muhammadijah, see Alfian, "Islamic Modernization in Indonesian Politics: The Muhammadijah Movement during the Dutch Colonial Period (1912–1924)" (Ph.D. diss., University of Wisconsin, 1969); Deliar Noer, *The Modernist Muslim Movement in Indonesia, 1900–1942* (London: Oxford University Press, 1973).

The second reason for Taman Siswa's predominance in East Java was the sympathy it gained among the East Javanese by the fact that its leaders, centered on members of the house of Paku Alam, not only rejected the present "kingdom" but had instituted the "reconstruction" of Javanese culture. Since the founding of the Islamic kingdom of Mataram in the sixteenth century, East Java had not once harbored the royal capital and palace of a Javanese kingdom. This region, where such court cities as Madjapahit, Singasari, and Kediri had once displayed the glory of Java, had come to be regarded as peripheral, and its people had become alienated from Central Java, particularly the Mataram kingdom and the descendants of its royal family, and were eager for a return to their ideal of glory. To them, the Taman Siswa movement, though born in Yogyakarta, must have offered the hope of fulfilling this desire.

The third reason was that people who were dissatisfied with Soetomo's "moderate cooperatist line" joined Taman Siswa as a vehicle of resistance to Soetomo's Indonesia Study Club and its successor, the Indonesian People's Party (Partai Bangsa Indonesia), which had exerted a strong influence in East Java since the mid-1920s. (This was pointed out to me by Mr. Abdurrachman Surjomihardjo in a conversation in March 1975.) As will be seen in the following chapter, confrontations frequently arose between the Soetomoist faction and the East Java branches of Taman Siswa.

66. "Persatuan Taman Siswa," *Wasita* first ser. 2, no. 1 (July 1930): 8. Note that Taman Siswa groups the schools at Madiun, Ngawi, Ngambré, and Bojonegoro, with those of Central Java, whereas the contemporaneous (and the present) administrative boundaries place them in East Java.

67. It is interesting that Taman Siswa's activities failed in the cities of Surakarta (Solo) and Semarang, the former being the seat of court of the Surakarta and Mangkunegaran houses, the latter the center of colonial administration and economic activity in Central Java. In the former case, the failure may be attributable to the antagonism between Solo and Yogyakarta: as Yogyakarta came to function

as a center for the nationalist movement in the twentieth century, so the houses of Solo and Mangkunegaran strengthened their ties with the colonial government and became increasingly conservative. In Semarang, on the other hand, it was deemed difficult to establish Taman Siswa schools in the face of the "people's schools" of the Communist Party and the Sarekat Rakjat, which had successfully been maintained since Tan Malaka's time. A Taman Siswa school was finally opened in Semarang on 1 July 1932. *Pusara* 2, no. 1–2 (March 1932): 8–10; *Pusara* 6, no. 7 (May 1936): 161.

68. Dewantara's only pronouncement on how branch schools were to be established was reportedly as follows: "Don't talk about this and that. Work unsparingly and with an open heart to find people of nationalist spirit who are not enslaved to fanatical ideas. Then form a committee and look for teachers and a schoolroom. If Allah bestows his blessings and pupils gather there, then a Taman Siswa school will be established." Ki Djoe Nitik, "Sedikit Riwajat," p. 264.

Both this formula and the stipulation of "eight years of silence" are pervaded by the spirit of the Javanese maxim about accumulation of kasektèn: *sepi ing pamrih, ramé ing gawé* (work hard, free from personal desires). For further discussion of this motto, see Benedict R. O'G. Anderson, "The Idea of Power in Javanese Culture," *Culture and Politics in Indonesia*, ed. Claire Holt, Benedict R. O'G. Anderson, and James Siegel (Ithaca, N.Y. and London: Cornell University Press, 1972), p. 39.

69. A history of Taman Siswa published by that organization in 1974 states that Selasa Kliwon was a "Religieuse Studieclub." Team Studie Taman Siswa, "Laporan Studi Sejarah Pendidikan Swasta Taman Siswa," vol. 1, mimeographed (Yogyakarta, 1974), p. 152. However, this term was first used in 1932 (in *Pusara* 2, no. 5–6 (May 1932): 39, and was probably coined to set Selasa Kliwon apart from such study clubs as those set up by Sukarno and Soetomo in the late 1920s, which were concerned with political and social matters. "Religious" can here be inferred to mean "Javanese spiritual life."

70. Early in the 1930s, Sajoga joined the office of the Supreme Council of Taman Siswa. After independence he remained on the editorial staff of *Pusara*, and contributed a lucid article on Taman Siswa's struggle in *Taman Siswa 30 Tahun*, published in 1952. He died in 1977. Sudarminta joined Taman Siswa in the late 1920s and thereafter remained a member of its leadership. Tauchid, after joining Taman Siswa in 1933, taught at the Banyumas school. After independence he was long a member of the Supreme Council and wrote several books related to Taman Siswa. At the same time, he was active as a leader of Sjahrir's Indonesian Socialist Party.

71. A detailed account of the activities of Sarmidi, Mangoensarkoro, and Tauchid in the period between the Japanese military administration and independence may be found in Benedict R. O'G. Anderson, *Java in a Time of Revolution: Occupation and Resistance, 1944–1946* (Ithaca, N.Y. and London: Cornell University Press, 1972).

4

ORGANIZATION: THE EAST
JAVA CONFERENCE AND THE
NATIONAL CONGRESS

We saw in the previous chapter how Taman Siswa grew through the 1920s: following the opening of the first school in 1922, the movement spread across Java and the east coast of Sumatra, encompassing a total of fifty-two branches by July 1930.

The process of expansion was one in which people across the Netherlands Indies saw the Yogyakarta school as a new cultural center and formed branches in their own areas. There were no organizers dispatched from the center to stamp the center's design directly on this process, and in consequence each branch represented a unique movement calling itself a Taman Siswa school. Nevertheless, these schools were not scattered at random but clustered around the center in Yogyakarta and subcenters at Surabaya, Malang, Jember, and elsewhere in East Java, Batavia and Bandung in West Java, and Medan on the east coast of Sumatra.

The loose unity of Taman Siswa was supported by two factors. First, the centers were linked by a network of relationships between nationalistic aristocrats which were based equally on their common interest and their common lineage, and which centered on the members of the Central Javanese house of Paku Alam who had founded Taman Siswa in 1922. All these aristocrats had associations with Budi Utomo and with the Selasa Kliwon society that had preceded Taman Siswa, and all shared a common desire to revive Javanese culture in the context of an Indonesian nation. To this end they were united in their will to create in Taman Siswa a counterinstitution to the structures of colonial rule.

The second factor was the people involved with Taman Siswa across the country: the organizers and administrators of the branch schools, the teachers, and the parents who sent their children to the Taman Siswa schools. By and large, these people responded extremely positively to the formation of Sukarno's PNI in 1927, to the adoption of the "Youth Pledge" in the following year, and to other elements in the new movement towards the "unity and solidarity" of the Indonesian nation.

In the late 1920s and early 1930s, a fresh and vivid "spirit of the age" welled up in the form of a self-awareness of "Indonesia"— particularly in its connotations of territory, nation, and language—in place of "the Netherlands Indies" and of the "community" that was presumed to be formed on that basis. It manifested itself also in calls for the overthrow of the structures of colonial rule and the independence of the Indonesian nation. These structures of colonial rule were the instruments by which tropical agricultural products and minerals were plundered through the requisitioning of land and labor, and which allowed the "drain of wealth;" in short, they were the system of colonial bureaucracy centered in Batavia.[1]

Contemporary nationalists put forward a succession of ideas and systems which they believed could oppose the colonial system, engendering an ever-widening debate. Through the "freedom of information" that had of necessity been brought to the colony in the process of bureaucratization and rationalization of Dutch rule in the twentieth century, the Indoesian nationalists came into contact with cooperativism, the Swaraj and Swadeshi movements, the modernist movement and the secular state in Islamic countries, Sun Yat-sen's Three Principles of the People, European parliamentary democracy, and a host of other ideas and systems, and were sensitive to all that they considered might contribute to the formation of a counterinstitution. Though the result was seemingly chaotic, no more than a display of learning, this was nevertheless a path that had to be trodden in the formation of the idea of nation-state.

The common denominator in this plethora of ideas was the principle that a new, independent state should be founded on the basis of a "Sovereign People" (*Kedaulat Rakjat*). The concept of Rakjat was another important symbol that showed the spirit of the age and provided the legitimating principle of the nationalist movement.

In the whirlpool of this spirit of the age, Taman Siswa's role was unique. As an educational institution, it advocated the establishment of "education for the People" and "education for the nation;" and as a result it was constantly aware of its opposition to the educational machinery run by the colonial government and constantly seeking to define the ideal Indonesian and the ideal type of national education system. It stood, moreover, for national principles of social order that rivaled those of colonial society. In both these causes Taman Siswa advocated the revival of the precolonial culture. From the mid-1920s, former activists in Budi Utomo who had grown dissatisfied with its "conservatism" and people sympathetic to the causes of Sukarno's PNI one after another became involved in the activities of the Taman Siswa schools. Sukarno was the propagator of the spirit of the age; Ki Hadjar Dewantara was its embodiment.

In this way, the branches of Taman Siswa were loosely linked by a network of personal relationships among those who had led the movement since its founding; and at the same time they shared the fact of embodying the spirit of the age.

This chapter examines the situation that developed within Taman Siswa against this background. Specifically, it details as far as is possible the activities within the movement in response to its expansion in the late 1920s and early 1930s through the successive opening of new branches.

Two developments that reflected this expansion marked the period. First, Taman Siswa began to assert itself vis-a-vis the Indonesian nationalist movment as a whole. Of particular note is its influence on PPPKI, a loose federation of Indonesian nationalist groups. In this context we shall examine how Taman Siswa redefined its role in the People's Movement. Second, Taman Siswa attempted to unite and strengthen its organization. An important milestone in this process, which climaxed in the First National Taman Siswa Congress in July 1930, was the East Java Taman Siswa Conference held in Malang in late January and early February of the same year. We shall examine why and how this attempt was made.

Taman Siswa and PPPKI

The PPPKI was formed by an assembly of representatives of nationalist groups who met in Bandung on 17–18 December 1927.[2] The impetus had been provided by the PNI (Perserikatan Nasional Indonesia, later renamed Partai Nasional Indonesia), which advocated the "unity and solidarity of Indonesia," and which sought through the PPPKI to bring about such unity and solidarity among the groups involved in the nationalist movement. Those who answered the PNI's call to discuss problems relating to the whole Indonesian people and as far as possible to reach a consensus over those problems were the Partai Sarekat Islam (PSI, the successor to Sarekat Islam), Budi Utomo, Pasundan (a Sundanese organization), Kaum Betavi (a Batavian organization), the Sumatran Union, and the Indonesian Study Club of Surabaya, which together with PNI equaled a total of seven organizations. These organizations included all of the major political forces since the collapse of the Indonesian Communist Party (PKI) early in 1927: regional and ethnic groups; the political arm of Islam, represented by PSI; and the nationalistic, intellectual elite of the new age, the PNI, and the Surabaya Study Club.

Thereafter, the PPPKI made appeals for "unity and solidarity" in Jakarta, Bandung, Yogyakarta, Surakarta, Surabaya, and other cities across Java which were strongholds of its constituent organizations, and from 30 August to 2 September 1928 the First PPPKI Congress was convened at Surabaya. This "demonstration congress" attracted 2000 participants to hear speeches by Soetomo, Mr. Iskaq Tjokrohadisoerjo (PNI), Sukarno, Mr. Singgih (Budi Utomo), Ali Sastroamidjojo, and others; and on 31 August Dewantara spoke on educational problems.[3]

Dewantara's speech contained four essential points: that national education meant education for the People, in particular for children rather than adults; that it should aim to foster independent people; that, in consequence, "grants with strings attached" must be refused; and that an independent central foundation should be set up to implement national education. The first three had long been stressed by Taman Siswa, but the fourth was a concrete proposal to the PPPKI by Dewantara that included a call for the establishment of a unitary central body. A similar proposal had been made repeatedly in the early 1900s by Dr. Wahidin Soedirohoesodo, whose ideas had inspired the foundation of Budi Utomo; and the operation of a scholarship organization had eventually become one of Budi Utomo's major activities.[4] Dewantara had thus placed before this federation of nationalist movements an idea long-cherished among Javanese nobility: that of raising a scholarship fund for the benefit of young students.

Following Dewantara on the speaker's podium, a representative of the Muhammadijah schools criticized Dewantara's concept of national education as being rooted in the pre-Islamic past. From the mid-1920s, Muhammadijah had launched into secular education and, besides its religious schools, had opened various "Western-style" schools, which had proven particularly successful in the Central Javanese cities of Yogyakarta, Surakarta, and Pekalongan.[5]

Despite this criticism, the PPPKI congress resolved to appoint a committee to investigate educational problems along the lines of Dewantara's proposals and draw up a program for the implementation of nationalist education.[6] That same day, 31 August, the National Education Committee (Komisi Pengadjaran Kebangsaan) was established, consisting of three members—Mr. Singgih of Budi Utomo, Mr. Soejoedi of PNI, and Dr. Soekiman of PSI—and two advisers—Ali Sastroamidjojo and Dewantara. Singgih, Ali Sastroamidjojo, and Dewantara were all on Taman Siswa's Central Committee, and Soejoedi was also involved with the organization; and thus the National Education Committee of PPPKI became an organ for expressing Taman Siswa's educational ideas at the national level.

Dewantara appears to have long embraced the idea of establishing an educational system based on nationalist principles that could rival the colonial system. Although Taman Siswa was not widely publicized through the 1920s, Dewantara tried on many occasions through contacts with individual nationalist leaders to secure their agreement on the ideas of national education and to establish a unified educational system based on these ideas. He recounts in his memoirs how, in 1921, the year before setting up Taman Siswa, he had attempted to reach a consensus with Soetopo Wonobojo of Budi Utomo and Soerjopranoto of Sarekat Islam over the establishment of a national library. Although this attempt failed, he continued after the founding Taman Siswa to discuss the unification of national education with Dr. Soemowidigdo and Djojosoegito of Muhammadijah, Darsono of the Sarekat Rakjat, and leaders of the PSI.[7] Dewantara and other Taman Siswa leaders must therefore have welcomed the forum for discussion of nationalist education that was created by the establishment of PPPKI.

The PPPKI's National Education Committee twice met at the Taman Siswa headquarters in Yogyakarta, on 3 and 24 March 1929, to discuss concrete proposals for establishing a national education system.[8] The resultant three-point report was presented to PPPKI's Consultative Committee (Madjelis Pertimbangan) on 27 March. It proposed first, that PPPKI should set up a national education center, Concentratie Pengadjaran Nasional (CPN); second, that PPPKI should set up an educational fund (*onderwijsfond*) which would be administered by the CPN; and third, that PPPKI should consider setting up immediately an educational system up to the middle-school level. Each proposal was accompanied by a written statement of opinion bearing the signatures of Soejoedi, Dr. Soekiman, and Singgih.[9]

The proposal to set up the CPN was the embodiment of an idea contained in Dewantara's address to the PPPKI assembly. The statement of opinion asserted, among other things, that the CPN should be set up in Mataram (Yogyakarta); that its task should be to set up national schools, establish an educational foundation, prepare the necessary textbooks and curriculum, and take other available steps; and that anyone who accepted the principles of national education that had been set forth should be free to join CPN.[10]

In 1928 and 1929, PPPKI held various meetings and conferences—notably in Bandung (on 16 December and 25–26 December

1928), Yogyakarta (29–30 March 1929), and Jakarta (1–4 August and 1 September 1929)—where problems facing the nation were discussed, including the abolition of regulations controlling political activity, the improvement of economic conditions, and the promotion of the co-operative movement.[11] These meetings culminated in the Second PPPKI Congress, which was held in Surakarta on 25–27 December 1929 and featured national education among the principal topics on the agenda.[12] During the congress, the National Education Committee's three-point proposal was adopted: PPPKI gave its formal blessing to the institution of the CPN and the establishment of an educational foundation.[13] And in the process, through the PPPKI, Taman Siswa took firm grasp of the reigns of leadership of the educational movement.

The PPPKI was short-lived, however, for it did not survive the emergence of Sukarno and other new leaders and the rapid burgeoning of national awareness. With the arrest of Sukarno and other leaders of the PNI in late 1929, existing differences between member organiza-tions of PPPKI swelled into discord.[14] The main lines of antagonism were drawn between Islamic and non-Islamic forces, and between advocates of cooperation and noncooperation with the colonial govern-ment. So intricate was the balance of these forces that once their anta-gonisms were exposed, it was difficult for them to reunite. For example, PNI was non-Islamic and noncooperatist; PSI was Islamic and non-cooperatist; and Soetomo's Surabaya study club (which from the late 1920s came to function as a political party) was non-Islamic but cooperatist. Even more grave than the antagonisms between the consti-tuent groups of PPPKI were the antagonisms that germinated within the PNI following Sukarno's arrest. These surfaced during 1930, and in late 1931 the PNI split into the Partindo of Sukarno and Sartono, and the PNI-Baru of Hatta and Sjharir. Through this process, PPPKI's activities became increasingly nominal.

These antagonisms and divisions reflected the formation at this time of a succession of political parties, each with its own party rules and platform. At the party level, where the spirit of the age of "unity and solidarity of the Indonesian People" should have found concrete expression, the opposite, discriminatory effect was produced as indi-viual parties became more cohesive internally through the tightening of party organizations and the definition of policies.

Naturally, this situation was reflected within Taman Siswa, although the details are far from clear, as Taman Siswa suspended publication of its journal from late 1929 to mid-1930. Nevertheless, it is evident that Taman Siswa increasingly felt the need to achieve greater internal cohesion by replacing the loose unity it had.hitherto enjoyed with a tighter organizational structure. As a result, while continuing in the role of the main driving force of national education that it had played at the two PPPKI congresses, Taman Siswa systematically gave substance within itself to the ideal of "unity" that it had presented there.

THE EAST JAVA CONFERENCE

In July 1929, the Wonokromo branch of Taman Siswa led by Soedyono Djojopraitno called for the assembly of a national Taman Siswa congress. When the congress eventually assembled in August 1930, a number of important changes had taken place both inside and outside Taman Siswa and the nationalist movement, including the Surakarta congress of PPPKI, Sukarno's arrest and the discord within PPPKI, and a number of events involving Taman Siswa that will be detailed shortly. The most important of these as far as the national congress is concerned was the meeting of the East Java Conference, where the problems facing Taman Siswa and its raison d'être were discussed in detail.

The Conference Agenda

The Conferentie Taman Siswa Djawa-Timur convened in Malang from 29 January to 1 February 1930. Held at the Taman Siswa school in the Jagalan district of the city, it was attended by about fifty representatives of fifteen schools in East Java, all but the Genteng, Kraksaan, Ambulu, and Mojoagung schools, and by members of the Supreme Council from Yogyakarta.[15]

Nine items were on the agenda. Of these, four were related to organization (*organisatie*): (1) Procedure for opening new schools (proposed for discussion by the Wonokromo, Malang, Kencong, and Ciluring schools), (2) the establishment of a foundation and a committee of inquiry (proposed by Porong, Tanggul, and Bangkalan), (3) Taman Siswa's attitude towards politics (proposed by Pacarkeling), and (4) teachers' problems (proposed by Jember, Kencong, and Porong). Two more were related to education: (5) curriculum (*leerplan*) (proposed by Surabaya, Tanggul, Wonokromo, Kencong, and Bangkalan), and (6) teaching of the chronicles (*babad*) (proposed by Surabaya). The remaining three were miscellaneous topics: (7) Institution of holidays (proposed by Porong), (8) publication of a children's newspaper (*kinder-courant*) (proposed by Pacarkeling and Tanggul), and (9) construction of a children's holiday camp.

The conference opened on the evening of 29 January under the chairmanship of Poeger, the Malang representative. Because the delegation from Yogyakarta had not yet arrived, discussion began with the less important items (8) and (9).

The publication of a children's newspaper was approved as a measure which would further language education and promote cooperation. Isbandhi of the Pacarkeling branch would make preparations for publication of 250 copies weekly in the Javanese ngoko. Each branch would provide financial backing to cover expenses, which were estimated at ten florins monthly.[16] Carrying news stories and other reading matter, the newspaper would fulfill an important role in schools as a substitute for a library, which virtually none of the schools in East Java had at that time.

The idea of a children's holiday camp (*kindervacantie-kolonie*) was explained by Safioedin Soerjopoetro, who represented the Jember school. It involved setting up, with the cooperation of various nationalist groups, a recreation area like those run by the Dutch. This proposal was also accepted, with the resolve to instigate the construction of a camp in Malang.[17]

The second session opened on the evening of 30 January, again under Poeger's chairmanship, with the welcoming of Dewantara, Soenarjati, and Sudarminta, who had arrived from Yogyakarta. Discussion focused on the question of organizing Taman Siswa, and through Dewantara's speech followed by a question period, and Dewantara's advice (*nasehat*) on proposals made by the branch representatives, problems pertaining to items (1) to (3) were covered.

Organization and Funding

Dewantara's opinions on organization, stated at the conference, were as follows.[18]

(1) If Taman Siswa's principles were followed faithfully, the question of organization could not arise. Essentially, Taman Siswa emphasized the spiritual unity of man; and organization suffocated the spirit, crushed individuality. This danger of organization was also clear from the fact that European organizations generally became "mechanical" (*machinaal*). For this reason, the question of organization had never hitherto been considered within Taman Siswa.

(2) However, the Supreme Council had been wrong in thinking that the status quo would continue, and was forced to conclude that the organization of Taman Siswa was necessary. Firstly, Taman Siswa had grown very rapidly and now had many branches; and secondly, many of those branches still did not understand Taman Siswa's principles, which consequently had been contravened.

(3) For these reasons, the Supreme Council had now started to con-

sider the organization of Taman Siswa. This did not mean, however, the immediate establishment of regulations: organization should be carried out only as far as was necessary.

Dewantara's speech stated plainly the changes that had arisen within Taman Siswa between the mid-1920s and the early 1930s (the same arguments were repeated some six months later in the prospectus announcing the opening of the national congress). It also indicated that the Supreme Council was considering releasing Dewantara from Yogyakarta to allow him to assume command of the whole Taman Siswa movement.

Following Dewantara, Soedyono of the Wonokromo branch spoke. Making special mention of the relationship between Taman Siswa and PPPKI, he stressed that because Taman Siswa was due to become a constituent part of the CPN national education center (whose institution had just been formally agreed upon at the Second PPPKI Congress in Surakarta), it should strive to organize itself before joining the CPN.

Like Soedyono, many of the Taman Siswa activists in East Java were unknown youths of humbler birth and more than a decade younger than the Selasa Kliwon group. They brought to Taman Siswa the spirit of a new age, and at the same time, they found in the spirit of Taman Siswa guiding principles for their lives.[19] What Taman Siswa did for them was to relocate in the framework of Javanese culture a new, universal ideal of man that denied the role of the old nobility of Mataram—they were being mobilized lock, stock, and barrel to support the colonial bureaucracy—and the legitimacy of their palace culture, which had become debilitated through continued "involution."

It was for such reasons that Taman Siswa's appeal extended beyond the boundaries of Central Java, particularly those of the principalities (*vorstenlanden*) of Yogyakarta and Surakarta, where Javanese aristocratic culture still predominated. And while attracting widespread support among nationalists across Java, Taman Siswa won greatest acceptance in East Java, where the Mojokerto branch led by Soedyono was particularly active throughout the late 1920s and early 1930s.

The second generation of Taman Siswa, as typified by Soedyono, lacked the common origins and common experiences of the Selasa Kliwon group, experiences which included early involvement in Budi Utomo and residence in The Hague. Rather, they were bound by their common perception of the spirit of the age and their common interest in actualizing that spirit through the activities of Taman Siswa. The more widely Taman Siswa spread and the more the various other political groups assumed a semblance of organization, the more they required that their own unity in a single coherent organization should be guaranteed and, if possible, that their comradeship should continually be internalized. In response to the initiative of the young activists of East Java, the Selasa Kliwon group led by Dewantara attended the East Java Conference and eventually went on to sponsor the national congress.

Following the speeches by Dewantara and Soedyono, the conference embarked upon the main issue of organization. Discussion began with the question of the Supreme Council's authority. Several proposals were made, all of them addressing the question of how to deal with those schools across the country that deviated from Taman Siswa's principles, how to effect a self-purification (*membersihkan badan sendiri*). One proposal was to establish a standing inspectorate (*inspectie*), another to vest certain powers in the Supreme Council.

Kadiroen[20] of the Malang branch suggested that the Supreme Council should have the right of censure (*recht van afkeuring*); Safioedin, the Jember representative, went further in proposing that it should be given the right to intervene (*ingrijpen*). The Bangkalan representative Ismadi proposed that, in view of the frequent abuse of the right to self-determination (*zelfbeschikkingsrecht*), the Supreme Council should be given several powers; and a similar opinion was offered by Ngoesoemanadji of Ciluring. Finally, the Kencong representative Soekadi proposed that administration and finance should in general be centralized, and the conference appointed him to draw up detailed proposals on this line for the national congress.[21]

The last to speak on organization was Dewantara, who welcomed the fact that discussion at the East Java Conference had proceeded along lines compatible with the Supreme Council's thinking, and that when the time came to draw up the Taman Siswa's regulations, three points would cover the essentials:[22]

(1) If you are contemplating a certain act, first search your own feelings and thoughts [*perasaan dan fikiran*].
(2) If you need a model, look to the customs [*adat-istiadat*] current among the People.
(3) If you still cannot decide, ask an older friend.

The discussion then moved to the second topic on the agenda, the establishment of a foundation. The Porong representative proposed that a central foundation be set up under the administration and supervision of the Supreme Council; and in conclusion it was accepted that each branch should contribute five percent of its gross revenue each month to this central fund.

Educational and Political Movements

The third topic on the agenda was Taman Siswa's relationship to political activities. Discussion took place deep in the night, from 3:00 to 4:00 A.M., having been preceded by a two-hour preliminary conference of representatives that began after the completion of the second item on the agenda at 1:00 A.M.[23] What took place at this preliminary conference is not clear, but in the conference proper, discussion focused on Taman Siswa's relationship with the Surabaya branch of the PNI.

First, Isbandhi of the Pacarkeling branch reported that the Surabaya chapter of PNI had decided to ban admission of Taman Siswa teachers to the party, and he raised the question of Taman Siswa's response. A number of delegates, including Soewarno from Porong, Safioedin from Jember, and Soenjoto from Malang, proposed asking the Surabaya branch of PNI to explain itself.

On the question of political involvement, opinions differed: Safioedin held that Taman Siswa's objectives would be realized through active participation in a political movement, while Soenjoto argued that political and educational movements should be kept separate and that each individual should choose to become involved with one or the other.[24] Taman Siswa's stance had hitherto been that an individual was free to engage in political activities provided he did not bring politics into the classroom. Soewarno and Safioedin believed that Taman Siswa should maintain this stance.

Discussion was then adjourned to the next day without a conclusion being reached. Immediately before the conference rose, Dewantara offered the following opinion.[25]

> Taman Siswa has so far never laid down prohibitions of this or that on the understanding that teachers would take care not to bring politics into the classroom. The most fitting attitude for the teacher is that of the *pinandita*. That is, he should distance himself from politics. Politics is the place for the satria (*kesjatria*). However, I am also attracted to Safioedin's proposal, and wish that we should maintain our original stance lest it be thought that we are making concessions. But we should agree that heads of schools alone should not be involved in politics.

Pinandita mentioned here meant "pandita," the teachers who, as Dewantara himself had discussed in 1928 (see chapter 3), in ancient times had headed asrama, pondok, pawijatan, and other schools, and who were believed to reveal the secrets of religion and the universe. The satria, of course, were those at the hub of the kingdom who would go out to fight. In other words, Dewantara drew a clear distinction between the satria of the political world and the pandita of the nonpolitical world, evoking the traditional relationship between rulers and intelligentsia in Java.

The discussion of political activities was taken up again on the third day of the conference. Before the debate, Dewantara reiterated the burden of his speech of the previous evening and asked the conference to resolve that restrictions be placed only on the heads of schools. There then followed a proposal by Kadiroen that delegates be asked to express their opinions freely. The outcome of the debate, however, was the adoption of a resolution that maintained Taman Siswa's existing policy and followed Dewantara's wishes:[26]

> Taman Siswa teachers may freely join the political group of their choice. They must bear in mind, however, not to identify education with politics. Heads of schools will be required not to become leaders of political groups.

Other Problems

The final session of the conference ran from 9:00 A.M. to 6:00 P.M. on 1 February and dealt with the topics not yet covered. First to be discussed was the fourth item on the agenda, the question of teachers. The problems raised were all practical matters bearing on the running of the Taman Siswa schools: (1) whether a check should be made of whether the teachers at each school were abiding by Taman Siswa's principles; (2) what to do about the shortage of teachers; (3) how to determine teachers' pay; and (4) how to maintain the same quality of education throughout the schools.[27]

On none of these questions did the conference reach a consensus. On the first, opinion was equally divided for and against a proposal by the Porong branch that a committee be established to check on teachers. On the second, debate centered on Poeger's idea that the expansion of Taman Siswa be temporarily halted, and on the proposal by Safioedin that teacher-training schools like that in Yogyakarta be established in other large cities such as Surabaya and Malang. On the question of teachers' pay, it was suggested that this should be determined according to the individual teacher's circumstances, with, for example, a monthly stipend of 145 florins for those with one child, 160 for those with two children, and an extra 5 florins for each additional child. Most delegates were in favor of the existing system, however, which left the decision to individual schools, since circumstances in each school differed. On the fourth question, debate centered on Safioedin's proposal that teachers should be circulated between Yogyakarta and the branch schools, and on the establishment of a uniform curriculum. The last word again belonged to Dewantara, who stressed the urgency of establishing a central fund in order to resolve these problems.[28]

The conference next deliberated the Kencong branch's proposal that Dutch be struck from the curriculum. It was the contention of Soekadi, the Kencong delegate, that the Dutch language was unnecessary to the establishment of a true Indonesian school. While this opinion gained no support, there was no objection whatsoever to Soekadi abolishing Dutch language instruction at the Kencong school. Many delegates expressed the fear, however, that should this proposal be adopted the school would attract fewer pupils.[29]

Dewantara's opinion, offered in conclusion, was that while man did not live by bread alone, bread was necessary for man to live. At present, Dutch was still necessary as a means of livelihood; and for them the use of Dutch was unavoidable. They could not be idealists living "with their heads in the clouds" (*nglangut di awang-awang*).[30] This was the pragmatic side of Dewantara. He was concerned also with the "practical benefits" of the Taman Siswa schools.

At this point the conference returned to the question of organization, with a debate on the topic of the school board (*instituutraad*). This also began with Soekadi, who complained that in many schools the board acted not as administrators (*pemangku*) but as overlords (*heerschlichaam*), with the result that teachers had difficulty in carrying out their duties. Many of the delegates agreed. As a result it was decided to petition the Supreme Council urgently to provide a clear statement of the functions and authority of the school board. At the same time, to investigate conditions in the schools concerned, two new members were appointed to Taman Siswa's East Java Council (Raad Djawa-Timoer): Sadikin of Mojokerto and Anwari of Surabaya joined the existing members, Soedyono, Poeger, and Notodipoetro.[31]

Delegates next turned their attention to item (6) on the agenda: the teaching materials used in Taman Siswa schools.[32] First, based on Dewantara's advice, the Surabaya branch proposed that a variety of Javanese chronicles be used as materials for teaching Javanese culture. The question of preparing textbooks for use in Taman Siswa schools was also debated, and a decision was reached to raise this question to the Supreme Council. For the present, the policy of allowing each school to choose its own textbooks would be maintained.

The final topic addressed by the conference was item (7) on the agenda, that of holidays. Soewarno of the Porong school proposed that the Taman Siswa school holidays be standardized. The matter was placed entirely in Dewantara's hands, and in response he proposed that Taman Siswa should have 255 teaching days and 111 holidays annually. These 111 days should include the end of the Fast, the Prophet's birthday and other days in the religious calendar, days considered holy in Javanese belief, and 8 February, the day Dipanegara died. However, the birthdays of contemporary figures, even monarchs, should not be holidays: no man's achievements should be evaluated during his life.[33] With this, at six o'clock in the evening, the conference ended.

The Significance of the Conference

The resolutions passed at the East Java Conference made the conference an important determinant of future directions in the organization of Taman Siswa and the definition of its character.[34] The organization of Taman Siswa meant centralization of its administrative system and the securing of a central fund to ensure that centralization. The idea of a central educational fund had originally been proposed at the PPPKI congress; and now Taman Siswa had adopted the idea of formulating a more definite plan for its own centralization.

On political activity, Taman Siswa cited as its ideal the pandita-satria dichotomy, but at the same time was ambivalent in its pursuit. The gap between ideal and reality was neatly bridged by means of "implemental skill."[35] And it was Dewantara who initiated the exercise of such skill in, for example, his extremely realistic attitude toward the inclusion of Dutch in the curriculum.

Dewantara also showed an inclination to resolve the question of organization through the network of human relationships rather than by instituting regulations. The three conditions he cited as basic principles for legislation (first look to yourself, next to popular custom, then to someone older) laid emphasis on such relationships, pointing to his belief that "order and tranquility" could be realized on the basis of these principles, and that Javanese culture contained the potential to make this possible. These beliefs were none other than the ideology of the Selasa Kliwon group.

On the other hand, the East Java Conference showed clearly that matters had progressed beyond these opinions of Dewantara. The problems raised were wide-ranging, from the qualities and political activities of the teachers, to the friction between teachers and school boards, the policy differences between schools, the shortage of textbooks and teaching materials, and the lack of uniformity in the curri-

cula of different schools. Regarding all these problems, the delegates of
the East Java schools agreed on the need for some kind of institutionalization. What they had in mind was not the building around Dewantara of a network of people capable of "implemental skill," but organization through regulations. Underlying their attitude was a rigorism
that required applying the rules equally to all.

Dewantara's Speech

One further matter that deserves mention in regard to the East Java
Conference is a speech delivered by Dewantara on 2 February, the day
after the conference. Speaking on the theme of national education (*Pengadjaran Nasional*), Dewantara made three major points: that Taman
Siswa was an educational system of the People; that it was concerned
with the cultural side of the nationalist movement; and that it held
as a principle the idea of overcoming the deficiencies of Western
education.[36]

On the first point, Dewantara stated that Taman Siswa was an
educational institution established for the benefit of the People and in
response to the needs of the People, and that its teachers were resolved
to devote themselves to the People. The spirit of Taman Siswa—of
devotion to improving the lot (*nasib*) of the People—had found support
not just in Java but in all parts of Indonesia. This meant that the People themselves felt an even greater desire for education. The colonial
government, on the other hand, had failed to provide adequate educational opportunities for the People, and what educational institutions
there were did not serve the People's interests.

On the second point, Dewantara argued that because its highest
priority was to serve the interests of the People, Taman Siswa had a
role to play in the People's Movement, whose objectives it shared. In
this sense, Taman Siswa was a part of the People's Movement, like
Budi Utomo at the time of its founding, Sarekat Islam, and the PNI.
However, just as man was made of body and soul, and approached
wholeness through the harmonious development of both aspects, so the
movement had two aspects which must be developed in concert. Of
these, the political groups emphasized the material livelihood (*penghi-
dupan*) of the People, while the cultural groups emphasized their spiritual life (*kehidupan*). Because groups on both sides must advance hand
in hand, all groups from Budi Utomo to the PNI were Taman Siswa's
"friends" (*kantja*).

This led Dewantara to Taman Siswa's relationship to politics,
which he saw in the following terms.[37]

Political movements aim to secure various rights, which can be likened to the task of building a fence (*pagar*) to protect the People's interests. But there are also duties to be performed within that fence. These are the duties of the social movements.

Taman Siswa hopes to become a farmer (*paman tani*) working inside this fence. He will plant seed there for the People. Then, in later days, the People may reap the fruits that will let them live their lives, particularly their spiritual lives, more forcefully.

This imagery of the fence and the farmer would hereafter be used repeatedly in the Taman Siswa movement.

The third point covered by Dewantara concerned Western education, which he claimed was grounded in the principles of rule (*regeering*), discipline (*tucht*), and order (*orde*). These unquestionably had a bad influence on the spiritual life of a child. The child grew up waiting for orders and fearing discipline. And as an adult he would be unable to act without being coerced or commanded. If Taman Siswa copied this method, it would be unable to bring up people with personality (*persoonlijkheid*). Taman Siswa's education should not be like the Dutch opvoeding, but should be called by the Javanese terms, *panggoelawentah*, *momong*, *among*, or *ngemong*. Strictly speaking, the Dutch words for education, *opvoeding* or *pedagogiek*, represented concepts that could not be translated into Javanese. Javanese education was based on "order and tranquility" (*tata-tentrem*) rather than compulsion, discipline, and order. Its aims were to watch over children so that they might develop naturally, to guide them in the proper way before they made mistakes, and to foster independent personalities.

In conclusion, Dewantara offered the people three maxims as "charms" (*fatwa*, *djimat*): *tetap, antep dan mantep*; *ngandel, kendel dan bandel*; and *neng, ning, nung dan nang*. He explained that the first meant that a man's value was determined by whether he was resolute in thought and spirit. *Tetap* and *antep* both indicated "steadiness," a quality which would give rise to *mantep*, "perseverance." The second meant that faith gave man a firm position, bringing "courage" (*kendel*) and determination in the face of adversity. The third meant that if a man was pure in thought and spirit, his heart would be bright, and this would lend him strength. With "purity" (*neng*), "brightness" (*ning*), and "strength" (*nung*), "victory" (*nang*) was assured.[38]

Each of these maxims was rhythmical, and by reciting them, Dewantara claimed, one could achieve harmony (*tata*) and tranquility (*tentrem*) of spirit. They were called "charms" (*djimat*) probably because they were regarded as sutra or spells.

This speech by Dewantara contains important indications of his thinking in 1930. The keynote of his speech was, as in 1922 at the time of its founding, that Taman Siswa rested on rejection of the colonial education system; but now Dewantara stressed Taman Siswa's kerakjatan ("People-orientedness") and expressed confidence in Taman Siswa's part in the People's Movement.

Secondly, Dewantara clarified Taman Siswa's mission as a cultural movement in relation to the political movements. All those who would build the fence, be they the Javanese aristocrats of Budi Utomo, the Islamic internationalists of Sarekat Islam, or the radical nationalists of the PNI, were "friends" of Taman Siswa. That he chose the Javanese word kantja to express this friendship was not because his audience was entirely Javanese but because of the word's connotations of "comrades who share the same fate," like husband and wife.

Thirdly, he abandoned his former practice of explaining Taman Siswa's educational philosophy in terms of the ideologies of the Montessori and Fröbel schools, asserting rather that Javanese and Western education should be understood in terms of different paradigms (the terms for education were, in his words, "mutually untranslatable"). That the three maxims Dewantara proposed at the end of his speech were "sutra" solely by virtue of being expressed in Javanese was also a striking illustration of the Javanese structures of understanding.

While these changes in Dewantara's thinking naturally derived from the changed situation of the People's Movement, they were also reflected in his audiences. In his speeches of the early 1920s (for example, his 1922 speech on the inauguration of Taman Siswa, or his speech of January 1923), the broader audience to which Dewantara addressed himself, made up of those he assumed to be the "consumers" of his educational ideas, was fully conversant with things Western. Thus he used Dutch to explain various concepts and advanced his own ideas with reference to Western thought. In Malang, on the other hand, though his audience was again made up of people associated with Taman Siswa, he spoke plainly in terms of Javanese concepts and elicited little concern over how to interpret them in Dutch.

The difference in these two styles of speaking reflected a shift in Dewantara's assumed audience (or those who should be assumed to be his audience) from an elite group including the colonial government, native officials, and the intelligentsia of prijaji background, to the People. In terms of political groups, it can be said to show a shift from the bearers of Budi Utomo to the membership of the PNI.

Such was the form in which Dewantara stressed Taman Siswa's kerakjatan. Kerakjatan was an important concept which expressed the spirit of the age and afforded the nationalist movement the legitimacy to overthrow the Beamtenstaat. From this point on, Taman Siswa's task would focus increasingly on how to incorporate the concept of kerakjatan into the paradigm of tata-tentrem presented by the Selasa Kliwon group. If it could succeed in this task, it would be able to establish its own legitimacy within the People's Movement. Such was clearly in Dewantara's mind when he said that Taman Siswa had a role to play in the People's Movement.

THE NATIONAL CONGRESS OF 1930

The East Java Conference had resolved that the Taman Siswa schools scattered across the archipelago should be organized, thereby bringing greater cohesion to Taman Siswa. This resolution, however, affected not only East Java but raised matters that required the common understanding of all concerned with Taman Siswa. This point was reiterated in the Supreme Council's announcement of the national congress.

The Announcement of the National Congress

On 1 July 1930 an announcement was issued in Dewantara's name as chief secretary of the Supreme Council. It stated that the congress would take place in Yogyakarta on the eight days from August 6 to 13, and recommended that members examine the proposed agenda of topics for discussion in advance, adding that the membership of Taman Siswa included school leaders (board members), teachers, and parents.[39] Separately, a list of regulations was issued, setting forth that the costs of participation should be borne by the individual branches, that the Yogyakarta headquarters would arrange food and lodging for participants during the congress, and that proxies would be admitted only if they carried proper credentials.[40]

Following these procedural announcements, the Supreme Council issued a lengthy prospectus for the congress. It covered the aims of the congress, the principles of Taman Siswa, a report on the East Java Conference, where topics similar to those tabled for the national congress had been discussed, and a list of topics for discussion proposed by the Supreme Council, together with the request that each branch should discuss the contents of the prospectus.[41]

The aims of the congress were presented in roughly the following terms.

(1) Taman Siswa had grown to the point that it now embraced fifty-two schools. In just the past few months, several tens of people had made personal sacrifices to contribute to the running of Taman Siswa schools,

several tens of people had similarly volunteered to become teachers, and several thousand parents had sent their children to Taman Siswa schools. At such a time it was extremely important and meaningful that people concerned with Taman Siswa should meet together under one roof.

(2) There were still many people who did not fully understand Taman Siswa's intentions and objectives. Consequently, the coming congress must be made a forum firstly for the spread of Taman Siswa's ideals among those involved, and secondly for the demonstration of these ideals to all those interested in national education.

(3) At the same time the congress must aim to purify Taman Siswa itself, to rectify its errors, and to discover a new route forward.

The statement of these second and third aims suggests the underlying presence of at least two real problems.

The first was that the expansion of Taman Siswa's sphere of activity had entailed various conflicts and confrontations, and criticisms had been leveled at Taman Siswa that its leaders felt obliged to refute. Internal friction had also reared its head, being blamed, for example, for the drop in the numbers of teachers and pupils at the Slawi school between 1924 and 1929.[42]

Friction and misunderstanding between Taman Siswa and the outside had arisen during the time of the PPPKI and the moves to establish a national education system. In April 1929, for example, a report appeared that, contrary to reports in the "European press," Taman Siswa had no intention to sell government lottery tickets as a means to secure funds.[43] In July the same year *Obor* had carried an article critical of Dewantara, to which Taman Siswa offered a rebuttal.[44] This newspaper was published by Soerjopranoto, Dewantara's elder brother and the founder of the Adhi Dharma school, which was then being run by Soekiman, chairman of the PSI. Then, in May 1930, a rumor circulated that Dewantara had withdrawn from the leadership of Taman Siswa and had been replaced by Sudarminta.[45] Taman Siswa also came under severe criticism from Muhammadijah over an internal incident of "impure association," as a result of which, in March 1930, two teachers and one female student had been expelled from Taman Siswa. Muhammadijah blamed the incident squarely on the fact that Taman Siswa had introduced the idea of "Western-style free association" into Indonesia's society of pious Muslims.[46]

These incidents, while apparently trifling, may well have spurred the Taman Siswa leadership to conclude that the time was ripe to strengthen their organization with a coherent set of regulations.

The second problem was more basic: how to define Taman Siswa's relationship to the political movement. This point had been taken up at the East Java Conference, where Taman Siswa had confirmed its official stance of being an educational movement clearly distinct from political groups. Its politically active members were deemed to be acting in a "private" capacity and were expected not to bring politics into the classroom. Nevertheless, Taman Siswa formed an important channel between Budi Utomo and the PNI, and many of its leaders were members of these parties, often in the leading positions.

The colonial government had meanwhile grown increasingly wary of the political role that Taman Siswa was playing, and from the late 1920s, when the PNI and PPPKI were formed, its fears were aggravated. From 1932, the confrontation between the government and Taman Siswa would become decisive. This confrontation focused constantly on the school in Bandung, where the government had been especially sensitive to the climate since as early as 1923.[47] One reason was that the forerunner of this Taman Siswa school had been run by Sarekat Rakjat; another was that Bandung was the stronghold of Sukarno's PNI.

In early 1930, the Bandung branch became the focus of the question of Taman Siswa's relationship to political movements and of problems concerning Taman Siswa and colonial authority. First, in February 1930, parents in Bandung complained that the school had ceased to function as a place of education. They claimed that there were too few teachers, and that everyone concerned with the school belonged to PNI, so that Taman Siswa appeared to be a branch of PNI. The school countered that in fact it had sufficient staff, and that Taman Siswa itself belonged to no other group whatsoever. The head of the school at this time was Soekemi, a founding member of PNI and a continuing activist in the party. He and Sukarno, who had also had a hand in the founding of the Taman Siswa school, deeply influenced the staff and board of the school. The parental criticism was, in effect, that because of this strong political orientation education was being neglected.

In the midst of this internal wrangle, late in February 1930, the colonial government arrested three of the school's teachers, and early in March issued a decision in the name of the governor of West Java banning them from teaching. The stated reason for the decision was that "they had engaged in political activities in school as members of the PNI," although clearly it was related to the arrest of Sukarno and others the previous year.[48]

Even though it could monitor the curricula of schools, like Taman Siswa, that it did not subsidize, the colonial government had no powers to prevent their establishment or to require licensing of their teachers. Consequently it did not interfere with the foundation, staff recruitment, curricula, facilities, or other aspects of "nonsubsidized education" (*het nietgesubsidieerd onderwijs*). The schools involved were referred to as "wild schools" (*wilde scholen*), implying that they were of low standards and of no concern to the government. I shall return to this discussion in more detail in chapter 6.

The arrest of the Bandung teachers as a threat to the "order and peace" (*orde en rust*) of colonial society further convinced Taman Siswa headquarters of the need to reassert Taman Siswa's principles and to clarify its stance with respect to the colonial government. In particular, it had to compare the government's *orde en rust* with the "order and tranquility" (*tertib dan damai*; *tata tentrem*) that had been its "loftiest ideal" since its founding in 1922, by tracing to their sources the ideas on which they rested. In other words, Taman Siswa had both to conceptualize and to achieve within itself an "order and tranquility" to rival that of the Beamtenstaat. The two problems that Taman Siswa faced, the first of overcoming internal dissension in the branch schools, countering external criticisms, and strengthening internal regulations, the second of clarifying its relationships to political movements and the colonial authorities, ultimately came down to the question of how Taman Siswa should build its own "order and tranquility" both ideologically and in reality. How, in other words, after its "eight years of silence," should Taman Siswa organize itself in order to ensure cohesion to the center? This was the burden of the announcement of the national congress.

Procedure and Opening Ceremony

The Taman Siswa National Congress opened as scheduled on 6 August 1930 in Yogyakarta. Forty-two branches sent delegates, including the Medan and Tebingtinggi (Deli) branches in Sumatra, two branches sent notices of absence, and two absented themselves without notification (Ambulu and Probolinggo).

Before the opening ceremony, on the morning of 6 August, a preliminary meeting was held. Delegates' credentials were checked, and as a result Tondowidjojo was refused admission as he lacked a formal document from the Talun branch, while Kadiroen was admitted to represent the Malang branch when confirmation of his credentials was received from that branch by telegram.

Small adjustments were then made to the order of proceedings, and there was discussion on procedure.[49] It was decided that: (1) Some discussions would be closed to the public, others open. The former would take place at Dewantara's home, the latter at Djojodipro's home. (2) The congress secretariat would consist of five members: Kadiroen,

Soekemi, Sajoga, Sudarminta, and Dewantara. (3) Resolutions made by ballot would require at least three-quarters of the total vote to be carried. Even motions that had been carried could be amended with the approval of a three-quarters' majority. (4) Each branch would have one vote. If a branch had sent several delegates, that branch would forfeit its vote if the delegates were not unanimous.

Dewantara then closed the preliminary meeting with a brief statement of the congress's purposes.[50] He stressed that as Taman Siswa grew, it must establish not only a spiritual unity but also a unity of organization. To achieve organizational unity, Taman Siswa needed the "forces of youth" (*tenaga muda*) that had newly joined the movement, and the congress's primary aim should therefore be to devise a means to organize Taman Siswa by absorbing these forces. As they had shown at the East Java Conference, these forces had the will and the vitality to systematize Taman Siswa's centripetalism. The hope that Dewantara placed in the "forces of youth" was expressed by the presence of both Kadiroen, who had skillfully kept the minutes of the East Java Conference, and Sajoga, who had just graduated from the Taman Siswa school in Yogyakarta and was literally a trueborn "disciple of Taman Siswa, on the congress secretariat."[51]

The third and fourth procedural items, by which motions would be carried with the approval of three-quarters of the delegates, appears to have been a compromise between the customary decision by consensus (*mupakat*) and the democratic system; but it was also a formula that allowed the possibility of arbitration by powerful leaders.

The opening ceremony took place in public on the evening of 6 August.[52] Among the many present were several Dutchmen, including Dr. Pigeaud, who was director of the Java Instituut and the leading Dutch scholar of Javanese culture, and Van der Plas, then an official in the office of the adviser on Netherlands-Indies affairs, who was later involved behind the scenes in the maneuvering to restore the colony to the Dutch during the war of independence that followed Japanese military rule.[53]

After a gamelan performance, Dewantara rose to greet the assembly. He noted that its expansion to encompass fifty-two branches showed that Taman Siswa was growing amidst the Indonesian People (*Rakjat Indonesia*), and that its principles, not being rooted in a narrow regionalism, were becoming widely accepted by the entire nation. Discussions at the congress would, he expected, focus on the problem of organization (*organisasi*), with the object of achieving the unity within Taman Siswa that had been discussed earlier at the East Java Conference. It was important in considering organization that there should be no conflict with Taman Siswa's principles, particularly the fundamental right of self-determination (*zelfbeschikkingsrecht*), which would be greatly obstructed by Western-style organization. Here, as at the preliminary meeting, Dewantara asserted the need to meet simultaneously two mutually opposed requirements: to achieve organization and to check that organization.

Following Dewantara, Pronowidigdo, the vice-president of the Supreme Council, greeted the assembly. Then came a demonstration of Javanese dance by Taman Siswa students, which is said to have impressed the audience deeply. *Wasita* reported that "what was seen were children whose lives were yet unsullied [*wutuh*]."[54]

Ever since 1922, *wutuh* had been a central theme in Dewantara's references to the evils of colonial rule. His fears had found their most poignant expression in his article, "Associatie antara Timur dan Barat," discussed in the previous chapter, where he charged that colonial rule was destroying the spirit of Indonesians. Under colonial rule, naked hedonism and materialism had permeated society, with the result that traditional ethics and morality had been undermined and the traditional culture was on the road to collapse. To halt the decline, efforts had to be made to rebuild the culture through self-denial and self-discipline. Only when these efforts had succeeded would a basis exist for association between Eastern and Western cultures.

Among Taman Siswa's proclaimed educational goals was that of creating bearers of a "pure" (*wutuh*) culture, and the opening of the congress provided it with a favorable opportunity to demonstrate to a wider audience, through the performance of song and dance by its students, the nature of this goal and the fact that success was being achieved. In the mid-1910s, while in Holland, Soewardi and Soerjopoetro had given performances of Javanese music and expositions of Javanese culture at the request of the Dutch; now, they were succeeding across Java in raising others in the mold of their younger selves.

The remainder of the first evening was taken up with congratulatory messages from the representatives of various groups.[55] Mr. Singgih representing Budi Utomo praised Taman Siswa's activities, stating that only a nation that respected its own culture could survive and develop as a nation. He was followed by Sajuti Loebis of the Partai Sarekat Islam Indonesia (PSII) and representatives of the Mataram branch of the teacher's union, Persatuan Guru Hindia Belanda (PGHB), the Perkumpulan Seni Krido Bekso Wiromo (an association of performing artists), and the Katholieka Wandawa (the Catholic Fraternity)—all of whom congratulated Taman Siswa on its national congress and expressed their wishes for its future development. Replies were made for Taman Siswa by Soedarso of the Cianjur branch, Manadi of Bandung, Abdoel Gani of Jakarta, Ismadi of Bangkalan, and others. Finally, at 1:30 A.M., the opening ceremony ended.

The Taman Siswa National Congress began the following day, 7 August, and ended a week later with a picnic at Kaliurang and a *wayang kulit* performance. During the week, debate centered on the topics proposed in the prospectus, and after some amendment, resolutions were adopted establishing Taman Siswa's principles, its various bodies and their authority; and various leaders and committee members were elected. The motions adopted by the congress were to shape the framework of Taman Siswa from the 1930s and determine the substance of its activities. The resolutions affecting organization in particular showed that Taman Siswa had entered a new stage of activity. We shall look first at the debate on Taman Siswa's statutes (*statuut*).

The Statutes

Proceedings began at 9:00 A.M. on 7 August with a closed session chaired by Pronowidigdo.[56] First to speak was Tjokrodirdjo, who spoke of the familial unity of Taman Siswa.[57] He pointed out that the Mataram branch had made sacrifices in bearing a large part of the burden of the overall running of the Taman Siswa schools. In this sense the Mataram branch had carried out the duties and responsibilities of an elder brother towards its younger siblings. Now, however, with many of those siblings reaching the same maturity as the elder brother, their relationship should become that of fellow adults. "Bonds grounded in authority" (*wengku-winengku*) must be forged like those operating in a close-knit family. This should be the ethos underpinning Taman Siswa's organization. The union resulting from this organization should be neither social nor political, but a union in which people could empathize (*dirasakan*) with each other from heart to heart (*ati sama ati*).

Tjokrodirdjo's speech on organization (*organisasi*) was thus pervaded by references to familial relationships, the first time within Taman Siswa that the concept of family (*keluarga*) had been championed. This concept first found expression in the context of Taman Siswa's organization, with which it was linked inseparably as parts of the same whole, and over which it always occupied the superordinate position.

Next Dewantara rose to speak.[58]

> My feeling now is that in order further to protect and foster Taman Siswa, which is my own child, I should entrust it to the National Congress. At the recent East Java Conference an extremely desirable course was set, which should be fully respected. As far as Taman Siswa's principles [*azas*] are concerned, however, I do not wish to see any changes, for it is on these

principles that Taman Siswa was born and has grown to the present day. Without these, Taman Siswa's existence would become meaningless.

In these words, Dewantara declared the "inviolability" of Taman Siswa's seven principles, which he had proposed when the first school opened in 1922 and had elaborated the following year. This attitude had pervaded the thinking of Taman Siswa's leadership since the days of Selasa Kliwon.

The congress then proceeded to debate general matters pertaining to Taman Siswa's statutes.[59] The first article of the statutes was a statement of the seven principles, and after several questions over the wording, it was adopted unanimously as set out in the prospectus and as Dewantara had requested at the start of the congress. Thereby, the principles that had been presented in 1923 were readopted, with slight changes in phrasing, by the Taman Siswa National Congress.

Next, Articles 2 through 7 of the statutes were adopted after partial amendment, and were as follows.[60]

Article 2: Name. The name shall be Perguruan Nasional TAMAN-SISWA berpusat di Mataram (Taman Siswa National Education Centered on Mataram).

Article 3: Characteristics. Taman Siswa is an independent body (*badan merdeka*) in almost the same sense as a religious institution (*wakaf*), and a self-supporting organization in almost the same sense as a foundation (*stichting*). This does not mean, however, a government-approved foundation. An "independent body" is not one owned by a particular individual or group but a body operated independently on the basis of regulations that have been established with common approval.

Article 4: External form (*Badan Lahir*). Taman Siswa National Education is a body made up of a unity of branches, and shall be organized on the basis of regulations decided by the national congress (*Konggeres*) or by referendum.

Article 5: Internal bonds (*Badan Batin*). Taman Siswa is a great sacred family (*keluarga besar jang sutji*) tied by the bonds of its principles. No alteration of these principles will be allowed. These are the food that gave Taman Siswa life and that supported its growth thereafter. In these spiritual bonds, the Taman Siswa of Mataram is the "mother" (*ibu*) and Ki Hadjar Dewantara is the "father" (*bapak*).

Article 6. Each body within Taman Siswa shall carry out its own share of duties. The relationships between these bodies shall not be defined by power relationships, but must be what is known in Javanese as *wengku-winengku*, that is, they must carry out their duties under each other's influence.

Article 7. All of Taman Siswa's internal regulations must be decided on the basis of a *demokrasi* that considers the good of its component parts, however small they may be. But this democracy must not cross the bounds or stand in the way of order and tranquility overall. If necessary, therefore, Taman Siswa shall be able to exercise a "dictatorship" (*dictatuur*).

In defining the model for the organization of Taman Siswa as one of a "family" formed around the center of Mataram (Yogyakarta) as "mother" and Dewantara as "father," Article 5 formulated the ideal expressed in Tjokrodirdjo's opening speech, of people being able to "empathize with each other from heart to heart," in terms of a familial community. This represented a shift in the basis for association within Taman Siswa from comradeship to familiality.

Taman Siswa's public declaration of familial unity was important not only as a self-definition, however, for in setting forth for the first time the idea that the internal order of an organization should be sustained by familiar bonds, and in providing a clear model for the form of future Indonesian organizations, it was epoch-making within the nationalist movement. Hitherto, other organizations and groups— whether they styled themselves *partij* (party), *sarekat* (association), or *persatuan* (union), and to whatever degree the forces of unity and cohesion that functioned within them were based on the principles of gemeinschaft (and in practice these principles pervaded many of them, often extending beyond the bounds of the particular party or group)— had all turned to the outside world, particularly Holland, for a model of organization once they had defined their raison d'être.

In this way, in the course of the People's Movement, a "culture" was created in which human relationships in society were understood in terms of fictitious family relationships, and in which overall order and tranquility could be realized through the formation of a conical structure of chains of *bapak-anak* (father-child) relationships. Through this advocacy of the familial community, Taman Siswa made a major contribution to the Indonesian nationalist movement as originator and driving force for the formalization of the appellations "Bapak" and "Ibu," which were expressions of just such an understanding of human relationships.

In 1952, Dewantara discussed these appellations in the following words.[61]

We used the terms "Bapak" and "Ibu" because we considered that the terms of address currently in use, "Tuan" [Sir], "Njonjah" [Madam], and "Nonah" [Miss], and the corresponding Dutch terms, "Meneer," "Mevrouw," and "Juffrouw," and also the terms in use in Java, such as "Mas Behi," "Dén Behi," and "Ndoro," which implied superiority and inferiority of status, should be abolished from Taman Siswa. We introduced the use of the terms "Bapak" and "Ibu" not only for when pupils spoke to teachers but also for when younger teachers spoke to older ones. We never once spelled this out as a "regulation," but this kind of appellation soon came to be used in educational institutions across Indonesia. Not only that, after the Indonesian Republic became independent, it was even suggested that these terms should be used formally by younger officials in addressing older officials.

As discussed earlier, the appellation "Ki" of Ki Hadjar Dewantara expressed his comradeship with those who similarly styled themselves "Ki." Dewantara, however, was "Bapak" as well as "Ki."

In this light, Taman Siswa can be seen to have defined itself as what Anderson termed, in the context of nationalism, an "imagined community."[62] This amounted to an expression by Taman Siswa of a "pure form" of nationalism. While continuing to define itself as a gemeinschaft, Taman Siswa on the one hand expanded its projected image of community beyond the bounds of Java to Indonesia, and on the other it reinforced the centripetalism of the community and defined its center.[63] This meant in effect counterposing the *keluarga besar* that was supported by spiritual bonds (*perikatan batin*) against the Beamtenstaat that was supported by zakelijkheid. Taman Siswa was presenting itself ever more openly as a counterinstitution.

The establishment of the center and cohesion about it were further reinforced by the concept of *wengku-winengku* in Article 6. In this connection, the Supreme Council had urged the congress that "no branch should pursue its own rights. To achieve the overall order and tranquility of Taman Siswa as a family union (*familie verbond*), each branch must maintain an attitude of *wengku-winengku*."[64] This meant that each branch must accept the authority of the center and act in accordance with that authority, while at the same time constantly asking itself whether its actions complied with that authority: it meant that each branch must be bound up in a chain of authority. In other words, each member of the Taman Siswa family should identify himself in relation to the center, the father of Taman Siswa, and give expression to his own kebidjaksanaan within the conical structure of relationships in the family. In this way, the keluarga besar would be constituted of chains of kebidjaksanaan.

After acceptance of these seven articles, the congress proceeded to debate matters arising from Article 7.[65] The central point in the debate concerned, of course, who would choose the "dictator."

First, the Supreme Council explained the need for a "dictator." Although, as far as possible, Taman Siswa should be run on democratic lines, there should also be a limit (*tutup*) to the exercise of democracy.

This limit would be constituted by the "dictatorship." It should therefore be decided when dictatorial rights should be exercised and what should be the powers and duties of the "dictator." Also, Taman Siswa's "dictator" should not be regarded in the same light as Western dictators, who were born of the lust for power. "Our dictator will be chosen by us. He will not be a dictator 'for a moment' [*voor een oogenblik*] but one who constantly holds the right of dictatorship and exercises that right. Therefore he will bear the 'burden of accountability' (*verantwoording schuldig*)."[66]

Debate turned to the question of whether the Supreme Council or the national congress should choose the "dictator."[67] Though a majority were in favor of choice by the congress, a motion to this effect failed to win the three-quarters of the vote required by the procedural regulations made on the first day. Debate was then held over to a closed session on the following day, 8 August, when first ballot of the day again saw the motion win a majority of votes, twenty-three for and ten against, but still not the required three-quarters. With the issue seemingly deadlocked, Dewantara stated his opinion: "It is inappropriate that such an important matter as this should be entrusted to the judgment of a handful of people." This was enough to shift opinion in favor of choice by the congress, and in the day's second ballot the motion was passed by a twenty-six to eight margin.

The congress next addressed the question of whether the "dictator" should automatically be a member of the Supreme Council. The Bandung branch proposed that he should be, for if he were not the danger of confrontation would exist between the "dictator" and the Supreme Council. The Jakarta branch seconded the motion, and the congress gave its approval.[68]

Lastly, a vote was held to choose the "dictator." With thirty-two votes for, two against, and two abstentions, Dewantara was elected.[69]

Organization

The congress turned next to the composition and powers of the various bodies within Taman Siswa, the structure and administration of the branches, and the arbitration of disputes, then moved on to discuss the powers of leadership (*kekuatan penguasa*).[70]

Authority exercised within Taman Siswa had to be based on "self-determination" and "order and tranquility." Consequently, all regulations had to be made in consideration of the good of all Taman Siswa members, of even the smallest minority. And "rules for peace" (*anggar kedamaian*) had to be established in accordance with nine points.

(1) As long as there is even one member opposed, a resolution should not be adopted.

(2) When such opposition prevents adoption of a resolution on a matter on which a decision must be reached, the matter should be left for at least twenty-four hours and then debated again before a decision is made.

(3) For a motion to be passed, the approval of two-thirds of the voters is necessary. Matters approved without a two-thirds majority should not come into effect until after one month.

(4) Anyone dissatisfied with a council's decision may appeal to a higher council, but in the interim he must comply with the decision.

(5) Anyone who deliberately contravenes a resolution that is in effect must be relieved of his duties. In such a case, appeal will not be allowed.

(6) The Taman Siswa congress and the Supreme Council shall have the right to suspend from his duties anyone who disrupts order and tranquility and fails to change his attitude despite having been warned.

(7) Failure to comply with the decisions of the congress or the Supreme Council will be regarded as a breach of item (6).

(8) When order and tranquility are disturbed and cannot readily be restored, the Supreme Council can, if necessary, in consideration of Taman Siswa's principles, its statutes, and its general rules, and being accountable to the Taman Siswa congress, establish a "dictatorship" (*hak-leluasa*; *dictatuur*).

(9) The dictator shall also have the right to pardon wrongdoing.

These rules were all directed towards the centralization of Taman Siswa's organization. While molding the whole as a "sacred family" (*keluarga sutji*), they also had the purpose of conveying the will of the "dictator" (Dewantara) from the heart of the Supreme Council to the regions, the regional branch groups (*golongan*), and the individual branches, and they paid special attention to the handling of departures from Taman Siswa's spirit. This basis was to prove effective in supporting Taman Siswa's stubborn resistance to the Wild Schools Ordinance in a struggle that began two years after the First National Congress.

Nevertheless, the fine detail in which the method of decision-making was set forth, for example, the stipulation of decision not by a simple majority but by a two-thirds majority, or the rules provided for electing a "dictator," reflects strangely in the light of the keluarga besar ideal, for such express provision of democratic procedures was diametrically opposed to Taman Siswa's "familiality" (*kekeluargaan*). It also suggests that Dewantara and the rest of the Selasa Kliwon group had been compelled to adopt "Western democracy."

The introduction of "Western democratic procedures" was effected, however, in such a way as to provide a counterbalance to Taman Siswa's spatial expansion. And at the same time it showed Taman Siswa's adaptability: the "implemental skill" constantly expressed by a system of kebidjaksanaan. It revealed, in other words, a structure of understanding that, in certain circumstances, kebidjaksanaan can be expressed by the introduction of Western principles, and that the more the system can incorporate disparate elements, the greater its power becomes to concentrate kasektèn.[71]

The premise for this was that "the essence of existence" was immutable, that what changed in various ways was its manifestational form. It was assumed, in other words, that "Western democratic procedures" could not function in such a way as to undermine radically this system of kebidjaksanaan. In reality, however, the more Taman Siswa extended spatially and the more loudly it advocated the national education of the Indonesian People, the more apparent became the tension and contradiction between these two disparate principles. This in turn raised the serious question of whether the Javanese structures of understanding that underpinned Taman Siswa could function effectively within the wider boundaries of Indonesia.

Selection of the Supreme Council

After passing a motion on school holidays based on the decision taken at the East Java Conference, discussing a proposal by the Bandung branch for a unified curriculum, and placing the teacher-training course in Yogyakarta under the Supreme Council's control, the congress proceeded to the selection of the Supreme Council.

For this, Pronowidigdo of the Supreme Council took over the chair of the congress from Poeger. Pronowidigdo declared that not only had the congress succeeded in producing the anticipated results, it had also revealed the current of a new age and the rise of young forces. In these felicitous circumstances, the existing Supreme Council would step down from office and be dissolved.[72]

Dewantara then spoke in his capacity as "dictator."[73]

> The composition of the Supreme Council has not changed since the founding of Taman Siswa. Now, however, the moment has come when it must be changed. With the expansion of Taman Siswa, the old forces must be exchanged for new, young forces. It has now become plain, moreover, that these new, young forces are truly worthy of trust. They are forces worthy to lead Taman Siswa.

Following this speech, congress embarked upon a debate on the composition of the Supreme Council and heard proposals from the Porong branch of East Java and the Mataram branch. The Porong proposal was that the congress should choose only the Central Committee (Badan Pusat) of the Supreme Council, which would in turn select its remaining members. Mataram's counterproposal was that all members be elected by congress. In the ensuing ballot, the Porong proposal secured the three-quarters of the vote required for adoption, with twenty-nine votes for and nine against.[74]

First to be elected to the Central Committee of the Supreme Council were three elders of the Selasa Kliwon group who had served Taman Siswa since its founding and who received a standing ovation: Pronowidigdo, Tjokrodirdjo (Semarang), and Ki Hadjar Dewantara. These three then chose the six other members of the council. In the order in which their names are numbered in the congress report, these were: Sadikin (Mojokerto), Soedyono Djojopraitno (Wonokromo), Safioedin Soerjopoetro (Jember), Poeger (Malang), Kadiroen (Malang), and Sarmidi Mangoensarkoro (Jakarta).[75]

The process by which Taman Siswa acquired the trappings of organization saw the rise of a new generation of leaders made up of young activists mainly from East Java. Throughout the process of the East Java Conference and the First National Congress, this second generation retained the initiative. Their idea was to strengthen cohesion around the various subcenters, while at the same time promoting the centripetalism of the whole system. And their approach was characterized by a rigorism involving strict self-judgment and strict differentiation between self and others, which stemmed from their belief that they were the true embodiment of the "spirit of the age" (which was manifested in awareness of the community of Indonesia and the spirit of the People's Movement and kerakjatan).

Secondly, the leadership in Yogyakarta imposed order on this drive towards organization by defining Taman Siswa as "a great sacred family." For them, organization was a means to endorse and maintain the unity of this family.

Thereafter, these two themes were developed in concert within Taman Siswa. In the next chapter we shall examine this development through the views advanced by Soedyono Djojopraitno, the most influential of the East Java leaders, and by Dewantara.

NOTES

1. A lucid analysis of the drain of wealth and its influence on Javanese society can be found in Clifford Geertz, *Agricultural Involution: The Process of Ecological Change in Indonesia* (Berkeley and Los Angeles, Calif.: University of California Press, 1963), pp. 38–123.
2. J. Th. Petrus Blumberger, *De Nationalistische Beweging in Nederlandsch-Indië* (Haarlem: Tjeek Willink & Zoon, 1931), p. 251.

3. Ibid., p. 255.
4. Nagazumi Akira, *The Dawn of Indonesian Nationalism: The Early Years of Budi Utomo, 1908–1918* (Tokyo: Institute of Developing Economies, 1972), pp. 29, 90–92.
5. For greater detail on this period, see Alfian, "Islamic Modernization In Indonesia: The Muhammadijah Movement during the Dutch Colonial Period (1912–1942)" (Ph.D. diss., University of Wisconsin, 1955), pp. 300–320.

    It is clear from this dissertation that although Muhammadijah was formed in 1911, over a decade earlier than Taman Siswa, it did not branch into secular "Western-style education" until after Taman Siswa appeared on the scene. Apparently, Muhammadijah was stimulated to enter this field by Taman Siswa's success.

    Secondly, the Muhammadijah schools were concentrated in the large cities of Central Java and had barely penetrated into East Java, where Taman Siswa had its greatest number of branches. In this context, it should be remembered, as mentioned in Chapter 3, note 65, that East Java was the stronghold of Nahdatul Ulama (NU), a self-proclaimed orthodox Islamic group that was opposed to Muhammadijah. In this respect, NU, made up of pesantren-based kijai and ulamas who had unshakable confidence in Javanese culture, had probably established a symbiosis with Taman Siswa. At the same time, Taman Siswa tended to reject the present *kraton* culture—whereas Muhammadijah had its origins in the Kauman clan of religious officiants at the Yogyakarta court—and this too must have struck a chord with NU's opposition to Central Java and the Mataram court culture.
6. Blumberger, *De Nationalistische Beweging*, p. 255.
7. Ki Hadjar Dewantara, "Persatuan National Onderwijs," *Wasita* first ser. 1, no. 6 (March 1929): 172–173.
8. "Verslag dari kumisi Pengadjaran Kebangsaan," *Wasita* first ser. 1, no. 7 (April 1929): 212.
9. Ibid., p. 208.
10. Ibid., p. 211.
11. Blumberger, *De Nationalistische Beweging*, pp. 258, 261.
12. Ibid., p. 267.
13. Ibid., p. 269.
14. A lively account of contemporary events by an interested party is: Soekiman, *Apakah P.P.P.K.I. dapat diteruskan? Noncoöperatie atau Coötie? Nationalisme, Islamisme, Internationalisme* (Jakarta (?), 1931).
15. "Verslag Conferentie Taman Siswa Djawa-Timur (29 Januari–1 Februari 1930) di Malang," *Wasita* first ser. 2, no. 1 (July 1930): 11.
16. Ibid., pp. 12–13.
17. Ibid., pp. 13–14.
18. Ibid., pp. 14–15.
19. On the atmosphere at this time and the attitudes of those who joined Taman Siswa I learned much from Mr. Muhammad Said (in several interviews in Yogyakarta in July 1975 and in Leiden in November 1976). Pak Said, as he was known, studied at the HBS (Dutch-style high school) in Semarang with the intention of becoming a doctor; but on deciding that it was more important for him to become "a guru, a doctor who takes care of people's hearts," he joined the staff of Taman Siswa. In the post-Independence period, he became well-known as charismatic leader of the Jakarta school. He died on 18 June 1979. A history of Taman Siswa written around Said, his thinking and personality, is: W. Le Febre, *Taman Siswa ialah kepertjalan kepada kekuatan sendiri untuk tumbuh . . .* , trans. P. S. Naipospos (Jakarta and Surabaya: Penerbitan dan Balai Buku Indonesia, 1952).
20. Kadiroen was secretary of the East Java Conference, who produced an accurate and vivid report of the proceedings.
21. "Verslag Conferentie Taman Siswa Djawa-Timur," p. 17.
22. Ibid.
23. Ibid., p. 18.
24. Ibid., pp. 18–19.

25. Ibid., pp. 19–20.
26. Ibid., p. 22.
27. Ibid., pp. 22–24.
28. Ibid., pp. 24–25.
29. Ibid., p. 25.
30. Ibid., p. 26.
31. Ibid.
32. Ibid., pp. 26–27.
33. Ibid., pp. 27–28. Even today, Taman Siswa maintains the policy that "portraits of existing figures shall not be displayed." Dewantara's former living room in Yogyakara, for example, contains portraits of himself, Sarmidi Mangoensarkoro, and Tagore, and a picture of Semar; but the Jakarta home (and office) of Said (as of 1975) contained only a portrait of Sukarno. Since offices normally contain a photograph of president Suharto, I asked Said about this. He replied, "It has been a precept since Dewantara's time that living people should not be idolized."
34. As will be seen later in this chapter, at the First Taman Siswa National Conference held in the summer of that year, the chairman's group's proposal was substantially based on the agenda of the East Java Conference.
35. The term "implemental skill" is used to express the utilitarian aspect of kebidjaksanaan, which was discussed in chapter 1.
36. "Pengadjaran Nasional. Pidatao K. H. D. pada Openbare-Vergadering di Malang (2 Februari 1930)," *Wasita* first ser. 2, no. 1 (July 1930): 32–37.
37. Ibid., p. 33.
38. Ibid., p. 37.
39. K. H. Dewantara, "Permulaan Kata, dari Directie Wasita," *Wasita* first ser. 2, no. 1 (July 1930): 1–3.
40. "Daftar Pakerdjaan-Agenda dan Peraturan Umum," *Wasita* first ser. 2, no. 1 (July 1930): 5–6.
41. Atas Nama madjelis Luhur, Secretariaat: Ki Adjar Dewantara, "Prae-Advies Madjelis Luhur." *Wasita* first ser. 2, no. 1 (July 1930): 39–48, and no. 2 (July–August 1930): 49–72.
42. See the discussion of the Slawi branch in Chapter 3. See also "Taman-Siswo Slawi," *Wasita* first ser. 1, no. 6 (March 1929): 196–197.
43. "Sinpo, April 11," *I.P.O.*, 1929, p. 81.
44. "Djanget, July 4," *I.P.O.*, 1929, p. 42.
45. "Sinpo, May 22," *I.P.O.*, 1930, p. 393.
46. This incident involved teachers and a female student who absented themselves overnight while on an excursion with one of the Taman Siswa branches. "Sedio Tomo, March 11," *I.P.O.*, 1930, p. 408; "Bintang Mataram, March 21," *ibid.*, p. 32; "Suara Muhammadijah, March 21," *ibid.*, pp. 85–86.
47. In the background to the founding of the Taman Siswa school at Bandung was the existence of the so-called Tan Malaka school, which Tan Malaka opened in Semarang in 1921. A detailed account of the school can be found in Noriaki Oshikawa, "Tan Maraka no shisō to kōdō: 1896–1922" [Thoughts and deeds of Tan Malaka: 1896–1922] (Graduation thesis, Tokyo University of Foreign Studies, 1974).
48. "Persatuan Indonesia, March 10," *I.P.O.*, 1930, pp. 395–396.
49. "Verslag Konggres Taman-Siswa (6 sampai 13 Agustus) di Mataram," *Wasita* first ser. 2, nos. 3–6 (August 1931): 125–126.
50. Ibid., pp. 126–127.
51. Sajoga was born in Kudus in 1910. He graduated from a Dutch-Native school (HIS) and, in 1928, from the Taman Siswa teacher-training school (see also chapter 3, note 77). Gunseikanbu, *Orang Indonesia Jang Terkemuka di Djawa*, (1943), p. 403.
52. "Verslag Konggres, Receptie," *Wasita* first ser. 2, nos. 3–6 (August 1931): 127–130.
53. Opened on 4 August 1919, the Java Instituut based its activities in Surakarta. It

published the magazine *Djawa*, whose objective was "to develop native culture in the widest sense of the word" (R. C. Kwantes, ed., *De Ontwikkeling van de Nationalistische Beweging In Nederlandsche-Indië* (Groningen: H. D. Tjeenk Willink, 1975), p. 73).

54.   "Verslag Konggres, Receptie," p. 129.
55.   Ibid., pp. 129–130.
56.   "Verslag Konggres, Besloten Vergadering (Jang Pertama)," *Wasita* first ser. 2, nos. 3–6 (August 1931): 130–138.
57.   Ibid., pp. 131–132.
58.   Ibid., pp. 132–133.
59.   Ibid., pp. 133–134.
60.   "Peraturan Taman Siswa," *Wasita* first ser. 2, nos. 3–6 (August 1391): 88–89.
61.   Ki Hadjar Dewantara, "Azas-azas dan Dasar-dasar Taman Siswa," *Taman Siswa 30 Tahun* (Yogyakarta, 1952), p. 61. "Bapak" and "Ibu" are still the most widely used terms of address for elderly men and women of high standing.
62.   Benedict R. O'Gorman Anderson, "The Imagined Community," mimeographed (1978), p. 4, suggests that:

> what is common to all nationalisms is their frame of reference: they are all *"imagined, limited communities"* of a very particular kind. *Imagined*, because in even the smallest nations, members will never know most of their fellow-members, meet them, or even hear of them, yet in the minds of each lives an image of their communion. *Limited*, because even the largest imagined communities, encompassing tens of millions of people, have finite, if elastic boundaries. No nation imagines itself coterminous with humanity. Nations are explicitly non-universal, without the global pretensions of the great religions, liberalism, Marxism and so forth. *Communities*, because, regardless of the actual degree of inequality and exploitation that prevails within nations, they are always imagined as deep horizontal comradeships.

An important point in this connection is that Taman Siswa even had its own cemetery for its members.

63.   This expansion to the whole of Indonesia is shown in Article 2 of the statutes, in which the Indonesian spelling "Siswa" replaces the Javanese "Siswo" in the formal title of the organization. It is also notable that the word *rakjat*, through its non-Javanese origin and its abstract nature, contributed to the expansion of Taman Siswa's activities to new boundaries and new space. When Taman Siswa advocated "education for the People," the image of "the People" this invoked automatically transcended the boundaries of Java to encompass the "Indonesian People"across the length and breadth of the colony.
64.   "Verslag Konggres, Besloten Vergadering (Jang Pertama)," *Wasita* first ser. 2, nos. 3–6 (August 1931): 135.
65.   Ibid., pp. 135–137.
66.   Ibid., p. 135.
67.   Ibid., p. 138.
68.   Ibid., pp. 138–139.
69.   Ibid., p. 138.
70.   "Peraturan Taman Siswa, B. Peraturan Besar," *Wasita* first ser. 2, no. 3–6 (August 1931): 96–97.
71.   This discussion is based on Benedict R. O'Gorman Anderson, "The idea of Power in Javanese Culture," in *Culture and Politics in Indonesia*," ed. Claire Holt, Benedict R. O'G. Anderson, and James Siegel (Ithaca, N.Y. and London: Cornell University Press, 1972), pp. 13–25.
72.   "Verslag Konggres, Selasa 12 Agustus," *Wasita* first ser. 2, nos. 3–6 (August 1931): 156.
73.   Ibid., pp. 156–157.
74.   Ibid., p. 157.
75.   Ibid.

5

KERAKJATAN AND THE SACRED FAMILY

Through the East Java Conference and the First National Congress of 1930, Taman Siswa equipped itself with an organization through which to present the united front of Persatuan Taman Siswa and to lay the ground for the opening of new branches.

Following the national congress, the number of new branches rose sharply. Twenty-nine new schools were opened in 1930, thirty in 1931, thirty-seven in 1932, thirteen in 1933, ten in 1934, and seven in 1935.[1] As of November 1934, Taman Siswa encompassed a nationwide total of 172 branches, 14,602 pupils, and 533 teachers; for May 1935 the recorded figures were 187 branches, 11,235 pupils, and 602 teachers; and for June 1937, there were 184 branches, 9015 pupils, and 459 teachers.[2] In that Taman Siswa had 52 branches immediately before the First National Congress, it is clear that the congress triggered a massive expansion of the movement, particularly during the period from 1930 to 1932.

This expansion brought Taman Siswa a greater role in the People's Movement; and increasingly Taman Siswa came to emphasize, both internally and to the outside world, its own kerakjatan. This was shown in its assertions that the Taman Siswa teacher's duty was to devote himself to the People and to become one (*manunggal*) with the People.

THE PUBLICATION OF PUSARA

Reorganization of Publication

With the combined issue for July and August 1930 (volume 2, number 2), publication of *Wasita* was suspended. It resumed a year later with the August 1931 issue, volume 2, number 3–6, bearing the new title, *Wasita dan Pusara Taman Siswa* (also referred to as *Wasita-Pusara*). An editorial preface explained the layoff as the unavoidable result of a personnel shortage at Taman Siswa headquarters in Yogyakarta. It also announced that Dewantara would retire from the job of editing and publishing *Wasita*, which would be taken over by the Malang branch. Thirdly, the rapid growth of the "Taman Siswa movement" (*pergerakan* Taman Siswa) had created the need for an official organ, which would be met by the publication of *Pusara* by Taman Siswa headquarters.[3]

The reasons for and substance of the switch from *Wasita* to *Pusara*, particularly the reasons for the publication of *Pusara* as its *officieel-orgaan* when Taman Siswa already had *Wasita*, are clear from the subsequent content of *Pusara*. In short, it may be said, as the preface to *Wasita-Pusara* indicated, that *Pusara* was inaugurated in response to the central leadership's need to secure control of and give direction to the Taman Siswa movement by announcing routine directives, and to expound Taman Siswa's spirit and objectives in accordance with the state of the movement. This was also shown by the difference in meaning of the old Javanese words *wasita*, "advice," and *poesara*, "a bond."[4]

Publication of Pusara

Two months after the publication of the combined *Wasita-Pusara* issue in August 1931, the heralded publication of *Pusara* began. Dated 31 October 1931, the first issue (volume 1, no. 1–2) proclaimed *Pusara* to be a "magazine for the unification and instruction of all members of Taman Siswa . . . a monthly journal published under the direction and editorship of the Taman Siswa Supreme Council in Mataram." Since then, except for the period between the Japanese military government and independence, *Pusara* has continued to be published as the official organ of Taman Siswa.

An inaugural message in the first issue stated that publication followed an examination of policy by the general leadership (*pemimpin umum*) from across the country at a Leaders' Conference (Konferensi-Pemimpin) held in Yogyakarta on 23–25 September 1931, and by members of the Supreme Council. The express purpose of *Pusara* was determined to be as "a guide [*pandu*] showing the path; a teacher [*guru*] imparting learning and education; and a guardian [*pamong*] keeping watch over the conduct of our daily lives," although it might also serve as a means for communication between branches and for the expression of members' opinions.[5]

Two points of "policy" received particular attention. One was the need for extreme caution, as on a rickety bridge (*oewotogal-agil*), in order to avoid a clash between Taman Siswa's principle of independence (*azas kemerdekaan*) and the principle of tranquility. In this, *Pusara* was intended to serve as a guide. The second was the instructional role of *Pusara*. Despite the existence of regulations setting forth a distinctive lifestyle for Taman Siswa's members, most still failed to understand it. Many were "unwittingly violating Taman Siswa's customary law [*hukum-adat*]." To resolve this situation, *Pusara* would be employed to propagate the spirit of Taman Siswa.

Through the early 1930s, at least until 1935, *Pusara* carried a lively variety of material, the substance of which can broadly be grouped as follows.[6]

The largest group consists of items giving basic, concrete information about Taman Siswa's activities. This includes details of the various activities of Taman Siswa schools across the country, reports of regional and national conferences, and announcements concerning the payment of dues to the central body.

The second group is made up of articles in which leaders discussed ideas and expressed opinions about Taman Siswa's educational policy, its objectives, and what was then called *ke-Taman Siswa-an* (the spirit or character of Taman Siswa). These articles constituted in effect an exposition of Taman Siswa's "customary law." In the period 1931–1933, Dewantara remained the principal editorialist, while in the quality and quantity of their writings Soedyono Djojopraitno from East Java, writing under the name of Gadjah Mada, and Sarmidi Mangoensarkoro, who was influential in West Java, also distinguished themselves. Other major contributors included Tjokrodirdjo, Darsono, Soewandhi, and Safioedin Soerjopoetro.

Thirdly, there were items providing information about educational ideas then current in the world or trends in the Indonesian nationalist movement. While fewer in number than those of the first two groups, these articles are interesting in showing the areas of Taman Siswa's concern at the time.

The fourth group is made up of articles dealing specifically with problems and events related to Taman Siswa that arose both inside and outside the movement. While many of the items in this group could also be placed in one of the first three categories, there is an important reason for grouping them separately: in the autumn of 1932, Taman Siswa entered into fierce conflict with the Dutch colonial government over the Wild Schools Ordinance, which became the focus of Taman Siswa's activities into early 1933.

The articles in the second and fourth categories represent two of the principal areas of Taman Siswa's activities in the early 1930s, endeavors that entailed repeated trial and error and sometimes spawned internal friction. The first of these is the subject of the remainder of this chapter.

Through the 1920s, from the time of its founding, Taman Siswa had presented its own logic for the creation of order in the nationalist movement, which provided the basis for its own continuing efforts to achieve organization. Pertinent to this were the *Pusara* articles on ke-Taman Siswa-an.

At the same time, Taman Siswa strove to maintain a visible role as counterinstitution to the "colonial order," and this brought it into conflict with the colonial government over the Wild Schools Ordinance. This conflict is covered by the *Pusara* articles of the fourth category and will be dealt with in chapter 6.

GADJAH MADA'S CONCEPT OF RAKJAT

Together with Ki Hadjar Dewantara, the most prolific contributor to the newly inaugurated *Pusara* was Soedyono Djojopraitno, who emerged as the "general leader" of East Java in the late 1920s and distinguished himself as a leader of Taman Siswa's second generation at the First National Congress.[7] Seodyono adopted the nom de plume Gadjah Mada, the name of the prime minister to Hajam Woeroek during the golden age of Madjapahit, whose services made Hajam Woeroek the greatest of the kings of that state.[8] Under this name, Soedyono wrote numerous articles during the 1930s, of which the seven-part series entitled "Didiklah kamu sendiri!" (Educate yourselves!) best expressed his basic views on the importance of the People and of serving the People, to which end strict self-denial and self-discipline were required. Published in *Pusara*, the first part appeared in volume 1, number 1 (October 1931), the last in volume 2, number 4 (June 1932).

Written in Indonesian, these articles were interspersed with many key words in Javanese. This style not only appealed to a wider audience than the earlier writings of Taman Siswa members, it afforded readers a considerably deeper understanding.

In the first article, Soedyono contrasted the terms *guru* and *onderwijzer*, setting the ideal Taman Siswa teacher clearly apart from the *onderwijzer*, the bearer of colonial education. He likened the Taman Siswa guru to the sun, which radiates its own light, and proposed conditions that the guru should meet.[9]

> As educators of a school that calls itself "national," we have an extremely important and valuable duty, a duty towards the life [*kehidupan*] of our nation, the soul [*bathin*] of our nation. To become truly aware of this duty, we must follow a certain course, to which we must first resolve to dedicate ourselves. If we do not, we shall become gurus in name only [*djumènèng guru*].

A guru is not an *onderwijzer*, one who demands to be called "Meneer" or "Sir" by his pupils and is always giving orders. A guru can be compared to the sun, which shines in all directions and gives strength [*daja*] to all living things: he gives the spiritual strength that benefits the lives of children. The fact that a guru can be compared to the sun means that when a man cannot himself radiate light, he is not qualified to be a sun.

Next, Soedyono distinguished between the external and internal qualifications of the "true national guru."[10]

"National" education is provided with external and internal conditions in order to develop the nation and land of Indonesia and make them independent. The external conditions are all the strengths that make children stronger in mind and body. These include exercises such as gymnastics, the art of self-defense, dance, and soccer, and studies such as arithmetic and language. The internal strengths are all those endeavors that strengthen our lives, such as purification of the heart, and the uplift of self-confidence, courage, and moral character.

At present, our nation has been put in a weak position both internally and externally. This is hardly surprising in that we are in the position of a colony.

In the realm of science, where phenomenal strides are being made in various fields, our nation can be said to be like a child, because our People [*Rakjat*] are in many fields still ignorant [*gelapnja pemandangan*]. In this, our nation should make the utmost endeavor to keep abreast of other nations. Let us recall the ages when Hindu and Islamic "cultures" [*cultuur*] developed. In those times, with every passing year, eminent scholars must have visited our shores from India and Arabia. Why must we now make our own efforts to acquire Western science and technology?

The same is true of physical training. We must actively learn from elsewhere the exercises we think suitable and adopt them for ourselves.

After thus asserting that the active study of Western science and technology would provide the external conditions, Soedyono went on to emphasize that the internal conditions could be met only by the transmission of their own culture.[11]

Internal conditions, on the other hand, are extremely important, for they are the very foundation of all education.

In the asrama of Hindu times and the pondok of Islamic times, it was to matters of spiritual life [*kehidupan*] that the pandita and the guru attached paramount importance.

In the wayang there is a scene in which a satria strives to equip himself with the strength to overcome the temptations that raksasa will place in his path after he has left the asrama. The path he seeks is not the worldly path of grief and pleasure but the path leading to his father through mastery of the flesh and strengthening of the spirit.

In his search for Dewa Rutji, Sang Sena was a model of resolution in pursuing an objective.

In the age of Islamic culture, too, the name of Moemin is mentioned in various writings as one who overcame all manner of adversities in pursuing his aims.

In this way, almost all scriptures record conditions for the education of the spirit, that is, conditions for strengthening one's faith and raising one's moral fiber.

Gadjah Mada, Hajam Woeroek, Empoe Sedah, Empoe Kanwa, Jesus Christ, Soehita, Mangkubumi, Dipanegara and others are our champions [*djago-djago*] in these matters.

For this reason, we must study as thoroughly as possible the skills [*pengetahuan*] of "creativity" and "the ability to think," in order to fulfill these spiritual conditions.

The wayang episode referred to here is from the *Tale of Abijoso*. This character had earlier featured in the disputes between Tjipto Mangoenkoesoemo and Soetatmo Soeriokoesoemo that ran from 1918 to 1923: Tjipto had regarded Abijoso as the ideal satria, seeing in him a model of "firm will and independent mind."[12] Such, too, must have been Soedyono's view.

This view also accords with the citation of Gadjah Mada, Dipanegara, and the rest as "champions," men who, while outlaws in the eyes of authority, could become invincible warriors at the head of revolt when occasion required. Standing outside the existing order, they disciplined themselves in mind and body through their own efforts.[13] It was not, however, as outlaws that Soedyono portrayed them but as satria of "firm will and independent mind." And as a model of the path to acquisition of "strength," Soedyono cites the example of *Dewa Rutji*, a wayang play in which the satria hero finds the divinity within himself.

In sum, this first article presented the Javanese concept of kasektèn and linked it with the ideal of the satria.

In the second, third, and fourth parts of "Educate yourselves!" Soedyono turned to the situation created by Dutch colonial rule. The burden of the second article (December 1931) was as follows.[14]

Insofar as we are people living in this world we at least have the same understanding of good and bad, right and wrong, nobility and baseness, rights and duties.

But our fatherland Indonesia fell and became a colony, being turned into a market and a farm that "imperialists" controlled. We were even told by a people calling themselves more civilized [*lebih sopan*] that we were not yet mature enough to have our own country. This was not because we were of little value in this world but because we were said to be not yet fully equipped to know the workings of Western "imperialism." In Hindu and Islamic times, the exchanges between our fatherland and other peoples led to the development of a Hindu kingdom and an Islamic kingdom *of*, *by*, and *for* ourselves (Modjopahit, Mataram) and at the same time allowed the freedom for development of Hindu and Islamic "cultures."

Whether or not they are aware of it, there are among us some who believe that Western imperialism also gives us the room to develop Western "culture" involving national government *of*, *by*, and *for* our country and People. But while Hindu and Islamic "imperialism" was spiritual [*kebatinan*] in an entirely religious sense, European imperialism is worldly and materialistic, devoted to gluttony.

We must be aware of the advantage we have as teachers in nationalist schools of using our weapon of precise knowledge. Just as X-rays penetrate the body, so we must see through all things Western that have infiltrated our fatherland to their skeleton of imperialism. What I have called our weapon is not to satisfy one's hunger or to seek selfish pleasures but to pursue constantly the scientific skill [*pengetahuan exact*] to acquire knowledge. Neither is it to seek "intellectual" degrees ornamented by such titles as Mr., Dr., or Ir., but to become a man of wisdom. In short, it is not to be manipulated at the will of others but to become a person who can think and act on the basis of the facts of social life.

People acquire greater knowledge not just by sitting at a school desk and learning from a teacher; at all times, and in all places, we continually acquire knowledge. If we can continue to acquire knowledge in this way, our level will rise in the People's eyes, and People's trust in our national education will continue to grow.

In emphasizing the importance of becoming a "man of wisdom" (*manusia jang bidjaksana*) rather than acquiring the titles of the Dutch educational system, Mr., Dr., Ir., and so on, and in defining a "man of wisdom" as one able to confront squarely "the facts of social life," Soedyono expressed by the word *bidjaksana* the perspicacity to see the correspondence between these titles of the "neo-prijaji" and the traditional titles of nobility, like Raden and Raden Mas. Such insight required the penetrating power of "X-rays," an analogy which was linked to the "sun" in the first article not only by the imagery of radiation (*tjahja*) but by the fact that such radiation, like the wahju, "emanates from within," and, in line with the original meaning of *bidjaksana*, is able to penetrate "things kept secret." Soedyono also argued that becoming a "man of wisdom" would raise the teacher's "level" (*deradjat*) in the eyes of the People and strengthen the People's trust in national education: clearly, the ultimate judges were People themselves.

In the third article (February 1932), Soedyono depicted his image of colonial rule, the essence of which is as follows.[15]

The aims of Western imperialism in our fatherland are not the prosperity and peace of the People but to guard the interests of the imperialists. If the several million People of Indonesia did not produce wealth, the colonial government would have no reason to exist.

The conditions necessary for the colonial government to rule are as follows.

The first is the colonial spirit [*de kolonial geest*]. Over several hundreds of years, and several tens of generations, this spirit has spread among the People and penetrated the marrow of their bones, becoming a part of them. Proofs of this are too numerous to mention. The following are a few examples.

1. In the pages of *Aksi* a pure Indonesian scholar recently described the history [*babad*] portrayed by Ronggowarsita as "flatus" [*entoet beroet*]. According to him, the only true history books are those written by scholars [*doctor-doctor*] devoted to learning. However, this is a false argument, for every historical account is based on the ideology of the person who wrote it. This is true even of seemingly academic works.

2. There are many nationalists who, though their assertions may be revolutionary to the point of rejecting the colonial government's educational system, send their own children to study in Holland. They have been poisoned by the colonial spirit.

3. There is the view that "without the H.I.S. we would follow the path to extinction." This argument is also based on the same spirit.

4. The claim that the colonial government has improved cities and roads, developed communications, and built factories for the benefit of the People overlooks the fact that all these things were accomplished by the sweat of the People. This argument also overlooks how miserable the People's present life is.

5. There is a tendency for certain people to give their children Dutch-style names, to make their children call them "pappi" and "mammi", and to adopt Dutch customs in their daily lives, as a result of which they feel superior and look down on ordinary people. This again is proof that they have been infected by the colonial spirit.

   This colonial spirit is like cocaine, eating into the hearts of the People of the fatherland.

This "colonial spirit" corresponds to the materialistic side of colonialism which Dewantara had criticized in 1929 in "Association between East and West" (see chapter 3). Both Soedyono and Dewantara stressed that colonial rule had brought hedonism and materialism, which had engendered "obeisance to Western civilization" and destroyed the People's lifestyle and spirit. But Soedyono went further, directing his "X-rays" not only toward the Dutch colonists but also toward Indonesians, revealing the spiritual make-up of "nationalists" who did not act according to their word. His unsparing directness was an expression of his sense of danger that colonialism was "like cocaine, eating into the hearts of the People;" and at the same time it showed the intensity of self-assertion of a satria who has "come to emit his own light."

In the fourth article (March 1932), Soedyono's analysis of colonialism looked specifically at "The use of words," based on his own experiences of education under the Ethical policy. The burden of this article was as follows.[16]

Colonial education is like this. A photograph of Queen Wilhelmina hangs prominently on the classroom wall, and the teacher teaches [that] this is the person who rules the Indies. August 31, her birthday, is a holiday, and the children sing "Wilhelmina" and "Holy Blood of Holland." Before they are old enough to know what is happening, children come unconsciously to worship Holland. This is why the government fears and opposes the fact that Taman Siswa schools conduct classes as normal on August 31.

When I learnt Dutch at school, the teacher would point at a picture of an Indonesian and say *"Dat is een man"* [That is a man], then at a picture of a Dutchman and say *"Dat is een heer"* [That is a gentleman]. He would show the distinction between *dame* [lady] and *vrouw* [woman] with the same kind of pictures. When we came to *"Dat is een dief"* [That is a thief], the thief in the picture was portrayed as a peasant [*kromo*].

In this way a sense of inferiority [*minderwaardig*] was implanted in the children, and the distinctions between gentlemen and men, between ladies and women, were made racial distinctions.

In history classes, the history we were taught was that of Holland, a small European country, while in "history of the Indies" our heroes (Imam Bonjol, Dipanegara, . . .) were portrayed as "traitors." The progress of Dutch imperialism was praised as industrial and economic development, which, we were taught, would greatly benefit the People.

These colonial teachings were all inculcated into us before we were aware of it. We all firmly believed that political systems, customs, and educational systems of European origin were all superior, and that we should take them as models and follow them.

We must understand that the colonialists' idea of the *mission sacre* of Western civilization not only reveals the West's arrogance towards the East but that it is only the surface of Western imperialism, which in fact spreads Western capital into the East.

To negate and to overcome such a system, it is absolutely necessary that children should never again be given an education that is based on this sort of colonial spirit. It is necessary to educate children so that a national spirit is fostered among them, a spirit that reconfirms the pride and worth of the nation.

Here Soedyono shows plainly that the teaching of Dutch under the Ethical policy served to reinforce "the myths of white racial superiority" that supported Dutch colonial rule.[17]

Based on this perception of the situation, the final three parts of "Educate yourselves!" represented a groping toward "What the teacher should be." The fifth article (April 1932) opened with an explication of the pandita's function. It first discussed how, in ancient times, people drew a sharp line between pandita and *ratu* (king).[18]

> The spiritual teachers [*pendeta, wali*] depicted in our chronicles [*babad*] stood above the king [*radja*] in the eyes of the People. Although the People served the king with words and behavior expressing the highest possible esteem, these things were external: no one knew their hearts. With their guru, on the other hand, they opened up their hearts, trusting him completely. The meeting of guru and murid was a meeting of spirit with spirit.

The relationship of Manunggal Kawula lan Gusti referred to here is that established not between the king and his subjects but between pandita and the People. It depicts passive resistance to the king in the form of false deference. The words "no one knew their hearts" (*dalam dadanja . . . siapa tahu*) further imply that the king was unable to see into their hearts, that he lacked the necessary witjaksana, and that he no longer possessed the wahju. As the true embodiments of Manunggal Kawula lan Gusti in such a kingdom, the teachers and their pupils were the principal bearers of resistance to the king. Soedyono discussed this situation in the following terms.[19]

> Our chronicles frequently relate that when the People rose in rebellion and brought about revolution [*revolusi*], their gurus always occupied important positions. This alone is evidence that, in our society, education [*keguruan*] is the foundation of our nation's glory [*pokoknja keluhuran bangsa kita*], and that the teachers living amongst the People are society's very soul [*djiwa*].

This passage finds in the chronicles the "counterprinciple" expressed in the pandita-murid relationship and asserts that this principle is the essence of the nation. Soedyono is clearly referring to the fact that the pesantren and pondok were not only places where teacher and pupil lived together in quest of the arcana of the universe, but at the same time functioned as a counterinstitution to the kingship. He then goes on to assert that Taman Siswa should strive to establish this selfsame pandita-murid relationship, and that the Taman Siswa teacher should strive to acquire the qualities of the pandita.[20]

The fact that we are teachers of national education can, viewed in this way, be said to place upon us an extremely grave responsibility. We must be the fertilizer [*rabuk*] of our pupils and nurture their spirits. All of our words and deeds must be examples to our pupils. We cannot nurture our pupils' spirits with fine words of falsehood: we can do so only with words that stem from our hearts. Therefore we must first purify our own spirits in a nationalistic way.

Dewantara was absolutely right when he said "Though still young, we must have the hearts of panditas" [*harus telah berperasaan pandita*]. This means that, whether we want to or not, we must subdue our own passions [*hawa nafsu*] and at the same time equip ourselves with noble strength.

Soedyone's interpretation of Dewantara's "hearts of panditas" in terms of control of passion and acquisition of "noble strength" was in fact an expression of structures of understanding in Javanese culture about the concentration of kasektèn through suppression of pamrih.[21] For Soedyono, however, the ultimate judge of a man's ability to accumulate kasektèn was the People. And the means to acquire the heart of a pandita was through "self-discipline."[22]

Our time on duty is not just the time we are standing in the classroom. As long as we have life, we are on duty. Our supervisor [*controleur*] is not an inspector [*inspecteur*], a school superintendent [*schoolopziener*] or other official but the People themselves.

The better we understand that we are supervised by the People, the better we shall understand our value in society and the better we shall realize the importance of our duty towards the People and the fatherland. The more we realize this, the greater our strength [*tenaga*] will grow and the more complete our education will become. Happily, the People are beginning to realize the significance of national education. And this fact requires of us "self-discipline" in the broadest sense.

Soedyono thus saw the suppression of personal desires as being attainable not through austerities (*tapa*) practiced in some sacred spot away from society but through "self-discipline" practiced in the heart of society.

The sixth article (May 1932), which set out to clarify the substance of "self-discipline," began with an exposé of the "colonial spirit" to be found within Taman Siswa itself.[23]

The following matters form a trilogy [*trimurti*] of colonialist tendencies still to be seen within Taman Siswa.
1. We are still fond of using Dutch.
2. Our educational system has a bourgeois structure. That is, it imitates the educational system run by the colonial government. Even our textbooks are just the same [*sami mawon*] as in those schools.

3. We open our schools to only a small part of the children of the People, that is, just to the children whose families can pay tuition fees.

This situation should be overcome. Our aim is for a new society established on the foundation of the People.

To this end we must first distance the People from *kebelandaan* [Dutch-mindedness, being Westernized]. To do this we must cut away the veneration of Dutch language that haunts our minds. When we have done so we shall understand that Dutch definitely has no great role to play. As an international language, English is far more effective. Also we must have the courage to teach the sciences in Indonesian and in regional languages and make efforts to that end.

Soedyno's apparently tautological proposition that *kebelandaan* rests on the foundations of the Dutch language is reminiscent of Dewantara's earlier arguments on language and culture. At the same time his argument shows plainly that Taman Siswa was a movement to revive and regenerate the People's own languages. He saw kebelandaan, moreover, as being not just concentrated in the colonial bureaucracy but extending to the unwitting minds of nationalists. To totally negate kebelandaan, therefore, it was necessary to foster kerakjatan in order to unify both spiritually and physically the native society that had been sealed inside a Pandora's box.[24]

We must resolve to eat what the People eat, to wear what the People wear, to live where the People live. Thereby, the feeling will grow that we share the lot of the People.

To achieve this, "self-discipline" is needed. "Self-discipline" does not mean binding one's spirit of independence with organizations and regulations, but listening to the voice that comes from the bottom of one's heart. It is this that commands "self-discipline" of us. This voice speaks such words as "independence" and "order and tranquility" not as empty phrases [*frazes*] but as words full of meaning [*perkataan perkataan jang sungguh berisi*].

In Soedyono's definition of "self-discipline" as "listening to the voice that comes from the bottom of one's heart," this concept has much in common with that of kawitjaksanan, which, as we saw in chapter 1, was the expression of internal divine guidance.

In the final part of his article (June 1932), Soedyono presented several important ideas that served to locate the concept of kerakjatan within the context of the structures of understanding of Javanese culture.

He first asserted that "within us, there exists the the same character [*watak*] as within the world's heroes." He cited the names of Gandhi, "who, although a skinny little man, shook the world;" Lenin, "who, while no orator, provoked a great revolution in Russia;" Dipanegara, "who, despite being neither an outstanding warrior nor a man of high intellect [*berintellect tinggi*], ran the Dutch army to and fro for five years;" Dr. Sun Yat-sen, "who, unlike the Japanese emperor, achieved the great undertaking of bringing down the imperial government of China with neither warships nor planes;" and the Buddha, Christ, Muhammad, and Confucius, "who commanded hundreds of thousands of people without recourse to wealth or power." He then continued:[25]

> According to Marxism, leaders are born according to the needs of the time and the society. Even without Lenin, another leader would have led the proletariat; even without Gandhi, another leader would have stood at the head of the Indian independence movement; even without Sukarno, another leader would have advocated revolutionary nationalism; and even without Ki Hadjar Dewantara, another champion of national education would surely have emerged. In other words, in every country social structure changes as the economic structure changes, the proletariat and the *kromo* [impoverished] class gain ground, and new radical theories are formed.
>
> Our people have long talked of "the one in whom the wahju resides" [*sing kanggonan wahju*], and the dalang have told of "the one who is an incarnation [*sing katitisan*] of Sang Hyang Wenang." The meaning of the dalang's words is as follows. Whoever the one who is the incarnation of Sang Hyang Wenang may be, even if he be Petroek, for example, before him even kings and even the gods [*dewa-dewa*] must kneel. In other words, just as Soeratimantra shook the realm of the gods [*djonggring selaka*] because the gods ignored Artjapada's dishonesty, so eventually the most unlikely person will rise to his feet, shake himself, and begin to move. Such was the case with Lenin, Gandhi, and Semaoen, unlikely people who suddenly rose up, shook themselves, then shook the world of the imperialists [*djagad imperialis*].

Here, Soedyono combined the wayang and Marxist theory to assert that when one emerges who embodies the will of the Divine Soul and whose identity is proven by his possession of the wahju, then there is no power on earth that can stop him. "What, then, should we do now?" asks Soedyono; and in answering, he names one by one the contemporary leaders of Taman Siswa.[26]

> Should we become like Marx and Lenin and Sun Yat-sen and Semaoen? If we do not, shall we be unable to possess the wahju, to become incarnations of Sang Hyang Wenang, to acquire the power to see through things, to become self-disciplined? Nothing of the kind.
>
> We just have to be ourselves [*Kita hanja harus mendjadi kita sadja*]. This

means that Ki Tjokrodirdjo must be Ki Tjokrodirdjo, Ki Prono [Pronowidigdo] must be Ki Prono, Ki Hadjar Dewantara must be Ki Hadjar Dewantara, Ki Kadiroen must be Ki Kadiroen; and in the same way, Ki Sarmidi, Ki Poeger, Ki Sadikin, and Ki Safioedin must all be themselves. There is absolutely no need for us to use trickery or to imitate other people.

Soedyono went on to elaborate, and in so doing he expressed the central ideas running through "Educate yourselves!"[27]

We have no need to imitate anybody else. Like the heroes of this world, we are people, we have within us the same character [*watak*] as them. It is just that this character, which Sang Hyang Wenang gives us, does not appear on the surface. To embody Sang Hyang Wenang, to possess the wahju, and to acquire the power to see through society, we must be self-disciplined. Both Gandhi and Lenin were great leaders only because they suppressed their own passions [*hawa nafsu*] and devoted themselves to self-discipline. According to Marxism, changes in economic structure create leaders; but these leaders of the people also had unique personalities [*persoonlijkheid*].

According to the dalang who narrates the wayang, an incarnation of Sang Hyang Wenang will not emerge unless the gods ignore injustice. At the same time, Sang Hyang Wenang will not manifest himself unless there emerges a man with self-discipline, unless there emerges a man who will suppress his own passions and join the holy war. That Dewantara can be Dewantara is because he is the kind of Dewantara he is today; that Sukarno can be Bung Karno is because he is the kind of Sukarno who voiced his views in the Bandung court.

It is often asked "What would become of Taman Siswa without Dewantara?" and "What would become of the political movement without Bung Karno?" The answers to these questions are simply "Taman Siswa would still be Taman Siswa," and "The political movement would still be the political movement." How "unfortunate" it would be if the movements of the sixty million Indonesian People were to depend on just a handful of people. Only personality and self-discipline underpin the greatness of the People's leaders.

For this reason, Taman Siswa will continue to be Taman Siswa; and we must maintain our own personalities and be self-disciplined in order to teach the People not to follow Dewantara fanatically, and in order that national education should not be borne by Dewantara alone. We are not machines, and thus there is absolutely no need for us to become Dewantara. However, we must possess the same character [*watak*] as he has in national education. When we form the asrama of national education, we must lay aside all of our religious and political differences. Above all we must always "become one" with the children who are the prospective People of the future [*kita harus selalu "manunggal" mengutamakan sang anak tjalon rakjat di kemudian hari*]. When the children's interests are pushed aside by our interests, we must have the courage to tell ourselves, "Stop that!"

In this series of explanations—that he who suppresses his own interests, devotes himself to self-discipline and joins the holy war will surely embody the will of Sang Hyang Wenang; that each and every member of Taman Siswa can perceive that will by "listening to the voice speaking from the bottom of the heart;" and that this means "'becoming one' with the children who are the prospective People of the future," and who are now in the midst of the People—Soedyono clearly identified Sang Hyang Wenang, the Divine Soul, with the People and with the children who would be People of the future.

Seodyono concluded his article with several points for Taman Siswa teachers to keep in mind, which provide a model of the independent and self-disciplined individual.[28]

Because the children will eventually replace us, they are more important than us. All we can do for them is impart our nobility of character [*budi perkerti jang luhur*]. All we can do is educate the children to devote themselves to forming a society that accords with the ideals we hold. How they actually devote themselves will be left entirely up to the children.

To form the asrama of national education, should we not ignore our minor differences and stress our general similarities in an endeavor to assemble our like characters into one? To succeed in this, we need personality and self-discipline. And in order that we may abide by this, let us, at a time when we are alone and quiet, ask ourselves the following things and answer ourselves honestly.

(1) Did you join Taman Siswa with an awareness of the sacrifice involved; or was it because you could not find a comfortable job elsewhere? (Listen to the answer.)

(2) Do you reject and dislike being under supervision [*controle*] because you truly realize the right of self-determination [*zelfbeschikkingsrecht*] of "order and peace" [*orde en vrede*], or is it simply because being controlled does not suit your desire to put self first? (Listen to the answer.)

(3) Do you truly regard the people of Taman Siswa as one family? Or do you discriminate on the basis of things like "intellect" or lineage? (Listen to the answer.)

(4) Which are more important, your interests or the children's? If your own interests are disturbing the order and tranquility [*tertib damai*] of Taman Siswa, shouldn't your resign from Taman Siswa immediately? (Listen to the answer.)

(5) When you have voiced opposition at various conferences, was this really prompted by lofty desires [*kemauan jang mulia*], or was it simply the result of having consulted your purse? (Listen to the answer.)

(6) If you reject the regulations of the branch of Taman Siswa to which you belong, is it not because you wish to free yourself from them because they stand in the way of your own interests? (Listen to the answer.)

(7) Is *ke-Rakjat-an* truly your own? Do you look upon your pupils as your own children? If you still regard "Meneer" and "Juffrouw" as important, can it be that you are not truly free from aspirations to nobility [*keningratan*]? Do you truly not make distinctions between nations? And do you truly feel that you and the People are the same humanity? In other words, do you no longer need to be looked up to by the People? (Listen to the answer.)

We must ask ourselves these things, and other things too.

The answers to these questions can only be yes or no. And there is no need to tell your answers to others; they should be locked within your heart. These answers are for your own benefit. There is no meaning in speaking them or expressing them by pen, for lips and pen often only comfort the heart. Though the heart may say, "I am a thief!", the lips and pen will say, "No. I am innocent!"

Again, these are not formal matters, they are not matters about which oaths are sworn or "deeds" drawn up. Thus you should be able to set up and ask yourselves these questions in order to acquire self-discipline and personality.

Stylistically, Soedyono's "Educate yourselves!" had several notable features: (1) it was written in Indonesian with key words in Javanese; (2) except in a few instances (for example, the use of *inzicht* and *doorzicht* for "insight" or "discernment"), it invested Dutch words with negative connotations (in most cases with use of quotaton marks, for example, "intellect"); and (3) it made frequent use of imperative (beginning with the title) and declaratory forms. Soedyono's use of language reaffirmed that Javanese and Dutch were "mutually untranslatable" (see Dewantara's speech to the East Java Conference, chapter 4), and showed plainly his view that Dutch had undermined Javanese culture ("like cocaine, eating into the hearts of the People"). His use of the imperative and declaratory forms, moreover, gave the series the flavor of "combat orders."

Closely related to this style was the substance of the series, which emphasized the traditional location of the pandita and guru at the center of rebellion. By presenting his heroes (*pahlawan*), from Gandhi to Semaoen, more as satria than as pandita, he stressed, moreover, the satria spirit into which Taman Siswa teachers were to be reborn.

Most significantly, Soedyono's writing captured the spirit of the age, the ideas of "the People," "nationalism," and "national education," within the context of Javanese culture, thus allowing these ideas to take root and come alive within his readers. Soedyono stressed the need for each and every member of Taman Siswa, through self-denial and self-discipline (which were presented in the context of the suppression of pamrih), to be self-reliant (this was expressed as an injunction not to submit blindly to Dewantara but to let one's own personality (*diri sendiri*) blossom). At the same time, he emphasized that these individuals should be linked together through the notion of "becoming one" with the People.

The People were identified with Sang Hyang Wenang, the Divine Soul, whose attributes of invisibility and universality corresponded exactly with the Javanese conception of the People: invisible, because rakjat was an abstract concept with no equivalent in Javanese; universal, because rakjat extended beyond the boundaries of Java. The understanding that Divine Will would be manifested through one who would restore true order and tranquility when "the gods ignored injustice" also found corresponding expression in the notion that the People's will was manifested in the dynamism of the People's Movement to bring about order and tranquility (rather than to support the colonial *orde en vrede*). The People's will, moreover, was presented as being as absolute as that of Sang Hyang Wenang. Nobody, even members of Taman Siswa, could conceal his true nature from the People. Particularly in the seven questions with which it concluded, therefore, Soedyono's article also cast light back upon Taman Siswa's own teachers.

In the context of Taman Siswa, Soedyono's remarkable equation of Rakjat with Gusti in "Educate yourselves!" stimulated the second generation toward the revival of Javanism, encapsulated in the notion of Manunggal Kawula lan Gusti, that had originated with Soetatmo Soeriokoesoemo and the Selasa Kliwon group. Secondly, it emphasized satria over pandita qualities, setting as the ideal for the second generation the model of the pandito-sinatrio, the teacher who is ready to take up arms to protect the nation and the People. This standpoint was the legacy not of Soetatmo but of Tjipto Mangoenkoesoemo and Soewardi Soerjaningrat, protagonists in the Native Committee incident.

Lastly, in terms of language, "Educate yourselves!" fixed the concept of Javanese within the context of Indonesian, the language that was in the process of being created within the People's Movement, giving it clear-cut outlines and significance. Based on the paradigms of Indonesian, Javanese words (and some European words like "X-rays") gained "inflectional" forms.

DEWANTARA'S CONCEPT OF THE "SACRED FAMILY"

The period from late 1931 to mid-1932, when Soedyono Djojopraitno was writing "Educate yourselves!", was for Taman Siswa a time of increasing emphasis on kerakjatan and of tightening of organization. Soedyono and other essayists spoke repeatedly of forming a national education system to rival the colonial system. While Soedyono emphasized unity with the People and internalization of kerakjatan, however, Dewantara's writings showed subtle differences in tone. Dewantara stressed foremost the structure of Taman Siswa, as a "great sacred family" and explained the concept of Manunggal Kawula lan Gusti in terms of "becoming one" with this "family." He also reasserted Soetatmo's thesis that "democracy without wisdom will bring catastrophe." Ultimately, however, Dewantara's views were the other side of the coin to the assertion that Taman Siswa was a rival to the colonial educational system.

In the year between October 1931, when *Pusara* was inaugurated, and September 1932, when the Wild Schools Ordinance struggle began, Dewantara published more than ten articles in *Pusara*; the most coherently argued, entitled "Pertalian lahir dan batin dalam Taman Siswa" (Physical and spiritual union of Taman Siswa), appeared in successive issues in the autumn and at the close of 1931.

This article ascribed Taman Siswa's nature as a "sacred family" to its founding principles. "The spirit of independence [*kemerdekaan-diri*] that Taman Siswa stresses must not be divorced from 'order and tranquility' [*tertib dan damai*]. 'Order and tranquility' is our highest objective."[29] Behind this assertion lay an awareness of the dangers of "Western democracy," which Dewantara expressed using the earlier thesis of Soetatmo.[30]

> Making "order and tranquility" our highest objective while still attaching great importance to the spirit of independence means that central unity [*centrale eenheid*] must not be forgotten when decentralization is carried out. In other words, democracy must not be allowed to violate overall interests [*democratie jang ta boleh menjalahi kepentingan umum*]. Soetatmo, the first chairman of Taman Siswa, said "democracy without wisdom is a catastrophe for us all." In other words, there can be no tranquility when *wiraga* [order of conduct] is not accompanied by *wirama* [self-control, order of spirit]. However well the *saron* or *gendèr* or other instruments of the gamelan orchestra might be played, the *gending* music will surely be unbearable to the ear if they are not in unison with the melody and the overall *wirama*.
>
> The difference between Western democracy and Eastern democracy

lies in just this point. Western democracy attaches greatest importance to the freedom of the individual [*individu*], and the individual dislikes being subject to overall order, namely, to regulations. Eastern democracy, on the other hand, attaches greatest importance to establishing a unity of all individuals [*persatuannja semua individu*]. While this diminishes the independence of the individual, it means that he considers himself one with the whole and devotes himself wholeheartedly to the good of the whole. *In other words, master and servant become one* [**manunggal ing kawulo-gusti**]. (Dewantara's emphasis.)

Next, Dewantara explained how these ideas were reflected in Taman Siswa's organization.[31]

Taman Siswa is both a physical body [*badan lahir*] and spiritual body [*badan batin*]. . . . The fact that Taman Siswa has family bonds shows that it is a spiritual body.

In other words, *organisatie* points to our body; and *keluarga* [family] shows our spiritual unity.

Who are the members of our great sacred family? Normal organizations are bound by "articles and regulations" [*statuten dan reglement*], and anyone may belong who has paid his "dues" [*contributie*]. Providing he pays his dues and abides by the rules, he may do as he pleases. Solidarity among members of the organization can be found only in the fact that they attend "meetings" [*bervergadering*] where there are speeches and debates, motions are introduced, and after heckling, protest, and even bargaining, decisions are taken by a majority vote.

Our situation is very different from this.

The members of Taman Siswa are not people who occasionally speak at meetings, but people who work daily for us because they are bound together by "one ideal" at the bottom of their hearts, not because they are employed by Taman Siswa. . . . Such people should be called family members [*anggota keluarga*]. They must not think they are tied by regulations; they must sense that they are united by feelings of *purity [rasa* **kesutjian**], that is, by the bonds of the family name. They should not behave well because of what is called in Javanese *mangèsti persatuan*, that is, because of regulations; they should behave well because they are aiming for an ideal. (Dewantara's emphasis.)

Next, Dewantara explained again Taman Siswa's motto, *sutji-tata-ngesti-tunggal*, which indicates the Javanese year 1853, the year of Taman Siswa's founding.[32]

Sutji-tata-ngesti-tunggal does not simply indicate the years of Taman Siswa's founding ([the Javanese year] 1853). It is a mantra expressing our sacredness, it is our motto [*sembojan*], and it must become our symbol [*symbool*]. *Ke-sutji-an* [purity] is our soul [*djiwa*]; *tata* [order] is our body [*badan*]; *esti* [resoluteness] is our movement; and *tunggal* [becoming one] is perfection, that is, it is our objective.

Sutji-tata-ngesti-tunggal is the charm [*djimat*] of the independent man. With these words, all temptation and evil are dispelled, we stand firm, and we reach perfection.

Dewantara concluded by emphasizing that members of Taman Siswa's "family community" should be mindful not to harm their "sacred family" and suggesting that prospective members should join for a trial period of, say, one year before becoming full members. This was probably a practical suggestion to cope with the rapid growth that Taman Siswa was then experiencing. But the warning not to harm Taman Siswa would be repeated time and time again during the Wild Schools Ordinance struggle that began a year later.

While the article dealt mainly with Taman Siswa's internal unity, particularly its style of order, it also presented an understanding of democracy and a specific reference to Soetatmo's thesis that were carried over directly into Dewantara's "legacy," his article "Democracy and Leadership" written in 1959.[33]

Dewantara again stressed "external and internal unity" in an article entitled "On the nature and purpose of education," in which he summarized the history of educational thinking in Europe. Focusing on wisdom (*wijsheid*), the goal of education since the times of Socrates and Aristotle, he noted: "Wisdom is the path that leads to perfection, to the unity of mind and body." He also noted that while new educational ideas had recently emerged from a reconsideration of intellectualism, "these European ideas are by no means new to us. We can understand them all immediately, for they are nothing but our own educational ideas. The pedagogy that is now emerging as a 'new science' in European countries is nothing new to us, being simply what we have long maintained."[34] These references to the "Wisdom-Tradition," the "ultramodernity" of Taman Siswa's educational ideas, and the ideas of Annie Bessant, a leader of the Theosophical Society, bring immediately to mind the ideas that *Wederopbouw* and the Selasa Kliwon group were advocating before the founding of Taman Siswa.

The other side of the coin to Dewantara's view that Taman Siswa's "order" should be based on unity as a "sacred family" was his rejection of the government's educational system. His most scathing indictment of colonial education appeared in an article entitled "The P.G.B.H. protest, or the smashing of the colonial H.I.S system," published in the November 1932 issue of *Pusara*, which highlighted the disparate images of the People held by Taman Siswa and the government.[35]

> The distinction between national education and colonial education is as follows. The former has the purpose of imparting knowledge to the rakjat (staatsburgers) who carry the dignity of our fatherland and nation; but the latter has the purpose of giving a suitable education to those who assist the colonial government. Such a colonial education harms our People greatly. For example, because teachers have to be Dutch, the children become submissive to Holland and divorced from the lives of the People. What they are taught, moreover, is of no use to the lives of the People.

Dewantara also claimed that the colonial government had "shifted the brunt of the economic depression onto the educational system, cutting back sharply the quality and quantity of education." This was tantamount to making "no attempt whatsoever to return to the People's hands the taxes squeezed from them." Now, therefore, was the time for teachers in government schools to "return to the People" and devote their energies to "education for the People."[36]

In sum, Dewantara's writings of this period were characterized by his views that, while externally Taman Siswa should stand as a counterinstitution to the system of colonial rule, internally it should be organized as a "sacred family." In this ideal of the "sacred family," which he had expounded since the First National Congress, Dewantara was the "father" who stood at its center, at the apex of its conical structure, and was able to perceive "the People's will." Members of the Taman Siswa family had constantly to be in mutual sympathy with the "father," themselves perceiving and internalizing what he perceived.

In this connection, Soedyono's writings complemented those of Dewantara by clarifying what it meant to perceive the will of the "father" and by defining the conditions under which this could be achieved: the constant exercise of rigid self-discipline by each and every member. While Dewantara established the center of Taman Siswa's "sacred family," Soedyono drew with sharp, solid contours its outer boundary.

FURTHER ORGANIZATION

The ideas prevalent in Taman Siswa in the early 1930s, particularly those of Soedyono and Dewantara, found concrete expression in the systematization of the "sacred family" principle of order and in criticism of the colonial education system. They also reflected the various ideas and activities of the contemporary Indonesian nationalist movement: heightening of the sense of national unity, pursuit of the non-cooperation policy, and the groping for organizational principles.

Since the First National Congress, Taman Siswa had continued to strengthen its organization. In the process, almost as if it anticipated the Wild Schools Ordinance struggle that was to begin in October 1932, it completed its "battle-preparations." First, the branches of Taman Siswa were organized into regional groups (*golongan*), each under the leadership of an "instructor" (*instructeur*), and through this communication channels were opened between the branches and the Supreme Council.

In 1931, nineteen golongan were set up.[37] From the easternmost, in the East Hook of Java, to the westernmost, these were as follows.

(1) Golongan Belanbangan: This consisted of seven branches: Genteng, Srono, Sepanjang-Glnm., Kalisetail, Banyuwangi, Kalibaru, and Ciluring. The principal town was Banyuwangi.

(2) Golongan Argopuro: This consisted of fourteen branches: Jember, Tanggul, Pamekasan, Panji Situbondo, Situbondo, Bondowoso, Kalisat, Rampiduji, Ambulu, Klakah, Lumajang, Kencong, Probolinggo, and Kraksaan. Besides including such cities as Jember, Lumajang, Probolinggo, and Bondowoso, it contained the largest number of branches of all the golongan.

(3) Golongan Singosari: This consisted of four branches: Malang, Turem, Dampit, and Tosari. It centered on Malang, which at the time was contributing 50 florins monthly to Taman Siswa headquarters, the same sum as Surabaya.

(4) Golongan Jenggala: Centered on Surabaya, this group comprised six branches: Surabaya, Wonokromo, Porong, Bojonegoro, Sidoarjo, and Bangkalan.

(5) Golongan Mojopahit: This consisted of five branches: Mojokerto, Mojoagung, Plosso, Cukir, and Jombang. It centered on Mojokerto (that is, Mojokerto paid the highest contribution to the central fund of these branches).

(6) Golongan Daha: This comprised six branches: Tulungagung, Blitar, Kertosono, Kesamben, Talun, and Pare. Of these, Blitar was situated in the largest city, but in terms of their contributions, none of the branches could be called central.

(7) Golongan Madiun: This comprised three branches centered on Madiun: Madiun, Ngawi, and Ponorogo.

(8) Golongan Surakarta: This comprised the Surakarta and Pedan branches, both of which contributed only small sums.

(9) Golongan Mataram: Centered of course on Mataram (Yogyakarta), it also included the Prambanan and Godean branches.

(10) Golongan Kedu: This consisted of seven branches, none of which was particularly central in terms of its contributions: Magelang, Grabag, Blabak, Kedu, Salaman, Wonosobo, and Ngadirejo.

(11) Golongan Bagelèn: This comprised four branches: Purworejo, Kutoarjo, Karanganyar, and Gombong, of which Purworejo was central.

(12) Golongan Banyumas Utara: This comprised only two branches: Purwokerto, the major branch, and Probolinggo.

(13) Golongan Banyumas Selatan: This comprised six branches, none of which was particularly central: Sumpyuh, Kroya, Cilacap, Tambak, Sidareja, and Banjar.

(14) Golongan Tegalarum: This comprised four branches: Slawi, Tegal, Pekalongan, and Pemalang, of which Pekalongan was central.

(15) Golongan Pasundan: This was made up of eight branches: Bandung, Cianjur, Sukabumi, Garut, Cibeber, Cibatu, Subang, and Kalijati. As the major city, Bandung was the central branch; but during this period it is recorded as having made no contributions to the central fund. In terms of contributions, Cianjur was central.

(16) Golongan Jakarta: This comprised the Jakarta and Bogor branches. Jakarta contributed sums of 150 florins in August 1931 and 67.5 florins each in September and October, second only to the contribution of Mataram.

(17) Golongan Andalas: This contained four branches: Medan, Tebingtinggi, Galang, and Pankarangbaru. No contributions are recorded for Medan.

(18) Golongan Kalimantan: This comprised the Pakumpai and Banjarmasin branches, of which the latter's contributions are recorded as 12.5 florins monthly.

(19) Golongan Semarang: Only the Ambarawa branch is mentioned, and no contributions are recorded.

The names chosen for these golongan showed interesting tendencies. In Central and West Java, Kalimantan, and Sumatra, contemporary Indonesian toponyms were chosen in preference to Dutch-style names (such as Sumatra, Borneo, and Batavia). In East Java, the names of historical or legendary kingdoms were often chosen. Daha, Jenggala, Singosari, and Mojopahit were all historical names that had fallen into general disuse. Their adoption as names of golongan is clear evidence of a strong awareness of the local cultural tradition among Taman Siswa's followers in East Java.

This "centralization" (*sentralisasi*) of Taman Siswa was taken a step further during the Wild Schools Ordinance struggle, when a Supreme Council conference held at Tosari on 5–6 October 1932 established the twenty-two golongan and their "instructors" listed in Table 2.[38] Of these twenty-two, eleven were located in East Java (numbers 1–11 in the table), seven in Central Java (12–18), and four in West Java (19–

TABLE 2. THE GOLONGAN AND THEIR "INSTRUCTORS" (OCTOBER 1932)

GOLONGAN	INSTRUCTOR	RESIDENCE
1. Belanbangan	Abdulsjasmu	Banyuwangi
2. Argopuro	Oesman	Kalisat
3. Sero Giran	Usman Nafsiri*	Lumajang
4. Shungurin Saraka	Soehardjono	Lumajang
5. Singosari	Poeger	Malang
6. Mojopahit	Sadikin	Mojokerto
7. Daha	Soeratmoko	Kediri
8. Jenggala	Sisworahardjo (Kadiroen)	Surabaya
9. Jipan (East)	Sisworahardjo	Surabaya
10. Jipan (West)	Soetiarko	Cepu
11. Madiun	Soekemi	Yogyakarta
12. Mataram	Soedjanarko	Yogyakarta
13. Bagelèn	Unknown	Purworedjo
14. Kedu	Soeratmono	Magelang
15. Semarang	Ngoesmanadji	Ambarawa
16. Tegal Alum	Sutjipto	Selawi
17. Banyumas Utara	Hadisoenarto	Purwokerto
18. Banyumas Selatan	Achmad Sumadi	Purwokerto
19. Garut	Sardjono	Garut
20. West Priangan	Mangoensarkoro	Jakarta
21. Jakarta	Mangoensarkoro	Jakarta
22. Cirebon and Krawang	Abdul Gani	Cirebon

*Subsequently taken over by Soehardjono, who was concurrently Instructor of Shungurin Saraka.

22). Amongst those nominated as "instructors" were Poeger, Sadikin, Kadiroen, Soekemi, Sardjono, Mangoensarkoro, and other leaders who had been active in their respective areas since the late 1920s.

The second measure Taman Siswa took to strengthen its organization was to hold various conventions to familiarize the regional branches with the resolutions taken at the East Java Conference and the National Congress. In November 1930, a West Java Conference was convened at the Taman Siswa school in Kemayoran, Jakarta, while in the following March a Central Java Conference was held in Yogyakarta. Then, in September 1931, and expanded meeting of the Supreme Council, general leaders, and regional leaders was held in Yogyakarta. The matters discussed and conclusions reached at these conventions were again deliberated at the first and second annual conferences held in January and August of 1932.

Through this series of conventions, Taman Siswa strengthened and further centralized its organization. What this meant to Taman Siswa was touched on by Dewantara in his closing address to the Second Annual Conference of August 1932, when he spoke of "a great success" and "a new era." This he elaborated on in an article published later the same month. Subtitled "From Alam Wiraga to Alam Wirama," its burden was as follows.[39]

Looking back on the assembly, Dewantara was overjoyed that Taman Siswa had wholeheartedly accepted order and tranquility as one family. This had come about because members had willingly sacrificed themselves for the sake of building unity (*dengan ridla hati menghilangkan diri kita sendiri untuk menjusun persatuan kita*). Through this common experience of self-sacrifice, they had transformed themselves into "a bigger and purer body, free from all egoism" (*mendjelmanja diri kita kedalam badan jang lebih besar dan lebih sutji, terlepas dari segala egoisme diri*). Now the body of Taman Siswa was complete.

They were now entering their second *windu* (cycle of eight years), when, in their maturity, they must embark upon an "internal process" (*innerlijk proces*). They must not give way to anger, conceit, or ambition and disturb Taman Siswa's order, nor must they rebel against their chosen leaders (*ketua-ketua jang kita sendiri sudah memelihnja*). The turmoil of the previous assembly was now over; and judging from the success of the present assembly, there remained little fear of its recurrence. Dewantara now hoped that they would "move smoothly from the world of order and organization [*alam wiraga*] to the world of spiritual maturity [*alam wirama*]," and that, whatever crises might arise, this maturity would ensure order and tranquility.

This article captured the essence of the organizational problems with which Taman Siswa had grappled since 1930.

First, it showed that in the early 1930s Taman Siswa was attempting to build a common spirit of self-sacrifice for the overall good. Taman Siswa was seen as advancing to the stage at which its members would play within themselves a melody—the original meaning of *wirama*—that resonated and harmonized with the melody of the whole. At the core of this view was clearly the notion of Manunggal Kawula lan Gusti.

That such was the import of the "great success" and the "new era" meant that Taman Siswa's organization was no more than a variation on the "main theme" (*wirama*) that it began at its inauguration: however heated the debate on organization and however detailed regulations might be, these were to be viewed as variations on the main theme. Because regulations were the external expression of Taman Siswa's spirit, their individual provisions could not develop independently from this spirit.

How important it was that Taman Siswa's spirit should be shared by all of its members through debate, and that each member should feel and respond to that spirit within himself, was shown by the fact that many of the resolutions taken at the first and second annual conferences contained the selfsame provisions. This spirit was expressed in Taman Siswa's principles and in Dewantara's explicit rejection of rebellion against the "chosen leaders." Its essence, moreover, was precisely the "rebirth of Javanism" that the Selasa Kliwon group had cherished, the revival of Manunggal Kawula lan Gusti in an age of nationalism and democracy. In this sense, regulations expressed means and procedures for perceiving and responding to this spirit.[40]

Second, at the present stage of Taman Siswa's development, the extensive debate over organization and regulations was indeed cause for Dewantara to be "overjoyed." In the process, the "forces of youth" extolled at the First National Congress had been subsumed into Taman Siswa as a force for order. They had come to understand the need for self-sacrifice for the good of the whole and had become part of a "purer body," the "sacred family" of Taman Siswa.

Although Taman Siswa rejected the confrontational aspects of the contemporary nationalism by maintaining a pandita's stance, it succeeded in absorbing the vitality of the nationalist spirit through the satria ethics of self-discipline and self-sacrifice that marked Soedyono's writings. Because this vitality was combined with Taman Siswa's kerakjatan, it highlighted Taman Siswa's anticolonial character; and because it was channeled totally into the maintenance of order and tranquility, it further strengthened Taman Siswa's centralization. In this way, the People's Movement came to be subsumed into Taman Siswa as a movement for the creation of order.

Taman Siswa's "battle-preparations" were now complete. And immediately after the Second Annual Conference, its dramatic clash with the colonial government over the Wild Schools Ordinance began. Taman Siswa's tertib dan damai met head on with the government's orde en vrede.

NOTES

1. For years other than 1931 and 1935, figures are from "Statistik Murid-murid dan Guru-guru Persatuan T. S.,"*Pusara* 5, no. 2 (November 1934): 63–68; for 1931 and 1935, statistics are from "Statistik Murid-murid dan Guru-guru Taman Siswa," *Pusara* 6, no. 7 (May 1936): 161–165.
2. The totals of pupils and teachers in 1934, 1935, and 1937 are, respectively, for only 135 branches ("Statistik," *Pusara* 5. no. 2 (1934): 63–68), 136 branches ("Statistik," *Pusara* 6, no. 7 (1936): 161–165), and 113 branches ("Statistik Guru-guru dan Murid-murid Taman Siswa, 1935/1936," *Pusara* 7, no. 8 (June 1937): appendix).
3. 'Pembuka Kata Wasita-Pusara," *Wasita* first ser. 2. no. 3–6 (August 1931): 73–75.

4. *"Wasita"* has also been interpreted as meaning "the word of a pandita" (*sabda pandita*). "Kata Pendahuluan," *Wasita* second ser. 1, no. 1 (March 1935): 1.
5. Paniteran Madjelis Luhur, "Kata-Pembuka," *Pusara* 1, no. 1–2 (October 1931): 1–2.
6. Publication of the second series of *Wasita* began in 1935. From this time *Wasita* dealt with educational questions and educational ideas in general. Left with matters pertaining to Taman Siswa proper, the pages of *Pusara* lost their former luster.
7. Little is known of Soedyono Djojopraitno. He was born in 1903 in Java (probably East Java) and for a while taught in one of the colonial government's schools. In late 1923 or early 1924 he joined Taman Siswa, becoming a leader of the Wonokromo branch and headmaster of the school. Thereafter he rose in the movement and assumed an active part in its central leadership. In the late 1930s or early 1940s he withdrew from Taman Siswa, and during the Japanese military rule he belonged to the "Kaigun group," employed by the naval administration, and worked as editor of the *Asia Raya* newspaper. In November (or December) 1945, he attended the founding in Madiun of the PBI (Partai Buruh Indonesia, Indonesian Workers' Party), and in 1946 he was selected as the party's representative in the KNIP (Komite Nasional Indonesia Pusat, Central Indonesian National Committee). The founder and central figure in the PBI was Sjamsu Harja Udaja, Soedyono's junior by ten years, who in the 1930s had studied with Taman Siswa and organized the Taman Siswa alumnal association, PBMTS (Persatuan Bekas Murid Taman Siswa). This association was formally inaugurated at a congress in Surakarta on 6 February 1938. "Maklumat," *Pusara* 8, no. 3 (January 1938): 59.

   Like Sjamsu, Soedyono also joined the Persatuan Perdjuangan (Struggle Union), led by Tan Malaka, and appears to have been involved in the July Third Affair of 1946. From 1948, having moved to Jakarta, he helped edit the daily *Merdeka* run by B. M. Diah. As an ardent supporter of Tan Malaka since joining the PBI, he upheld the Partai Murba's opposition to the PKI (Indonesian Communist Party). In 1962 he wrote *PKI-Sibar Contra Tan Malaka* (Jakarta, 1962), a biting criticism of the PKI for proceeding with the insurrection of 1926 against the advice of both the Comintern and Tan Malaka, upon whose head it had then groundlessly laid the blame for its failure.

   Soedyono died on 30 January 1973. Although, according to Taman Siswa sources, Soedyono withdrew completely from Taman Siswa after independence, he in fact provided various forms of support until the end of his life.

   This account is based on: Kementerian Penerangan Rep. Indonesia, *Kami Perkenalan*, (Jakarta: Kementerian Penerangan,1950 (?)), p. 87; Atou Masuda, *Indoneshia gendaishi* [A modern history of Indonesia] (Tokyo: Chūōkōronsha, 1971), pp. 48–49, 168; an interview with Sajoga and others in Jakarta, 19 May 1975; and personal correspondence with Professor Benedict Anderson dated 30 July 1976.
8. That Soedyono used the pen name Gadjah Mada was confirmed by Sajoga and others in an interview in Jakarta on 19 May 1975. The identity of Gadjah Mada can also be deduced from circumstantial evidence. First, the content and phraseology of Gadjah Mada's writings are identical to those of articles Soedyono wrote in his own name; second, both men identified their places of writing as either Jenggala or Wonokromo; and third, in listing the names of Taman Siswa leaders in part seven of "Educate yourselves!" (discussed hereafter), Gadjah Mada omits mention of Soedyono—the most natural explanation for this being that Gadjah Mada was hesitant to include himself in the list.
9. Gadjah Mada, "Didiklah Kamu Sendiri! I," *Pusara* 1, no. 1–2 (October 1931): 4.
10. Ibid.
11. Ibid., pp. 4–5.
12. Takashi Shiraishi " 'Jinmingshūgi' ni tsuite" [On 'kerakjatan'], *Tōnan Ajia Kenkyū* [Southeast Asian Studies] 17, no. 4 (1980): 752–754.
13. The unique social role of the *djago* is analyzed in the following works. Benedict R. O'G. Anderson, *Java in a Time of Revolution: Occupation and Resistance, 1944–1946,*

(Ithaca, N.Y. and London: Cornell University Press, 1972), pp. 156–157; Onghokham, "The Inscrutable and the Paranoid: An Investigation into the Sources of the Brotodiningrat Affair," in *Southeast Asian Transitions*, ed. Tuth T. McVey (New Haven, Conn. and London: Yale University Press, 1978), pp. 118–119, 132.

14.   Gadjah Mada, "Didiklah Kamu Sendiri! II," *Pusara* 1, no. 6–7 (December 1931): 42–43.

15.   Gadjah Mada, "Didiklah Kamu Sendiri! III," *Pusara* 1, no. 11–12 (February 1932): 82–83.

16.   Gadjah Mada, "Didiklah Kamu Sendiri! IV," *Pusara* 2, no. 1–2 (March 1932):10–12.

17.   How "the myths of white racial superiority" functioned in Dutch colonial rule is discussed in Benedict R. O'G. Anderson, "Japan, the Light of Asia," in *Southeast Asia in World War II: Four Essays*, ed. Josef Silverstein, Southeast Asia Studies, Monograph Series, No. 7 (New Haven, Conn.: Yale University, 1966), pp. 17–21.

18.   Gadjah Mada, "Didiklah Kamu Sendiri! V," *Pusara* 2, no. 3–4 (April 1932): 21.

19.   Ibid.

20.   Ibid.

21.   See chapter 1.

22.   Gadjah Mada, "Didiklah Kamu Sendiri! V," p. 21.

23.   Gadjah Mada, "Didiklah Kamu Sendiri! VI," *Pusara* 2, no. 5–6 (May 1932): 33–34.

24.   Ibid., p. 34.

25.   Gadjah Mada, "Didiklah Kamu Sendiri! VII," *Pusara* 2, no. 7–8 (June 1932): 49–50.

26.   Ibid., p. 50.

27.   Ibid.

28.   Ibid., pp. 50–51.

29.   K. H. Dewantara, "Pertalian Lahir dan Batin dalam Taman Siswa," *Pusara* 1, no. 1–2 (October 1931): 2.

30.   K. H. Dewantara, "Pertalian Lahir dan Batin dalam Taman Siswa," *Pusara* 1, no. 6–7 (December 1931): 43–44.

31.   Ibid., p. 44.

32.   Ibid., p. 44–45. While the motto "sutji-tata-ngesti-tunggal" has meaning as it stands, each word also represents a number, the arrangement of which indicates a year in the Javanese reckoning (the year of Taman Siswa's founding). Such representation, called *tjandrasangkala*, is possible both with words and forms: at the Yogyakarta palace, for example, the nagas carved above the veranda (*pendopo*) indicate a specific year.

33.   See chapters 1 and 7.

34.   K. H. Dewantara, "Tentang Sifat dan Maksud Pendidikan, serta sedikit Keterangan dari Riwajat Paedagogiek di Europa," *Pusara* 1, no. 6–7 (December 1931): 47–50. Those whose ideas are cited include Spranger, Heymans, Freud, Foerster, Kerschensteiner, Maria Montessori, Annie Bessant, Elley Key, and Helen Parkhurst.

35.   K. H. Dewantara, "Protest P.G.H.B. atau Hantjurnja Systeem H.I.S. Kolonial," *Pusara* 1, no 3–5 (November 1931): 28–29.

36.   Ibid.

37.   "Masuknja uang iuran guna Kas Séntral Persatuan Taman Siswa Djuli sampai 19 November 1931," *Pusara* 1, no. 3–5 (November 1931): 38–39.

38.   "Instruktur-Instruktur Taman Siswa," *Pusara* 3, no. 2 (November 1932): 29.

39.   K. H. Dewantara, "Kesudahan Rapat Besar: Dari Alam-Wiraga ke Alam Wirama!" *Pusara* 2, no. 11–12 (August 1932): 77–78.

40.   Taman Siswa's spirit and the organization and regulations that are its external manifestations can be likened to the main theme and its development in a piece of gamelan music or Ravel's "Bolero."

6

THE WILD SCHOOLS
ORDINANCE STRUGGLE

From October 1932 to early 1933, Taman Siswa clashed head on with the colonial government during the course of the promulgation, enforcement, and repeal of the Wild Schools Ordinance. In this period in the history of the Indonesian nationalist movement, Taman Siswa showed pertinacity in resistance and the strength to survive, and greatly influenced the People's Movement.

United around the central leadership under Dewantara, Taman Siswa displayed in its struggle the spirit of satria who regarded the People as Sang Hyang Wenang. At the same time, it clearly maintained its *pinandita* or pandita-like qualities; and around the "pandita," the "satria" of the political world closed ranks to form a protective "fence." Among the "satria" of the People's Movement were not just the "non-cooperationists" but virtually all of the contemporary political parties. Religious groups, women's associations, and labor unions added their weight, and finally the "native members" of the Volksraad played a major role.

As a result of these developments, the colonial government repealed a law it had already enforced, an extraordinary occurrence in the history of colonial rule. Throughout the struggle, the Taman Siswa leadership stressed "order and tranquility" (*tertib dan damai*) above all else, while the colonial government cited the "order and tranquility" (*orde en rust*) of native education as its reason for enforcing the ordinance. The conflict thus highlighted the disparity between the two versions of "order and tranquility;" and ultimately the government failed to force its version upon Taman Siswa.

These developments showed that Taman Siswa's principles and the organization in which they were expressed were able, under certain conditions, to evoke and give order to a spontaneous burst of "vitality" from within Javanese society. Taman Siswa's principles and their expressional form harmonized and resonated strongly with the "vitality" of Java. Essentially, Taman Siswa could be seen as a movement to evoke and order this "vitality" within itself and, therefore, in a pure form. This in turn made Taman Siswa a highly effective model for the rejection of the "decadent, materialistic, egoistic culture that arose in the process of colonial rule" and the "reconstruction [*wederopbouw*] of the true culture of bygone days." In sum, in its struggle against the Wild Schools Ordinance, Taman Siswa exhibited fully and simultaneously both the "counter" and the "institution" functions of a counter-institution.

THE CONVERGENCE OF TWO COURSES

Birth of the Ordinance

On 24 September 1932, the colonial government issued in the name of Governor-General B.C. De Jonge the so-called Wilde Scholen Ordonnantie. Known correspondingly in Indonesian as Ordonansi Sekolan Liar, it was officially entitled Toezicht Ordonnantie Particulier Onderwijs (Supervision Ordinance Private Education), Staatsblad 1932 No. 494. "Private education" here meant education that was unsubsidized by the colonial government (*het particulier ongesubsidiëerde onderwijs*), which had been spreading rapidly since the economic crisis of 1930, partly as a result of cuts in the government's educational budget, and partly as a result of unemployed intellectuals and others seeking income from teaching.[1]

From the early 1920s, the Dutch colonial government had made repeated attempts to supervise "wild schools." Reports on "unsubsidized private education" began to appear in colonial government documents from 1922.[2] The first of these, a report to Governor-General Fock from J. F. W. van der Meulen, the director of education and public worship (Directeur van Onderwijs en Eredienst), dealt with Chinese schools, the "Sarekat Islam school in Semarang" opened by Tan Malaka on 21 June 1921 (the so-called Tan Malaka school), and the "teacher-training school run by Soewardi in Yogyakarta," an obvious reference to Taman Siswa. Meulen expressed the view that the Chinese schools were "conducting anti-Dutch education based on Chinese nationalism in West Borneo," while the schools in Semarang and Yogyakarta were "disseminating unconstructive principles among youth." In order to supervise this "antisocial education" (*antimaatschappelijk onderwijs*), he recommended that the teachers involved should be required to register with the administrative authorities, their curricula should be subject to supervision, and residents should be empowered to halt education within their regencies.[3]

The colonial government thus was clearly concerned about unsubsidized private education in the early 1920s, when Sarekat Islam was setting up schools in Semarang and elsewhere and Taman Siswa had opened its school in Yogyakarta. It was especially concerned about the danger that these schools were conducting "anti-Dutch education" or "antisocial education," and on 28 March 1923 it promulgated Ordinance No. 136.[4] This ordinance obliged all teachers, within six months of being appointed to an unsubsidized private school, to report this fact and the location of the school to the proper local government office (Article 1), and to answer any questions the government office might have about the school (Article 2).[5]

Even after the 1923 ordinance came into force, these private schools, which from that year came to be referred to as "wild private schools" (*wilde particuliere schooltjes*) in government documents, continued to attract attention. In September 1923, for example, the then director of education, K. F. Creutzberg, reported to the Educational Council (*Onderwijsraad*) that the "wild schools" required supervision and guidance in order to raise the quality of education.[6] A memorandum from Director of Education Meulen dated 1 January 1925 named as "wild schools" not only the Chinese schools, the Sarekat Islam school, and the Sarekat Rakjat schools in Probolinggo, Purwokerto, and Jatinegara, but also the Taman Siswa school and the Ardjuna school of the Theosophists; and it recommended legal measures to combat the "political danger" of these schools, particularly their use in spreading Communist propaganda, and their "abuses."[7] It warned that the Sarekat Rakjat schools were particularly radical.

Against this background, Ordinance No. 260 was promulgated in 1925 empowering local administrative authorities to order teachers to suspend classes for the sake of "public order." A circular issued by the government secretariat in July of the same year explaining the ordinance to the heads of regional government expressed strong misgivings about the Sarekat Rakjat Schools.[8] Eventually, the arrest of many Sarekat Rakjat leaders following the Communist-led uprising of 1926–1927 alleviated this particular concern; but the colonial government remained wary of the nationalist movement under such leaders as Sukarno, believing that the radical elements had become the bearers of the Nationalist Party. In this way, the focus of the "wild schools" question shifted from the Communist Party and Sarekat Rakjat schools to the Taman Siswa schools, which since Taman Siswa's founding had been considered to be antigovernment and in step with the nationalists.

At the same time, the educational authorities held Taman Siswa in high regard. In a report to the governor-general of 23 April 1929, the director of education, J. Hardeman, referred to the regulation of "politically dangerous education" (*politiekgevaarlijk onderwijs*). In his opinion, it would be inadvisable for the government to take legal measures to strengthen its supervision of "wild schools" while there were among them "schools like Taman Siswa, which, while nationalistic and not meeting the government's educational requirements, were well-intentioned, conducting education on the basis of their own ideals, and refusing subsidy on the basis of these same ideals."[9]

Not all opinion was so moderate, however. In the same period, hard-liners were calling for firm legal measures against "inferior private education" (*minderwaardig particulier onderwijs*). This stance was represented by the Council of the Indies in its recommendations of 4 October 1929.[10]

Hardeman's successor as director of education from May 1929 to May 1934, Dr. B. J. O. Schrieke, adopted the council's hard-line stance and made preparations for the introduction of appropriate legal measures. On 13 June 1932, in a report to Governor-General De Jonge, he put forward recommendations that formed the framework of the Wild Schools Ordinance.[11] Aimed at raising the educational level of the "wild schools," these proposals included changing the system of notification set forth in the 1923 ordinance to one of authorization. Heads of regional government would be authorized to issue or deny licenses to teachers, basing their decisions on investigations and reports made by inspectors (*onderwijsinspecteur*); and local authorities would be empowered to order an indefinite suspension of classes by teachers who were regarded as disturbing "public order."

Incorporated into a draft ordinance, these proposals came before the Volksraad and were adopted with partial amendment on 9 September 1932. Comprising 21 articles in five sections, the Wild Schools Ordinance was promulgated on 24 September as Staatsblad 1932 No. 494, and took effect on 1 October 1932.[12]

The 1932 ordinance stipulated that teachers at schools receiving no government subsidy whatsoever should obtain a license from the head of regional government in their area (Article 1), and when a new school was established, teachers should similarly obtain licenses (Article 10). Before issuing a license, the official concerned should question the inspector of education (*Inspecteur van het Onderwijs*) (Article 3), and both the standard of education offered by the teacher and his "non-disturbance of order and tranquility" (*geene verstoring van orde en rust*) should constitute the basis of the resident's decision (Article 4). For the sake of "educational needs" and "maintenance of public order," a resident was empowered to revoke a license (Article 7), and if necessary, officials of the region concerned could enter a school or classroom to carry out investigations (Article 8). Penalties for infringement of these provisions or submitting a false report were set at a maximum of eight days' detention and a twenty-five florin fine (Article 16).

These provisions gave the colonial government a hold over the "wild schools" and their teachers. While the 1923 ordinance had provided for a system of registration, the 1932 ordinance imposed a system of authorization, whereby the licensing of teachers was placed in the hands of provincial educational inspectors and administrative authorities, and the issue of licenses was decided on criteria not only of "educational standards" but also "public order and tranquility."

For Taman Siswa, this meant that local officials were empowered "to act arbitrarily" (*bertindak sewenang-wenang*), according to their views of whether Taman Siswa teachers were "dangerous or well-behaved" (*berbahaja atau baik tingkah lakunja*).[13] The choice of "well-behaved" and "dangerous" as antonyms, here cited from the history of Taman Siswa published in 1974, is indeed apt, for as we shall see shortly, confrontations between Taman Siswa and provincial officials and the colonial government over this ordinance often centered around whether Taman Siswa's attitudes were submissive or rebellious. The use of the word "arbitrary" (*sewenang-wenang*), moreover, to describe the government's powers suggests the antinomy between the government's "order and tranquility" and Taman Siswa's. In other words, although the ordinance came into effect "legally" through a process involving various reports and recommendations by the government, once in effect, it was enforced "arbitrarily" by provincial officials.

For the colonial government, the ordinance was a means to control the "wild schools," which were conducting "inferior education" (*minderwaardig onderwijs*) in comparison with "public education" (*openbaar onderwijs*), and which were being "misused" (*misbruikt*) to disseminate "political propaganda against authority."[14] But for Taman Siswa the ordinance was, in this contest, the legitimation of "wild" behavior by provincial officials, the justification for them to "act arbitrarily;" and it was thus an instrument for disturbance of Taman Siswa's "order and tranquility."

The Equipment of Taman Siswa

Taman Siswa's leaders appear for some time to have been taking note of the government's moves to control "wild schools." For example, in the "Kritiek dan Kommentar" column of the inaugural edition of *Pusara*, published in October 1931, Dewantara discussed two points relating to the new Wild Schools Ordinance that had been raised by the daily *Mataram* in its 7 September 1931 edition.[15]

The first point was that many people had recently opened schools to seek a living (*tjari makan*) or merely out of dilettantism. Dewantara agreed entirely, noting that while such places, which should be called "commercial houses, shops, or trades workshops for 'sale of knowledge'" (*rumah perniagaan, toko atau ambachtswerkplaats untuk 'mendjual ilmu'*), had always existed, they had increased with the present economic crisis. They were not worthy of the name "school," and their "teachers," though "pedlars of knowledge" (*tukang 'dagang-intellect'*), would never be "Sang Guru." Taman Siswa should give this situation serious consideration.

The second point concerned an order issued by the Binnenlandsch Bestuur (Interior Administration; the Dutch civil service) that village leaders should inform people of the dangers of the "wild schools." Dewantara responded that, on principle, Taman Siswa had never called its schools "HIS" or any of the other names used in the colonial education system; but even if Taman Siswa were slandered because of this, it should remain silent. Although Europeans were saying things about "wild schools," there was no need for Taman Siswa people to tattle on the streets about "wild men" (*wilde medemenschen*; a reference to the impression made by the Dutch). It was wrong, however, for the civil service to tackle this problem. Its roots lay in the government's lack of resources to provide sufficient schools for the needs of the people. And even though *Mataram* had published a *rectificatie* excluding Taman Siswa from the category of "wild schools" two weeks after presenting the government's standpoint in its columns, the fact should be recognized that even in Yogyakarta there were many private schools which, though *Mataram* and the Binnelandsch Bestuur would disagree, could not be called "wild."

Dewantara went on to report that disparaging announcements about Taman Siswa had been made by the residents and other officials in Magelang and Kalimantan. He issued a call to Taman Siswa's branches to report all governmental interference to the Supreme Council, and charged that members should "uphold [Taman Siswa's] strength and dignity and not behave childishly."[16]

In sum, while acknowledging the existence of "inferior schools and teachers," Dewantara countered *Mataram*'s support for the Wild Schools Ordinance by strongly criticizing the government for embarking on a course of control and by calling on the branches of Taman Siswa to step up their vigilance and to maintain their self-respect.

Two months later, the December 1931 issue of *Pusara* carried the full text of the 1923 private schools ordinance (Staatsblad 1923 No. 136).[17] No explanation was given, but the reason may have been connected with an inquiry in the "Question and answer" column of the previous issue concerning the right of government inspectors to investigate native schools and whether Taman Siswa must accept this. The reply cited Taman Siswa's duty under provisions of the 1923 ordinance, then continued: "We should treat [inspectors] as guests. The fact that they are guests means that they have no right to give orders or make changes concerning our curriculum or holidays. This is the difference between Taman Siswa and the schools that accept the government's subsidies."[18]

Thereafter, until late September 1932, Taman Siswa made no direct response to the Wild Schools Ordinance. During this time, however, it was strengthening and centralizing its organization and developing its criticism of the colonial government's educational system. This was the period when the articles by Soedyono (Gadjah Mada) and Dewantara, discussed in chapter 5, appeared.

Members of Taman Siswa were continually being reminded of the need to observe their own principles and regulations. In October 1931, teachers were urged not to take on extra teaching at outside schools, for such would be a dereliction of their proper duties and give precedence to monetary gain, thus contravening the spirit of Taman Siswa.[19] The following month, in announcing five "observances," one of the elders of Taman Siswa issued the warning: "Whoever violates our principles and rules and disturbs our unity should immediately be banished from the family of Taman Siswa."[20] As if on cue, Dewantara exercised his "dictatorial rights" to strike off the names of several members of the Cilacap branch on the grounds that they had damaged the organization (*merusakkan organisatie*) through "problems with money and women."[21] Other teachers left Taman Siswa voluntarily on the grounds of incompatibility, it being reported May 1932, for example, that Suwondo Sismokusumo and his brother from Ciamis had founded a separate school.[22]

Taman Siswa's stance embodied the ethics of the satria, the rigorous "self-discipline" stressed in Soedyono's writings, the basis of which had been laid in Dewantara's "Association between East and West," published in 1929. In "The Press and morality," published in March 1932, Dewantara expressed outrage that a nationalist party organ, *Suara Umum* (the publication of Soetomo's Partai Bangsa Indonesia), should carry "advertisements by Dutchmen seeking Indonesian concubines;" he was strongly critical that even nationalist newspapers should publish various indecent advertisements and photographs for the sake of money; and he stressed that it was "only natural in carrying through nationalism and idealism" that *Pusara* had always "flatly refused to publish such advertisements."[23] In the eyes of those who maintained their own discipline, it was not Taman Siswa that should be deemed "wild," but "the Dutchmen who do as they please on the streets." It was, moreover, the materialism of the West that had produced these *wilde medemenschen.*

While thus urging greater self-discipline, in the same period *Pusara* carried several articles on educational history and educational ideas in Europe. In December 1931, for example, Dewantara published an article summarizing the history of European educational thought (see chapter 5, note 34), while in this issue and the February, April, May, and July issues of the following year, a writer from Golongan Tegal Alum under the pseudonym P. H. S. published, as a summary of various Dutch works, biographies of fourteen great European teachers.[24] Another article, published in March 1932, dealt with the lives and educational ideas of Montessori and Jean Jacques Rousseau.[25] Such articles on foreign educational ideas continued to be published after 1932, with the Dalton system and Tagore's ideas receiving widespread coverage.[26]

Taman Siswa had, of course, since the time of its founding, taken note of the educational ideas of Montessori, Fröbel, Tagore, and others who were critical of modern Western culture. By asserting that these "latest" ideas were consistent with Taman Siswa's educational ideals and that some of them had in fact long been an integral part of Javanese culture, Taman Siswa showed its rejection of the existing public educational system.

The movement to give substance to this standpoint developed contemporaneously with the process of preparation of the Wild Schools Ordinance. It began with the realization that the curriculum of Taman Siswa's Mulo, which had been run in Yogyakarta since 1924 under the headmastership of Soewandhi, was merely a copy of the colonial government's course; and it emerged as a movement to enrich and "Taman Siswa-ize" this course. "Taman Siswa-ization" was expressed in the ideas of *zending* ("mission") and *redding* ("salvation") that had been proposed by Tjokrodirdjo and discussed extensively at the Yogyakarta congress in late February 1932. These terms signified the intention to realize the national spirit within Mulo education, that is, to achieve "the rebuilding of our own culture."[27] And throughout the Wild Schools Ordinance struggle, they featured prominently as expressions of Taman Siswa's critical stance toward the colonial education system.

Just as if the head-on confrontation with the colonial government that was to begin in October 1932 had been anticipated, the organizational, ideological, and educational developments that we have just examined—the strengthening of organization and the centralization of leadership; the advocacy of national principles and the shunning of Western culture; and the confidence in Taman Siswa's "ultramodernity," shown in the display of various educational ideas, and the antipathy to the colonial education system—equipped Taman Siswa for the struggle. Once the struggle began, Taman Siswa demonstrated clearly that its "equipment" had strength in depth and versatility.

THE WILD SCHOOLS ORDINANCE STRUGGLE

First Responses

THE WORKING COMMITTEE OF THE SUPREME COUNCIL

Taman Siswa's response to the promulgation of the Wild Schools Ordinance on 24 September 1932 was swift and thorough. On 29 September, in his capacity as "dictator," Dewantara convened a Working Committee of the Supreme Council (Madjelis Luhur Harian), which scrutinized the Wild Schools Ordinance clause by clause to determine Taman Siswa's basic attitude toward the legislation, then issued a "call," of which the burden was as follows.[28]

(1) The new ordinance empowered the government to control the form and substance of unsubsidized private schools, and placed the determination of criteria for control in the hands of local officials.

(2) Because the Taman Siswa schools were generally different (*pada umumnja berlainan*) in form and substance from Western-style schools, the application of this ordinance to Taman Siswa would inevitably lead to frequent misunderstandings between the government and officials on one hand and the pepole and organization of Taman Siswa on the other, and to wrong measures being taken. Therefore, the new ordinance would be an obstacle to Taman Siswa's "sacred task or mission" (*pekerdjaan sutji atau zendingsarbeid*).

(3) While there was no need to fear that Taman Siswa's educational facilities and techniques would not exceed the levels required by the new ordinance, the assessment of teachers' qualifications was bound to involve subjective considerations on the part of the officials concerned, particularly about whether teachers were "political" or "nationalistic." Wrong decisions would inevitably result from this.

(4) The same was true for other "wild schools" which, like Taman Siswa, were run according to their own principles. And while it was proper that "wild schools" without principles should be controlled, this could be fully achieved under the old ordinance of 1923. The new ordinance was therefore unnecessary and bad for "general order" (*ketertiban umun*).

(5) Because the government had prepared the new ordinance quickly and announced it suddenly, Taman Siswa had not had time to convene a congress. Therefore, in order to distance the People in general and Taman Siswa in particular from the potential dangers that would arise with the enforcement of the ordinance, dictatorial authority to define Taman Siswa's stance and set a course of action would be given to Ki Hadjar Dewantara (*memberi hak leluasa pada Diktator Ki Hadjar Dewantara*).

(6). Until the next congress, it was strongly recommended that all problems arising over the ordinance and involving members or organizations of Taman Siswa should first be discussed at the regional group councils (Madjelis Golongan).

In sum, the working committee rejected the 1932 ordinance and took steps to maintain Taman Siswa's "order and tranquility" by vesting full powers in Dewantara and by emphasizing the authority of the individual golongan. At the basis of this stance was the recognition that the "order and tranquility" that the government was seeking to impose threatened the "order and tranquility" that Taman Siswa was in the process of establishing. Through the following months Taman Siswa maintained this dual stance, on the one hand pressing the government to repeal the ordinance, on the other preserving its own "order and tranquility" by uniting under Dewantara.

DEWANTARA'S TELEGRAM

Taman Siswa's first expression to the government of its intention regarding the ordinance was in the form of a telegram Dewantara sent directly to the governor-general. Sent privately in Dewantara's name on 1 October 1932, the day the ordinance came into effect, and addressed to Governor-General De Jonge at his residence in Buitenzorg (Bogor), the telegram read as follows.[29]

> Your Excellency. The fact that an ordinance that will eat away the soul of [our] society and culture is to be brought into effect forcibly and without warning after the government's plans for educational expansion have failed is proof of the agitation and confusion of a government that has misunderstood the interests affecting the life and death of the People. Therefore, I give warning that even the defenseless will instinctively defend itself out of self-preservation [*zelfs onweerbaren instinctief uit zelfbehoud zich verweren*] and announce that we, in the same way, will offer the greatest degree of passive resistance (*lijdelijk verzet*) for as long as is necessary.

The telegram was, of course, in Dutch; but the September–October issue of *Pusara* carried an Indonesian translation. This was stronger in tone than the original, with the second part reading:[30]

I give warning that even a helpless creature harbors the noble sentiment to fight against danger in order to protect itself, and in the same way, we must also resist to our utmost and forever [*perlawanan sekuat-kuatnja dan selama-lamanja*] with silent power [*tenaga diam*].

With the Supreme Council's statement of attitude of 29 September and this telegram of protest, Taman Siswa pitched itself headlong into the battle for repeal of the Wild Schools Ordinance.[31]

The September 1929 issue of *Pusara* (volume 2, no. 12) was not in fact published until the following month, when it appeared together with the October issue (volume 3, no. 1). Its front page bore the words "October 1st, the day freedom of education died" (*hari wafatnja kemerdekaan pendidikan*); and the October issue took the opposite approach, with "October 1st, the day true freedom was born" (*hari lahirnja merdeka sedjati*). The next issue, December (volume 3, no. 2–3), proclaimed itself a "special issue on the educational ordinance" and was filled with articles on the Wild Schools Ordinance. Such a situation was to persist until the following February.

PASSIVE RESISTANCE

Having sent his telegram of protest to the Governor-General, Dewantara immediately issued an announcement to all members of Taman Siswa under the title, "To abrogate the ordinance immediately;" and on 3 October he issued an "Announcement to all leaders of the People's Movement about an educational ordinance."[32]

Dewantara's first announcement explained in detail the meaning and advantages of the "passive resistance" (*lijdelijk verzet*) referred to in his telegram, and clarified point by point the reasons leading to the adoption of passive resistance. This was an amplification of the substance of the Supreme Council's resolution and Dewantara's telegram of protest.

He first described passive resistance in broadly the following terms.[33]

To resist the pressure of the authorities, the People must use the power [*kekuatan tenaga*] of the People effectively. However loudly they shout their protests and petitions, without using their power these will seem to the authorities at best as the "whimpering of children." There are two ways of using power: actively [*actief*] and passively [*passief*]. The active method is used when two opposing forces have equal strength; the passive method is the means employed when one's physical power [*kekuatan lahir*] does not match that of the opposing force.

Passive resistance does not mean keeping quiet physically and spiritually [*diam lahir batinnja*]; it means keeping quiet and not changing [*mbegogok*] physically, but in spirit [*dalam batin*] firmly maintaining one's independence and not admitting the opponent's sovereignity [*tidak mengaku soeveriniteitnja si lawan*]. Passive resistance is this kind of opposition.

Dewantara went on to stress that passive resistance was "an extremely difficult method, because one must use spiritual power [*kekuatan batin*] and not lose hope, nor must one get angry, restless or submissive;" but even so, "silent power [*tenaga diam*] alone can deny the new ordinance and force the authorities to retreat."[34]

Turning to the ordinance itself, Dewantara explained his views on it and the significance of his actions. The ordinance, he felt, deprived parents and the People of the fundamental right to choose how to educate their children, and it attempted to assume control over schools that were run without governmental subsidy, that is, the private schools that the People had founded, that had been nurtured with the People's donations, and that were the People's property. The life or death of these "wild schools" hinged on how the ordinance would be applied. With the ordinance, the government had breached the political movement that formed a "fence" [*pagar*] around the educational movement and had come armed into its "field" [*ladang*].

Dewantara argued that because Taman Siswa was seen as the "vanguard" [*pemuka*] of the educational movement and the People were awaiting its instructions, he had decided to speak out "in order that the People should not be seized by the iron hand of the new ordinance." In doing so he ran a great risk, because many people would leave him if he were judged to have been wrong. But he accepted this danger and would immediately issue instructions in his own name, because "to accept this ordinance as just will mean the death of the People's freedom to conduct education according to their own methods and aims." All that would remain would be the school system run or subsidized by the government, and "colonial education" [*koloniale opvoeding*]. And there was no reason for him to go on living in a society that was "socially and culturally very narrow" (*masjarakat jang maatschapplijk dan cultureel amat sempit itu*).

His telegram to the governor-general, Dewantara claimed, was "an opening salvo" [*uluk-uluk*], it was "a warning," it was "an ultimatum," and it was his "farewell address" to the Netherlands Indies' society. It was also an expression to the enemy of the "satria spirit" [*pernjataan ksatryaan (ridderlijkheid)*]. He did not entreat the enemy, but informed him that he did not recognize the legality of the new ordinance [*tidak menganggap sjah akan adanja ordonnantie itu*].[35]

Finally, Dewantara stated that because the new ordinance required a swift response he had acted entirely in a personal capacity and that the Taman Siswa Association (Persatuan Taman Siswa) was entirely free to act according to its own views.

> I will comply fully with the decisions of Taman Siswa as a whole. If the decision of the whole differs from my standpoint, I promise that I will vigorously demand of the people who thought me right that they should not oppose the decision of the whole. Abide by the majority decision. If that is disagreeable to you, I suggest that you leave Taman Siswa's "organization" in order not to destroy its order and tranquility.[36]

Dewantara's announcement to Taman Siswa's members thus contained three elements: an explanation of passive resistance, a rejection of the ordinance, and a demand for internal unity. Passive resistance was explained by the Javanese word *mbaléla* ("to rebel"): but the attitude expressed was rather one of *nrima*, that is, "acquiescence without assent."[37] In the context of Javanese culture, Dewantara must have known that an announcement of passive resistance would be nothing less than an open declaration of hostility.

The reason for this declaration, for rejection of the ordinance, was couched in passionate terms: to resist the government's invasion of the territory of "peasants working their fields within the fence" (see chapter 4). Recognition of this led to his showing the "open hostility of a satria." Thus Dewantara himself in effect asserted that he had acted in the "political world" of the satria in order to defend the "nonpolitical world" of the pandita.[38]

The call to members of Taman Siswa was complex. While issuing his announcement as "dictator," Dewantara had sent his telegram of protest to the governor-general in a private capacity. Indeed, he insisted that he had acted "privately," and by so doing he claimed to have "run a great risk," the risk that many people would leave him. But he also sensed a greater danger that the organization of Taman Siswa would fall into disarray over the Wild Schools Ordinance. In the subsequent course of events, however, his fears were not realized.

Dewantara's "Announcement to all leaders of the People's Movement," issued on 3 October, was less a call for support than a clarification of his position. This he presented in nine points, which can be summarized as follows.[39]

> (1) "Passive resistance" avoids disturbance and opposes with silent force.
> (2) We must lay our foundations on truth, which religion and morality dictate.
> (3) To sharpen our thinking, hone our sensitivity, and keep our will firm, we must first cleanse our hearts. In other words, we must first distance ourselves from desire and anger.

(4) We must have "the courage of endurance." We must accept all things gladly, without anger, complaint, or curses.

(5) We must consider calmly our circumstances and our attitudes. We must compare and consider calmly our relationships with others, our strengths, and any changes therein.

(6) We should not discuss this situation publicly and in a big way, but choose a quiet time and place for talks just between leaders who know one another.

(7) We must always keep the children's interests in mind and not disturb their studies.

(8) If, as a result of application of the ordinance, a school is closed or a teacher ordered to suspend classes, a committee of inquiry (Commissie van Onderzoek) should immediately be formed on the People's side. If, as a result, it becomes clear that the fault lies with our side, we must strive to rectify it. If, however, as a result of inquiry, it becomes clear that the judgment of government officials was unjust, we must demand of the government that a government-controlled school be established in that area immediately in order that the pupils of our school may continue their studies.

(9) We must immediately set up a fund to help any who fall victim to the ordinance.

Finally, Dewantara appealed to "all leaders of People's Movement" to lend material and moral support and "not attempt to change our path, which is already set, but 'each go his own way to the same end' [*gescheiden samengaan*]."

Overall, these nine points reiterate the substance and significance of "passive resistance." The fourth, sixth, and eighth points expressed ideals that had supported Taman Siswa since its founding: acquiescence (*nrima*), freedom from personal desire (*sepi ing pamrih*), and consultation with elders (*tanjalah pada jang tua-tua*). Through the organization of committees of inquiry, the "order and tranquility" underpinned by these ideals was set against the government's authority.[40]

THE TOSARI CONGRESS

Responding to the swift reaction of Dewantara and the working committee of the Supreme Council, Taman Siswa's branches began to tackle the problem of the new ordinance at the golongan level.

The first response was from East Java. Even before Dewantara had issued his announcements, the Surabaya branch had called upon all branches of Taman Siswa to take emergency action (*momentactie*) in view of "the danger of the new ordinance," declaring that Taman Siswa's principles were unchangeable and that teachers should continue their educational activities as normal without fearing oppression.[41]

On 1–2 October, Golongan Argopuro convened a meeting in Bondowoso and resolved to follow the decisions taken at the East Java conference scheduled for the middle of the month.[42] On 3–4 October, leaders from East Java met in Surabaya and instructed branches in East Java to refrain both from taking decisions at the branch level until after the Tosari conference and from joining other organizations in opposing the Wild Schools Ordinance.[43] Before this, the Mojokerto branch had complained of the folly of making a "carbon copy" (*carbon-afdruk*) of the colonial education system.[44]

On 9 October, a joint conference of leaders of Central Java and Golongan Semarang was held. Resoultions were taken to step up Taman Siswa's educational "mission" (*zendingsarbeid*; *kewadjiban sutji*) of education, to strive further to improve Taman Siswa, and to abide by the Supreme Council's requests at the branch level; a call was issued to members not to join opposition outside Taman Siswa; and a conference of Central Javanese golongan was scheduled for 29 October.[45]

What emerged at these branch and golongan meetings was a movement to base local responses on the directions of the center. As if to focus this movement, on 5–6 October a Plenary Assembly of the Supreme Council (Madjelis Luhur Lengkap) was convened at Tosari, a summer resort located 1700 meters above sea level in the Bromo mountains of East Java. Originally, a conference of delegates from East Java was to have been held at this venue, but with the developing situation, an assembly of the Supreme Council was hastily convened in its place.[46]

The assembly began by declaring the new ordinance to be unlawful (*tidak sjah*; *onwettig*) on humanitarian grounds (*rasa kemanusiaan*). It then voted to endorse fully the stance that Ki Hadjar Dewantara had announced in the pages of *Pusara*. Next, to avert future dangers, it was decided that the Supreme Council would issue "general instructions" (*instruksi umum*) which all branches would be expected to follow. It was also resolved that when the Supreme Council considered it necessary for Taman Siswa's members to participate in joint activities with other groups, it would approve participation, provided such activities did not contravene the "general instructions."[47]

In this way, Taman Siswa announced publicly its formal adoption of Dewantara's stance. And through this it came to define the chain of command between the central executive and the branches. This made use of the organizational system that had been instituted in 1930: from Dewantara via the Supreme Council to "instructors" heading the twenty-two golongan, and thence to the branches.

Two weeks after the Tosari conference, on 29–30 October, a Conference of Taman Siswa Leaders (Konperensi Pemimpin Taman Siswa) was convened. In the interim, both the government and the nationalist movement had been stirred to act over the ordinance. In the following pages we shall examine in particular the government's negotiations with Taman Siswa, which brought into confrontation two divergent interpretations of "order and tranquility." The form of this confrontation and the differences between the two interpretations are revealed accurately in two documents: a report of a meeting between a high government official and Dewantara; and the record of the hearing of an arrested Taman Siswa teacher.

Confrontation of Two "Orders"

THE DISCUSSIONS BETWEEN KIEWIET DE JONGE AND DEWANTARA

Under the 1923 ordinance, the colonial government had on several occasions required Taman Siswa to submit reports on its educational ideals and educational system. These reports can now be found among secret colonial documents dating from 1924.[48]

From 1930, and particularly after the enforcement of the Wild Schools Ordinance, the number of reports related to Taman Siswa rose sharply. For example, Dewantara's announcement in *Pusara* and other documents setting forth Taman Siswa's attitude towards the Wild Schools Ordinance were translated into Dutch and reported to the governor-general.[49] One document that portrays most minutely the contemporary relationship between the government and Taman Siswa is a detailed report running to thirty-six typed pages which was presented to Governor-General de Jonge on 26 October 1932 by Kiewiet de Jonge, a government delegate on general affairs in the Volksraad, about consultations between himself and Dewantara.[50]

The talks between Kiewiet de Jonge and Dewantara had been held from 19–21 October. They were reported briefly in *Pusara*, which noted that their meetings had taken place over three days at Pondok Dewantaran in a friendly atmosphere. Since both men were speaking in a private capacity, the Supreme Council assumed no responsibility for what Dewantara had said. Discussions had been restricted to Taman Siswa's actions over the educational ordinance and the government's aims in enforcing it. Both had eventually agreed that some form of compromise was required, and for Dewantara this meant resolving the problem of requiring permission to open schools and conduct education.[51]

To learn the details of the talks, we must look at the report of Kiewiet de Jonge. The meeting had arisen out of an order given by the

Secretary General (Algemeene Secretaris) P. J. Gerke that contact should be sought with Dewantara in order as far as possible to resolve the "misunderstanding" (*misverstanden*) that had produced the passive resistance movement.[52] Kiewiet de Jonge received this order on 12 October and set out for Yogyakarta the following day.[53] Dewantara, however, was in East Java for the Tosari conference, so De Jonge returned briefly to Bandung, leaving again for Yogyakarta on the nineteenth. He succeeded in meeting Dewantara that evening for three hours of talks, which were followed by a two-hour meeting two days later on the twenty-first.

Before the talks, at the resident's office in Yogyakarta, De Jonge saw for the first time the September and October issues of *Pusara* and was shocked by the impassioned tone of Dewantara's opposition to the ordinance, which he felt was an overreaction. He took particular exception to the passages in the "instructions" to Taman Siswa members which read: "the government [has] come armed into the field;" "I do not recognize the legality of the new ordinance;" and "the telegram to the governor-general was . . . 'a warning,' it was 'an ultimatum,' and it was my 'farewell address.' " He was also shocked by Dewantara's call to leaders of the People's Movement to support Taman Siswa's stance that came at the end of Dewantara's "announcement." In the Dutch translation of Item 8 of the "announcement," an underline had been added, drawing attention to a passage that read: "If [as a result of investigations by the committee of inquiry formed on the People's side] it becomes clear that the judgment of government officials was unjust, we must demand of the government that a government-controlled school be established in that area immediately in order that the pupils of our school may continue their studies."[54]

Kiewiet de Jonge was anxious to discover whether Dewantara's series of statements had been purely personal and spontaneous or instigated by People's leaders and People's groups who saw a struggle against the Wild Schools Ordinance as a chance to call for united action to restore and strengthen the unity of the nationalist movement. If the former were the case, De Jonge judged that the misunderstanding could easily be resolved, but in the latter case it would be difficult. Even after his talks with Dewantara, however, De Jonge reported that he was unable to decide.[55]

(A) The First Meeting: Having arranged to visit Dewantara at his home at eight o'clock on the evening of 19 October, at six o'clock Kiewiet de Jonge received a telephone call from Dewantara inviting him to observe the weekly practice session of Javanese dance that was to take place that evening under the direction of Pangeran Tedjokoesoemo. He accepted, being interested in Javanese dance and considering the topic a good icebreaker for their conversation, and set off at once for the Taman Siswa School, which was under the same roof as Dewantara's home. There he was greeted by Dewantara and his wife, who explained to him, in turns, the significance of teaching Javanese dance to boys and girls.

When the practice ended eight o'clock, the two men stayed behind in the classroom, and De Jonge surveyed its meager furnishing of low tables standing on bare earth and an area of matting spread in front of them. "You mustn't say anything about the classroom," Dewantara told him with a smile. "These desks and classroom have already been criticized by Mr. Stroeve, who was the inspector of Western-style elementary education in around 1925. He said that children, even Javanese, must not sit on the ground, that the room was not big enough, and that there must be no communication between the classroom and the living accommodation. For us this last point is a matter of principle, because we have found it to have good effects." "You have apparently not taken the inspector's observations seriously," remarked De Jonge, to which Dewantara replied: "Because we received no subsidy, we did not need to comply. And it is one of our educational principles that children should not be taught in an environment that is more beautiful than their own home surroundings."[56]

Thus began the dialogue as detailed in De Jonge's report. This account was, the author cautioned, only a summary of their conversation, and, in that Dewantara had not seen it, the report was extremely one-sided (*zooverre eenzijdig*);[57] but overall, among the documents written by Dutch colonial officials, this report is extraordinary in its liveliness and the sense of presence it conveys. And insofar as it is accurate, it shows that Dewantara led easily into the conversation and thereafter continued to guide it.

Kiewiet de Jonge continued: "That seems to me an excellent principle. It can create the right atmosphere and prevent children from becoming more or less alienated from their surroundings." Dewantara replied immediately that it was also Taman Siswa's aim as far as possible to bring unity between school and home, and between education and society. Western-style schools, he continued, alienated Javanese children from their own traditions. This was why, on such points of principle, Taman Siswa had not followed the recommendations of the school inspector Stroeve. Almost unintentionally, De Jonge agreed: "That is your privilege by not being subsidized;" and Dewantara, as if expecting this remark, responded "Yes, but now, with the new ordinance, that privilege has been suspended." Then, giving concrete examples, he explained carefully why the ordinance was unjust and why he opposed it.[58]

The dialogue continued in this vein throughout the consultations. On the first day, the talks centered exclusively around the fact that the new ordinance placed the right to authorize teachers in the hands of colonial officials, specifically the residents in their respective residencies.

De Jonge first pointed out that he was speaking not officially but privately in an attempt to clear up Dewantara's misunderstanding by clarifying the government's intentions. "The new ordinance can perhaps best be likened to one on the inspection of foodstuffs," he said. If the education in unsubsidized schools were likened to foods, then what the government wished to do was to issue "prescriptions" (*voorschriften*) not just on its physical quality, the school buildings, and environment, but also on its spiritual quality, the curriculum. "In short, the government wants to cooperate so that, in both cases, people get good value for their money." De Jonge must have adduced this as the "best" comparision because of its persuasiveness for Dutchmen. But Dewantara responded: "But have people ever needed permission to sell food?"[59]

Here Dewantara countered the materialistic comparison with selling food and getting value for money with logic in the same vein: that from the standpoint of free competition and the balance of supply and demand, a seller is a seller by virtue of meeting the buyer's demand, and the choice of merchandise is determined by the market.

Effective though it may have been in persuading a Dutchman, the logic of this simile, the reduction of the problem to one of value for money, was probably the worst logic to use to try to win over the Taman Siswa leader (even if there were none that would have succeeded). Dewantara and other nationalists had long criticized materialism, and the word itself had assumed connotations of hatred as an expression of a totality of absurd and cruel experiences. Even though this simile may have seemed to De Jonge the "best" he could cite in justification of the new ordinance, it was to Dewantara no more than a good example of the materialism of Dutch culture.

The dialogue on the licensing of teachers under the new ordinance similarly failed to produce an agreement, with Dewantara asserting that the old ordinance of 1923 was sufficient for the government to attain its objectives, and Kiewiet de Jonge countering that the new ordinance did not aim to control schools like Taman Siswa that had well-established curricula and organizations, but those private schools with inferior objectives and curricula. (Again De Jonge asserted that the control of such schools was to prevent parents from wasting their money.) Dewantara replied that with the powers of authorization given to officials, there was the danger of deliberate discrimination against nationalist education: "Almost every day I receive news from one of our 170 schools and 1,000 teachers of how they are treated unjustly in all sorts of ways by the Bestuur and other officials."[60]

The dialogue continued with De Jonge seeking a path to compromise:[61]

"Do you distrust the government, then?"

"No," replied Dewantara, "but even if we trust the government, we cannot trust its officials."

"Then it is not the ordinance itself that you oppose, but only the way it is to be applied?"

When De Jonge went on to suggest, however, that Dewantara's insistence that regional officials, native as well as European, were using the ordinance as pretext for high-handedness, and that Taman Siswa was a prime target of the ordinance, amounted to no more than "unwarranted, private fears" and a "personal misunderstanding," Dewantara released his second arrow: "These fears are far from unwarranted. Everyone in the People's Movement understands this, and they have all shown sympathy with my views. It is not that I have not been put up to this by them, but that they recognize the justice of my position."[62] Thus Dewantara insisted that while his actions were spontaneous, he was supported by the entire People's Movement; and he firmly rejected the reduction of the problem to a personal level.

The first meeting ended with Dewantara promising to tell Kiewiet de Jonge his views on the government circular (*uitvoeringsvoorschriften*) on the execution of the ordinance that was then being drafted. When they parted, De Jonge said, "You are a true Javanese, sensitive to reasonableness and pure intentions." "Yes," Dewantara retorted, "only sometimes a little too sensitive, especially toward the opposites."[63]

(B) The Second Meeting: On the following morning, 20 October, Kiewiet de Jonge telephoned the deputy director of the department of education, Ter Laan, and was informed that the circular had been drawn up and approved by the governor-general. A copy had been sent to Kiewiet de Jonge in Yogyakarta, together with the modifications suggested by the adviser on native affairs, E. Gobée; it arrived the following morning, and De Jonge relayed it immediately to Dewantara.[64] In their second meeting, which began at eight o'clock that evening, the circular thus became the focus for their discussions. How this circular was drafted is unclear; but, as will be discussed shortly, about a month later, on 14 February, it was actually circulated to regional administrative offices.[65]

The second meeting again took place at Dewantara's home. Talk began casually on the topic of "*kain* Taman Siswa," a style of dress favored by members of the organization. Dewantara remarked that, far from being compulsory, such a uniform was totally undesirable. Taman Siswa was seeking a national-cultural basis (*nationaal-cultureele basis*) and a center (*middel-punt*), which would provide the strength to bring about an overall synthesis (*synthese*) while each and every one remained himself.[66]

They then turned to their main topic. Dewantara began by pointing out that "we shut out from Taman Siswa teachers of weak morality, especially those that misbehave themselves in financial or sexual spheres." He cited an example and talked about the trouble caused by teachers who had left Taman Siswa and founded their own school. (Though they are not named, this was undoubtedly a reference to the teachers of the Cilacap branch mentioned earlier in this chapter.) De Jonge pointed out that it was because of just such inferior schools that the new ordinance was deemed necessary. Dewantara replied:[67]

> That is clear from reading the circular. In particular the modifications suggested by Mr. Gobée make frequent reference to the old ordinance. Even with the circular, however, the licensing system is still for me a cage (*kooi*). The circular makes the cage more beautiful . . . even a gilded cage. It is fine that the cage has become more beautiful, but a cage is still a cage. . . . The licensing system is unacceptable to us on principle.

In their first meeting, Dewantara had declared: "For Taman Siswa, education is a religious task [*een religieuse taak*]."[68] He again referred to this "religious task" in the second meeting in reasserting that the new ordinance contravened Taman Siswa's principles. His insistence that "a cage is still a cage" appears to have brought his point home to de Jonge, who thereafter urged Dewantara to leave aside for the moment the question of modifying the ordinance proper and to state his views on the circular. Dewantara replied cautiously that he would speak only for himself, in order to help break the deadlock, and did not know what the Supreme Council or the conference of leaders of Taman Siswa would decide.[69]

He then went on, however, to speak at length rather of Taman Siswa's ideals, of its national-cultural principles, and its principle of not worshiping the living (based on which, Taman Siswa would not display portraits of the Dutch queen). Why, then, asked De Jonge, did he speak so much of Dipanegara, the hero of the Java War (1825–1830), and hang his portrait everywhere? "He was my wife's great-grandfather," replied Dewantara. "But we don't by any means speak just about Javanese heroes. I have, for example, long sought a good portrait of Willem de Zwijger, but there is none to be found."

"Shall I send you one?" asked De Jonge.

"With pleasure."

"Will you hang it up?"

"Certainly."[70]

Willem de Zwijger, William the Silent, was William I of Holland, founder of the House of Orange and liberator of the Dutch from Spanish rule. As the liberator of his people from foreign rule, Dewantara clearly considered him worthy of Taman Siswa's esteem. At the same time Dewantara skillfully used the same logic that he had used in 1913 in his pamphlet, *If I were a Dutchman* (see chapter 2) to expose the self-contradiction in the Dutch position.

Before returning to the subject of the circular, Dewantara told De Jonge various things: how "once a Javanese feels distrust, he will never forget it;" that "there are various nationalists who will not speak to a European;" and that "we [of Taman Siswa] stand at the center of concentric circles: family, relatives, associations, nation, mankind, etc."[71]

Having repeated his hope that the ordinance itself would be rescinded, Dewantara requested that if the circular were to be promulgated, formal translations into Javanese and Indonesian should be appended, because without these there was a danger that numerous unofficial translations would be produced and give rise to new difficulties. Kiewiet de Jonge agreed.[72]

At the end of his report, De Jonge summarized the main points he had gathered in his talks with Dewantara: that government officials, particularly the Binnelandsch Bestuur, did not deal satisfactorily with "native intellectuals" (*inheemsche intellectueelen*), and that they should be aware that, for the Javanese, "form and the nuances of form are not merely formal but have a very real significance."[73]

Although both Dewantara and Kiewiet de Jonge were speaking "in a personal capacity," the talks brought into relief the contradictory principles underlying the government's and Taman Siswa's view of "order and tranquility." Kiewiet de Jonge was probably one of the few Dutchmen in contemporary colonial society who was inclined to try to understand the Javanese and their culture. De Jonge was sent to clear up Dewantara's "misunderstanding," that is, to win Dewantara over, because it was believed that he would understand Dewantara's logic, and that for him to succeed in his mission, he would need to point out the contradictions and flaws in that logic or any underlying factual misconceptions. De Jonge's report of the discussions shows that he did his utmost to succeed: he awaited Dewantara's return from East Java, visited his home, and watched Javanese dance with him. He was also happy that Dewantara fully appreciated his "reasonableness and pure intentions." De Jonge's attitude was truly sincere: he expressed concern that his report had been submitted without Dewantara seeing it and that it would therefore be extremely "one-sided."

Dewantara understood De Jonge's position perfectly and was able to explain clearly and logically Taman Siswa's position regarding the implementation of the ordinance and to convince the Dutchman of its logical consistency. De Jonge's comment that form and its nuances are reality for the Javanese probably derived from Dewantara's response to the suggestion that Taman Siswa formed a class apart from other private schools, that is, that for such fine schools as Taman Siswa's the licensing of teachers would be merely a procedural formality. Dewantara had made the Dutchman aware of this not by explaining to him the essence of Javanese culture—not once does the report mention Dewantara using a Javanese word and then explaining its meaning in Dutch—but by expounding the realities of the arbitrary behavior by colonial officials that had resulted from the implementation of the ordinance (this is also shown by a comment at the end of De Jonge's report, about the need for measures to deal with regional officials of the Binnenlandsch Bestuur).

Dewantara also showed remarkable versatility and hospitality in entertaining his Dutch "guest." The report conjures up a scene of Dewantara, faced by the extremely serious (and tense) Kiewiet de Jonge, quietly and (contrary to De Jonge's original intentions) persuasively explaining his position. Not only was De Jonge unable to change Dewantara's position one iota, the more he pursued Dewantara's logic the clearer he saw the inconsistency of the new ordinance and the problems of the colonial government, particularly in the local administrative offices. It also became clear that "materialism" was the only argument De Jonge had with which to try to win over Dewantara.

Such "materialism" was an expression of Dutch zakelijkheid, and as such it can be considered a pillar of the Beamtenstaat. By rejecting the actual mode of behavior of colonial officials, Dewantara demonstrated that the new ordinance was acting to legitimate "arbitrary rule" and to strengthen the Beamtenstaat.

THE RECORD OF A HEARING

We shall next try to show that the arbitrariness of colonial officials that was frequently spoken of in the talks between Kiewiet de Jonge and

Dewantara formed, together with "materialism," one side of the coin of colonial rule. Pertinent to this is the record, published in *Pusara*, of the hearing of a Taman Siswa teacher who was arrested on a charge of violating the Wild Schools Ordinance.[74]

This record is included in a report on the hearing which the Cabang Cikoneng branch of Taman Siswa in the Ciamis area of West Java submitted to Taman Siswa headquarters. The hearing was held by officials of the Ciamis district court on 9 November 1932.

The defendant was one Kartawan, a young tjantrik of the Cikoneng branch. As we saw in chapter 3, in the pondok, pesantren, and other traditional schools of Java, tjantrik were those who had completed sufficient training to be regarded as heads of schools (in 1928 Dewantara described the thirteen "ranks" in these schools, from the lowest pupil to the highest teacher, of which tjantrik was fourth from the bottom); and in Taman Siswa, tjantrik were trainees under a system, introduced at the Yogyakarta school in around 1924, whereby graduates of general education courses elsewhere could be appointed as Taman Siswa teachers on completion of Taman Siswa courses in the theory and methods of education. We can speculate that a similar system was in operation at Cikoneng, and that Kartawan was a "student-teacher" receiving practical training under the guidance of a regular teacher.

With the enforcement of the new ordinance, the licensing of tjantrik became a frequent point of contention between Taman Siswa and local officials. In Taman Siswa's eyes, tjantrik were students, not teachers, and therefore not subject to the licensing stipulated by the ordinance; but local officials considered that because they were actually teaching they needed the proper license.

The Cikoneng incident was the first to involve arrest on the grounds of teaching without a government license. A second reason cited for Kartawan's arrest and prosecution, however, was that "the tjantrik's attitude towards the official [concerned] was 'improper,' that is, 'very impertinent'" (*sikapnja* (*optreden*) *tjantrik terhadap kepada ambtenaar dianggap "ta' senonoh" jaitu "zeer onbeschoft"*).[75]

The hearing opened on 9 November in the presence of the assistant resident as judge, the assistant *wedana* (subdistrict head) of Cikoneng as prosecutor, the secretary to the assistant resident, Kartawan as first defendant, and the head of the Cikoneng Taman Siswa school, Soekardi, as second defendant.

The record of the hearing was made by Soekardi and sent to Taman Siswa headquarters, and as such, it may be as "extremely one-sided" as Kiewiet de Jonge's report. Nevertheless, it can be considered a fairly accurate record of events. Based on this record, we shall trace the course of the hearing and the outcome of the incident. At the start of the record, Soekardi notes that the questioning was conducted entirely in Dutch, and all answers were given in "our language" (presumably Indonesian).[76]

The hearing began with the following exchange between the judge (the assistant resident) and the defendant (Kartawan).[77]

JUDGE: Is it true that you taught without a license?

DEFENDANT: It is true.

JUDGE: Why did you take it upon yourself to do such a thing? Don't you know that there is an educational ordinance stipulating that everyone who imparts education should give prior notice to the government ?

DEFENDANT: I know very well. Concerning why I didn't notify the government beforehand, I should like the headmaster, Mr. Soekardi, to be asked. Mr. Soekardi has declared that I do not need a license.

JUDGE: Very well. Let us leave that till later. But do you nevertheless admit, Mr. Kartawan, that when you spoke with the assistant *wedana* your attitude was extremely impertinent?

DEFENDANT: Before I answer yes or no to that, I would like ask something. What does "impertinent" mean?

JUDGE: It means that your attitude toward the assistant was not what it should have been [*bukan semestinja*].

DEFENDANT: That does not mean my attitude was "very impertinent." For myself, I do not need to show deference [*menghormat*] to anyone, nor do I wish to be shown deference by anyone. [*Here, the note "Check! Pusara editors" was inserted in parentheses.*]

JUDGE: What do you mean by that?

DEFENDANT: What I want to say is that when the assistant asked about things, he asked just as if he were asking something of a child. Also, when he came to our school, he did not first ask permission of me, whose home it is, but came in just as if he were coming into his own house. (*Check! Pusara editors.*)

JUDGE: (*Making no response to this, merely clearing his throat*) Next I shall ask the second defendant, Mr. Soekardi. Why did you say those things to Mr. Kartawan?

SECOND DEFENDANT: This is why. This person is not yet a teacher but merely a student. In other words, he is my student, and he is learning from me about teaching. He is what we call a "tjantrik." Therefore, I considered that he did not need to report to the government. (*Check! Pusara editors.*)

JUDGE: According to the law, however, it is laid down that anyone who teaches, whoever he may be, must report that fact to the government beforehand. And Mr. Kartawan has already admitted that he taught without holding a license [*kennisgeving*]. (*Oh? Then what about apprentice pharmacists, learner-drivers, and so on? Pusara editors.*)

SECOND DEFENDANT: Does that law apply only in Cikoneng?

JUDGE: The law applies in all districts of the Netherlands Indies; and it applies to all people, be they Dutch, Chinese [*orang Tjina*] (orang Tjonghoa, Pusara editors), Arab, Maduran, or be they Javanese or Sundanese. And because Mr. Kartawan has admitted breaking this law, he is sentenced to a fine of ten florins or imprisonment for five days.

SECOND DEFENDANT: Judge, you have come here representing the regency of Ciamis, but do you not know that there are here other tjantrik of Taman Siswa schools who are teaching without a license? They are in Banjar, they are in Parigi; in fact, tjantrik who do not have that [*license*] are in almost all branch schools of Taman Siswa.

JUDGE: I didn't know that. Thank you for telling me. Well now, Mr. Kartawan is sentenced to punishment of a fine of ten florins or imprisonment for five days, and the case is closed. Do you have the money?

SECOND DEFENDANT: Just a moment, please. I have a question. Who is it who should pay the fine or be imprisoned? I bear the responsibility for what my student has done, so naturally I should be the one to whom this law is applied.

JUDGE: Very well. Then I grant an eight-day postponement for you to decide who should receive the punishment. (*Wise, just, and not mechanical! Pusara editors.*)

JUDGE: (*Pointing to the two defendants and addressing the assistant wedana*) Assistant wedana, who shall be subject to the decision? [*Here the record is all in Dutch.*]

ASSISTANT WEDANA: In my record of the hearing, Mr. Kartawan is the accused. I have no concern whatsoever with Mr. Soekardi. [*This is also in Dutch. A comment is added: "Mechanical! Pusara editors."*]

SECOND DEFENDANT: One moment, please. Certainly, my student has made a mistake; but that was because I caused him to make a mistake. Therefore, basically I am at fault; I should be punished, and there is no reason for my student to be punished because he did not understand anything.

JUDGE: You may consult over who will be punished. For the moment, I will enter Mr. Kartawan's name on the judgment. Is that all right?

SECOND DEFENDANT: There's something else. As Mr. Kartawan said earlier, the assistant wedana entered his home without first asking permission, just as if he were entering his own home. Now I ask you. Does a police officer really have the right to do such a thing? In other words, can he enter someone else's home without leave?

JUDGE: A police officer has the right freely to enter a school building.

SECOND DEFENDANT: I would like it to be known that my home is not a school building [*gedung sekolahan*] but a school-house [*rumah perguruan*], a place where a teacher lives. In other words, that building is a dwelling, it has an owner, it has someone with rights over it. Nevertheless, as far as I know, the assistant wedana has twice already entered my house without permission. Is such a thing proper?

JUDGE: The police officer did not at that time enter your home; he entered a classroom [*leslokaal*]: that is, he entered a place where a teacher was teaching students; he did not enter Mr. Soekardi's place. (*Mistaken and misused!* [Misbegrijp dan misgreep], *Pusara editors*). Moreover, a police officer has the right freely to enter a place of learning. His purpose is to inspect [*mengamatiamati*], not to interfere [*merintangi*].

SECOND DEFENDANT: Sir, I don't believe that [*Saja ta' pertjaja, tuan*].

JUDGE: What's that? You don't believe it? Are you saying you don't believe what I say? You be careful! [*Wees voorzichtig!*]. That is an insult to me [*Dat is een beleedging voor mij*]. You'd better remember this. The police have the right freely to enter your house [*rumah tuan*]. This means that if there is an incident of some kind in the future, for example, gambling or something, you yourself will be arrested.

SECOND DEFENDANT: And I would like you to understand clearly that my house is not a house that people enter and leave at will, and that my school [*perguruan*] is not a gambling-house [*speelhuis*]. [*Throughout the record, the Taman Siswa school is referred to by the Indonesian word* perguruan—*a guru's school*—*while* sekolah, *a loan word from the Dutch, is used exclusively for government-run schools. Also, the Dutch word* speelhuis *is used.*]

JUDGE: Thank you. And that ends the case.

SECOND DEFENDANT: You're welcome.

Soekardi's report goes on to state that in the eight-day period following the first hearing, the assistant wedana visited the school (*rumah perguruan kita*) three times to urge him to pay the ten-florin fine. Each time he replied, "I have plenty of money but I won't pay." On 17 November 1932, when the "time for consideration" (*bedenktijd*) had expired, he again set out for the assistant resident's office, in the company of M. Sardjono, the "instructor" of Golongan Garut, and Kartawan. While these two remained outside, Soekardi entered the office to resume his talks with the assistant resident. The record again indicates that the official spoke in Dutch, Soekardi in Indonesian.[78]

SOEKARDI: Mr. Assistant Resident. Do you remember me? The eight days have passed and I can't pay the fine, so I've come to surrender myself. I wish to be put in prison.

ASSISTANT RESIDENT: Er, your name?

SOEKARDI: I am Soekardi.

ASSISTANT RESIDENT: Mr. Soekardi, this is not your affair.

SOEKARDI: Mr. Assistant Resident, this is clearly my affair.

ASSISTANT RESIDENT: I say it is not your affair. It was Mr. Kartawan who broke the law; it was Mr. Kartawan on whom judgement was passed. Therefore, he pays ten florins or he goes to prison.

SOEKARDI: Don't you remember that the last time you gave us a postponement of eight days and told us to decide who would pay the fine or go to prison? Isn't that so?

ASSISTANT RESIDENT: That is so. But Kartawan's name has already been entered on the judgment, not your name. I cannot alter the judgment. Tomorrow, therefore, at half past nine, Mr. Kartawan must either pay the fine or go to prison.

SOEKARDI: In that case, what if I were to pay the ten florins?

ASSISTANT RESIDENT: Whoever pays, it will be recorded on the judgement that Mr. Kartawan paid.

SOEKARDI: Then what you're saying is that you don't mind if someone else pays the fine, but no one else must go to prison.

ASSISTANT RESIDENT: Mr. Soekardi, Do you want to go to prison? (*Mistaken! Pusara editors.*)

SOEKARDI: Of course, that is what I am asking.

ASSISTANT RESIDENT: That is not possible. Having you taken leave of your senses? [*Ben ik niet wijs?*]. Mr. Soekardi, I am a busy man. Mr. Kartawan has broken the law, he has admitted it, and he will pay or go to prison. Do you understand?

SOEKARDI: May I consult someone else about this incident?

ASSISTANT RESIDENT: I do not wish to speak any more about this to anyone. I do not wish to meet anyone. I invited you in because you are the chief. This affair is now settled. You can go.

SOEKARDI: Thank you. Tomorrow morning, will Mr. Kartawan be taken from Cikoneng? Or should he make his own appearance?

ASSISTANT RESIDENT: He should present himself at nine-thirty at the public prosecutor's office [*kantoor djaksa*].

This concluded Soekardi's second meeting with the assistant resident, but his report continued as follows.[79]

> What does the reader think of the assistant resident's words? I leave this to all of you to decide. I am still young and cannot offer a comprehensive and complete opinion or comment; but when I faced the assistant resident I trembled continuously, not from fear but because of my young blood. In breaking his promise, the assistant resident's behavior was truly inconsistent.

From 18–23 November 1932, Kartawan was interred in Ciamis prison. The final section of Soekardi's report details the work he did, the food he ate, and the clothing he wore in prison.[80]

Overall, the report is a remarkable document. It states that the government side spoke only Dutch and the Taman Siswa side only Indonesian. In the section covering the "court" hearing, the Dutch is translated into Indonesian, while in the exchange between Soekardi and the assistant resident, the original Dutch is cited. Both sides must have understood each other perfectly and yet conversed in their own different languages.

Stylistically, the report has a zakelijkheid quality, confining itself in "businesslike" manner to a verbatim account of the dialogue. However "one-sided" the report may be, it maintains this style consistently, even in the final section on prison conditions, which, though detailed, reports only the bare facts.

This style brings out clearly the paradoxical nature of the hearing: that it was in fact the colonial officials who were on trial before Taman Siswa. In their exchanges it was always the assistant resident and assistant wedana whose logic was exposed as "inconsistent" and who, as a result, became angry and agitated. At the hearing the assistant resident stated, "For the moment, I will enter Mr. Kartawan's name as defendant on the judgment;" but eight days later he told Soekardi, "Kartawan's name has already been recorded on the judgment. . . . therefore . . . Mr. Kartawan must either pay the fine or go to prison." When confronted with his contradiction, he replied: "Whoever pays, it will be recorded on the judgment that Mr. Kartawan paid" (Dewantara criticized such thinking as Dutch "materialism"); "I do not wish to speak any more about this to anyone. I do not wish to meet anyone." Involuntarily, the assistant resident revealed his dismay and his fear of becoming entangled further; and his final "You can go" had the ring of an entreaty.

Soekardi and Kartawan, on the other hand, handled the situation like satria. Each made it clear where his own responsibilities lay and asserted himself boldly and fearlessly; and at the same time they kept in close touch with both the local leadership (the "instructor" Sardjono accompanied them on their second visit) and the central leadership of Taman Siswa. To the end, their belief that they were right remained unshaken: Soekardi's claim that "I have plenty of money but I won't pay" was not simply an act of rebellion against the "materialism" of the officials but also an expression of this belief.

The reports of Dewantara's discussions with Kiewiet de Jonge and of Kartawan's trial reveal, firstly, Taman Siswa's readiness to stand against the colonial government on matters of principle: the nonseparation of the teacher's home and classroom, and the operation of the tjantrik system. In the latter case, Taman Siswa was even held to be in breach of the law.

Secondly, they show that Taman Siswa's stand against the Wild Schools Ordinance invoked "arbitrary" behavior by local officials. Dewantara spoke convincingly of this to Kiewiet de Jonge, and in Kartawan's case the assistant resident clearly sought to justify his "arbitrariness" through zakelijkheid in his handling of the documentation.

Thirdly, in announcing their distrust of local officials, both Dewantara (*"wantrouwen"*) and Soekardi (*"tak pertjaja"*) rejected "the proper attitude" (*sifat semestinja*), namely, those attitudes of deference and respect towards officialdom that were required by the *hormat* system. As such, the stand taken at Cikoneng provided a concrete example of Dewantara's "passive resistance" (*lijdelijk verzet*), which, in the context of the hormat system, was nothing short of open rebellion. In this way, Taman Siswa rejected the culture that supported the colonial government's "order and tranquility."

In sum, the two records show the emergence of a conflict between Taman Siswa and the colonial government over the principles underlying their respective versions of "order and tranquility." They show further that while the supporting ideology of "the white man's burden" was bankrupt and, consequently, the colonial bureaucracy was functioning as an instrument of naked oppression to maintain the government's "order and tranquility," Taman Siswa's "order and tranquility" possessed a logical consistency at both the center (Dewantara) and the periphery (Soekardi) and, because of its manifest centripetalism, was considered far more appropriate for the Javanese.

Throughout their dialogue, the assistant resident spoke in Dutch, Soekardi in Indonesian. That the Dutch was often logically muddled while the Indonesian was coherent in a sense symbolized both the existence and the nature of the conflict between the two versions of "order and tranquility."

Building The Fence

THE LEADERS' CONFERENCE

On 29–30 October 1932, about a week after the consultations between Dewantara and Kiewiet de Jonge, a leaders' conference (Konferensi Pemimpin dari Persatuan Taman Siswa) was convened in Yogyakarta with the aim of formulating Taman Siswa's response to recent developments, including the Tosari conference, the meeting between Dewantara and De Jonge, and reports from local branches and golongan councils.[81] Discussion covered five points, on which Taman Siswa's views were reconfirmed.

First, the Wild Schools Ordinance was found to contravene Taman Siswa's stated principles of independence (*kemerdekaan diri*), the establishment of order and tranquility (*tertib dan damai*) and its own educational system (*among-systeem*), and expansion of education opportunities for the People (*memperlebarkan pengadjaran pada rakjat*).

Second, the government was seen to be neglecting its duty to expand educational opportunities for the People and at the same time to be hindering the People's own educational activities.

Third, even though the discussions between Dewantara and Kiewiet de Jonge had been effective in conveying Taman Siswa's views to the government, particularly concerning the need to curb the arbitrary behavior of local officials, Taman Siswa recognized no change whatsoever in the government's basic policy.

Fourth, the crisis now faced by the unsubsidized private schools could only be resolved by the abolition of the Wild Schools Ordinance. The government's stated objective of supervising private schools was seen as being fully achievable through the ordinances of 1923 (No. 136) and 1925 (No. 260).

Fifth, whether or not the new ordinance could be abolished would depend on the firmness of attitude (*tetap teguhnja sikap*) of those who rejected the ordinance on the grounds of their rights and purity (*hak dan kesutjian*).

Finally, the conference adopted a three-point resolution. First, all members of Taman Siswa should, in the spirit of Taman Siswa and by methods that conformed with Taman Siswa's principles, remain firmly opposed to the new ordinance. In every case, however, the Supreme Council alone had the right and duty to decide what attitudes and actions should be taken. Second, for the next five months, from the present until 31 March 1933, no branch of Taman Siswa should establish new branches or employ new teachers. And third, instructions (*instruksi*) would be issued, when necessary, with the aim of achieving the overall order and tranquility of Taman Siswa.

A Dutch translation of these resolutions was also published in *Pusara*.[82] A note gave the reason for this as being "to forestall anyone from producing a distorted translation of our opinions."[83]

The second of these resolutions is particularly noteworthy. Clearly, Taman Siswa had spelled out a policy of avoiding confrontation with the government for a period of five months. In a letter to Kiewiet de Jonge written on 1 November, two days after the conference, Dewantara commented as follows about this policy, which he said was a response to De Jonge's good intentions and to his opinion that some form of compromise was necessary.[84]

> Within the coming six [*sic*] months up to 31 March 1933, we expect that the government, in consideration of our interests, will repeal the new ordinance. Based on this expectation, we have issued instructions that no new schools should be opened and that no new teachers should be employed until 31 March 1933.

De Jonge appended this letter together with a copy of the announcement of the leader's conference to a statement of opinion, dated 7 November, which he presented to the group of government delegates for general affairs of the Volksraad.[85] The burden of this statement was, first, that Dewantara's hard-line stance was unchanged, and that the "passive resistance" he advocated was continuing unabated. Dewantara's resolve appeared to be unshakable. Second, the announcement of the leaders' conference had a dual significance: that the resistance movement was growing; but that it was prepared to allow time for a satisfactory solution to be reached. Third, support for Taman Siswa was expanding to include virtually all nationalist groups. To restore tranquility, the licensing system should be replaced by the old system of notification through which the government's aims would ultimately be achievable. Fourth, to this end, it was desirable that the Volksraad should take an active role.

De Jonge's statement of opinion thus viewed the resolutions of the leaders' conference not as a compromise but as grounds for fearing that the resistance movement would spread; and, in full recognition of Taman Siswa's views, the statement proposed a method to settle the affair. The period of five months was seen as a "grace period" granted by Taman Siswa to allow the government to consider this method.

What prompted De Jonge to prepare such a statement is also clear from the foregoing summary. It was in part that on more than one occasion since his meeting with Dewantara, he had experienced personally Taman Siswa's obstinate powers of resistance; and in part it was that Taman Siswa's resistance had evoked an upsurge of vitality among the nationalists.

SUPPORTING ACTIONS

Although Dewantara did not specifically request support from the various nationalist groups after the enforcement of the Wild Schools Ordinance in October 1932, many of them called meetings about the ordinance from mid-October through November. The November–December 1932 issue of *Pusara*, a special edition on the ordinance, opened with an article entitled "Orientation" by the Taman Siswa leaders' group. It discussed the response of nationalist forces to Taman Siswa in the period of less than two months since the enforcement of the ordinance, depicting clearly the contemporary situation and Taman Siswa's view of its own position. The article ran as follows.[86]

> In the past few months, *Pusara* has devoted most of its space to the serious task of protecting our tranquility, namely, the task of rejecting the new educational ordinance. Other articles have had to be omitted. But after repairing our broken fence [*pagar kita jang dadal*] (in cooperation with our colleagues outside of Taman Siswa), we hope immediately to be able to come to grips with our own domestic affairs.
>
> We say "immediately" because the political group [*kaum politiek*]— the army that protects our tranquility—is now awake and ready to fight. We have sounded the "alarm" in the dead of night when they slept soundly and we have awakened them. We pray that this fight will succeed and that we—the farmers [*kaum tani*]—can return to the fields [*kembali keladang*] to fulfill the proper tasks of farmers, of tilling the soil, sowing seed, giving water, and clearing weeds.
>
> With a sense of joy we have seen and experienced that all People's groups [*semua golongan Rakjat*] are taking the same orientation. There is not one part that is moving away from us. [Here there is a footnote saying, "Apart from 'the Ajat group.' Corrector."[87]] All of the People and all People's groups have looked in our direction and have come to us asking the meaning of our SOS, that is, our distress call [*noodsein*]. We have explained things to them clearly and fully, and they have cooperated with us in resisting the danger. Regardless of politics, religion, or social group, all have now bound themselves together with cords to form a solid fence [*pagar jang amat rapatnja*]. Many people are now saying that while there had hitherto been only a unity of feeling [*persatuan-rasa*], there is now a unity of power of all the People [*persatuan tenaga dari segenapnja Rakjat*].

This is a lesson showing a method by which we, the People, can combine our power. As a result of this method, there was no struggle for power, no rivalry for election, no contention to exert influence, no conflict of any kind, and, moreover, as now, the People's power was perceived and demonstrated.

Why should this immense unity of power have materialized? Those who rang the alarm were as much nonpartisan men of understanding [*seorang jang faham*] as they were men who are considered the result of the workings of mystical power [*daja kebatinan*]. But whoever they were, it is fitting that we of Taman Siswa should praise God [Tuhan], for, being so destined [*dititah*], Taman Siswa has become the cause of a movemement of the People, who seek peace and happiness.[88]

The proof of the People's power is apparent in the unease in the European [Dutch-language] press and in the fact that Kiewiet de Jonge visited Ki Hadjar Dewantara. . . .

Taman Siswa's view that the situation will change has been consistent from the outset. Having become one with the People, we shall "go together" [*gescheiden samengaan*] with them.

It was thus in the context of its struggle against the Wild Schools Ordinance that Taman Siswa saw its self-image in terms of the nonpolitical-political, pandita-satria dichotomy, the image of farmers, whose fields are protected by a fence, as being most clearly realized. It also saw the realization of "the People's power," which made it a center surrounded by the People, as a manifestation of God's will, or destiny (*titah*). The title, "Orientation," chosen for this article was probably intended to refer to the movement provoked by the Wild Schools Ordinance; but more specifically the article showed the orientation of "the People's power," which was concentrating around the focus of Taman Siswa.

The first political group to respond to the new ordinance was the PSII, the Partai Sarekat Islam Indonesia. On 1 October 1932, the day the ordinance came into effect, the party issued an announcement at Bandung in the names of its vice-president, Abikusuno Tjokrosujoso, and its secretary, S. M. Kartosuwirjo. Addressed to "the entire Indonesian People and the newspapers," it stated that the new ordinance obstructed the right and duty of the People to educate themselves, and that a conference would be convened immediately to discuss the problem.[89] Held in Bandung on 5–6 November, this conference resolved to hold mass rallies against the ordinance on 11 December in Java and 18 December in Sumatra, and to embark on mass action from 1 April 1933 if the ordinance were still in force. This was in line with Taman Siswa's policy, and was said to have been intended to protect the PSII schools, of which there were several.[90]

Following PSII, which responded to the Wild Schools Ordinance simultaneously with Taman Siswa, various other groups began to take action. In order of date, these were as follows.

On 9 October, a rally of private-school teachers from East Java was reported to have been held at the Mulo Siswo Utomo school in Surabaya under the name of the Comité van Actie Wilde Scholen (Wild Schools Action Committee).[91] It is not clear, however, what kind of "action committee" this was.

Also on 9 October, the Isteri Sedar (Aware Wives) met in Jakarta and adopted a resolution to the effect that far from improving the condition of private schools, the new ordinance would hinder the People's own educational activities.[92]

On 9–10 October, the teachers' union, PGHB, adopted a resolution in the name of its executive council stating that: "The new ordinance will not improve the educational situation in Indonesia."[93]

On 16 October, the Partai Indonesia (PI) convened in Jakarta. Citing details of the educational budget for 1929, Sartono, a member of its central committee, pointed out that while 48 florins per head was apportioned for the education of Dutch children, for Indonesians the figure was only half a florin per head. To enforce the new ordinance on top of this, he believed, could only worsen further the People's educational circumstances.[94] It was also stated that the PI's formal position would shortly be decided, to which end a party congress met in Yogyakarta on 27 November. There, the new ordinance was condemned as restricting the People's right of educational choice, impeding the development of national education, and revealing the true face of imperialism in Indonesia; and it was announced that PI would (1) support and aid the position of People's education (*Perguruan Rakjat*) headed by Taman Siswa, (2) fight for the repeal of the ordinance by means of mass action (*massa-aksi*), and (3) appeal to all the People to step up the fight against imperialism.[95]

On October 22, the Madjelis Guru "Perguruan Rakjat" (Council of Teachers of "People's Education") met in Jakarta and issued a statement to the effect that they would (1) win the fight against the ordinance by means of spiritual force (*kekuatan batin*) and the power of silence (*tenaga diam*), (2) act in concert with other groups and schools that shared the same objective, and (3) support Ki Hadjar Dewantara's stance.[96] This "council" was probably an association of teachers of the "unsubsidized schools" against which the ordinance was directed.

On October 29, the Nganjuk branch of Budi Utomo voted to support Dewantara wholeheartedly and sent a text of the resolution to

Budi Utomo headquarters with an appeal that it should issue a similar declaration of support.[97] This prompt appears to have been taken, for the educational affairs committee of Budi Utomo issued a communiqué stating that the ordinance blocked the path to spontaneous development by the People and that the government should repeal it.[98]

The following day, October 30, saw a gathering in the central cinema in Malang of more than eight hundred representatives of thirty-three various political parties and groups, who, in the name of the Komité Menentang Onderwijs Ordonnantie H. B. Malang (Malang Committee Against the Educational Ordinance), issued an "Announcement to all the Marhaens of Indonesia." The burden of this was that the committee shared Dewantara's views on the new ordinance and would therefore fight in wholehearted support of Dewantara for the abolition of the ordinance.[99] The thirty-three groups included virtually all of the major political parties and groups then in East Java; and their coming together meant that an expanded unitary organization on the lines of the PPPKI of the late 1920s was formed around the nucleus of Taman Siswa and Dewantara.

This movement in opposition to the ordinance and in support of Dewantara gained further strength in November. Early in the month, the central executive committee of the Partai Bangsa Indonesia (Indonesian People's Party), a party led by Soetomo, announced in its official organ, *Suara Umum* (dated 3 November), that it opposed the ordinance because it hampered the progress of the People, that it supported one hundred percent the passive resistance advocated by Taman Siswa and Dewantara, and that teachers in the party's schools who could not subscribe to this policy should leave the party immediately.[100] In view of the fact that the party had long been at odds with Taman Siswa in East Java, this announcement was epochal, a public concession that Taman Siswa and Dewantara stood at the center of the struggle against the ordinance.

On 6 November, after a meeting at Blora in the north of Central Java, teachers from private schools in the vicinity announced their support for Taman Siswa's policy and that they had provisionally formed an organization called Perikatan Pengadjar-pengadjar Perguruan Liar Seluruh Indonesia (PPPLST; All-Indonesia League of Wild Schools Teachers).[101]

The same day saw the convention of 343 delegates of Pagujuban Pasundan, a Sundanese organization, in the Gedung Persatuan Rakjat (People's Unity Building) in Tasikmalaya, West Java, where they declared their opposition to the ordinance.[102]

On 10 November, the Perhimpunan Peladjar Peladjar Indonesia (PPPI; Association of Indonesian Students) met in Bandung. They declared that the ordinance served to "keep the Indonesian People permanently ignorant" (*Rakjat Indonesia tetap tinggal bodoh*), protect the interests of capitalists who required cheap, uneducated labor, and weaken the Indonesian independence movement; and they resolved to fight until the Wild Schools Ordinance was abolished.[103]

On 12 November, the PPPKI assembled in Yogyakarta, where it resolved to support Taman Siswa fully, to take mass action to this end in December, and to call upon all groups belonging to PPPKI to lend both material and moral support to Taman Siswa's activities. On 2 December, PPPKI convened again in Surabaya. One thousand delegates representing twenty-five organizations reaffirmed the resolutions to abolish the ordinance and support Taman Siswa.[104] Since its formation in 1927, PPPKI had failed to function as Sukarno had hoped it would, as an organization for national unification, but now, in the midst of Taman Siswa's struggle against the Wild Schools Ordinance, it displayed a united front.

On 13 November, at a Chinese assembly hall called THHK in the town of Pekalongan on the north coast of Central Java, 350 representatives of Indonesians, Arabs, and Chinese participated in a conference of Tiga Bangsa Berserikat (Union of Three Peoples), and announced their opposition to the ordinance.[105]

On the same day, in Jakarta, a committee was formed calling itself the Komite Penjokong Perguruan Kebangsaan (National Schools Support Committee). Its stated objectives were to protect the various national schools and to assist the "victims" (*korban*) of the ordinances.[106]

From 18–20 November, Muhammadijah held a congress in Yogyakarta. Since the mid-1920s, it had established numerous schools, mainly in the cities and towns of Java, and along with Taman Siswa it was a major target of the new ordinance. The congress decided that Muhammadijah could also not accept the ordinance and would act in concert with other organizations and schools that shared its objectives. Nevertheless, reflecting it hitherto conciliatory line towards the colonial government, its response was far more moderate than was Taman Siswa's.[107]

Through late November, opposition to the ordinance continued to spread. On 17 November, the Dinijah school for girls at Padang Panjang in West Sumatra declared its opposition. Established in 1923 by a local woman named Rahmah El Yunusiyyah, this "wild school" played a significant role in the modernization of Minangkabau women.[108] Its declaration showed that the movement to abolish the ordinance had spread beyond Java.

On 19–20 November, the ulamas, Islamic scholars, entered the fray. At the Spoed Konferensi Persjarikatan Ulama di Madjalengka (Emergency Conference of the Association of Ulamas in Majalengka), held in Majalengka in West Java, they resolved that, for a period of six months, new teachers would not be appointed in schools run by the Association of Ulamas, nor would new schools be established; but that they were prepared to take fresh action if the ordinance was still in effect after this period, and that they would support fully, both materially and spiritually, all organizations opposed to the ordinance.[109] This resolution brought the Association of Ulamas into step with the decisions of the Taman Siswa Leaders' Conference.

On 20 November, alliances against the ordinance were formed in Jember, East Java, and in Blora, Central Java. In Jember, twelve organizations including Partai Bangsa Indonesia, Partindo, and Taman Siswa formed a Comité Kepentingan U(Oe)mum (CKO; Committee for Public Well-being), which resolved to support Dewantara's stance one hundred percent and to do its utmost to abolish the ordinance.[110] This was another prime example of organizations such as Partindo, Muhammadijah, and Partai Bangsa Indonesia massing around the focus of Taman Siswa. In Blora, a Komité Menentang "Wilde Scholen Ordonnantie" (Committee Against the Wild Schools Ordinance) was formed and a declaration of opposition to the ordinance was issued in the names of its members.[111]

The foregoing sketch of the burgeoning opposition to the ordinance through October and November 1933 is far from the full picture. Among the many acts of opposition for which the dates are uncertain are the declaration of opposition by Catholic groups, the formation in Surabaya by Nahdatul Ulama groups of a Comité Mentjapai Kebenaran (Committee to Seek the Truth), and the declaration of opposition by Pakumpulan Kawula Ngajogjakarta (PKN), a body of farmers led by Yogyakarta nobility.[112] Organized in 1930 at the initiative of Pangeran Surjodiningrat, a prince of the Yogyakarta Sultanate, PKN attracted widespread support among the peasantry of the vorstenlanden, who were suffering the effects of the depression. By the time of its second congress, which was held in Yogyakarta in July 1932, and at which Dewantara was a guest speaker, PKN membership exceeded 180,000.[113]

Newspapers published in Java were also opposed to the ordinance and carried critical articles by such names as Soekiman, Hatta, and Volksraad delegate Wiwoho.[114]

This situation endorsed directly the opinions expressed by the Taman Siswa leadership in "Orientation." Day by day, Kiewiet de Jonge's fears had become reality. Opposition to the ordinance and support for Dewantara had gradually spread beyond the nationalist parties to Islamic groups, teachers' unions, peasant organizations, like PKN, that were based on "traditional bonds," and Chinese associations.

Against this background, from mid-November the government began to retreat, and the affair moved rapidly towards settlement. The stage for this was the Volksraad. Since the ordinance had originally stemmed from a decision taken by the Volksraad, the best way for it to be repealed without, in Kiewiet de Jonge's words, "harming the government's authority," was to return it to the same place for redeliberation.[115]

The Settlement

NOTIFICATION OF LOCAL OFFICIALS

The notification to local officials about enforcement of the ordinance, which had been discussed by Dewantara and Kiewiet de Jonge on 19–21 October, was not formally issued until over a month later, on 24 November 1932. Sent on this date by the first government secretary to the heads of regional government, it was officially entitled, "Rondschriven: Uitvoering toezicht-ordonnantie particulier onderwijs" (Circular: Enforcement of the ordinance on supervision of private education), but was normally referred to as the "*Circulaire.*"[116] This was followed by an "Instruction from the Director of Education and Religion to inspectors of education concerning the enforcement of the Wild Schools Ordinance."[117]

Both these documents sought to redress the excesses of the supervisory authorities in enforcing the ordinance. The circular mentioned specifically the teacher-training schools (*kweekschool*) of Taman Siswa and Muhammadijah, and stated that their graduates should be issued teaching licenses without question.[118] The "instruction" also cited the name of Taman Siswa, which was said to provide education according to its own principles and methods and to be an educational institution with its own standards.[119] While urging caution upon local officials, particularly with regard to Taman Siswa (and Muhammadijah), however, both documents aimed to perpetuate the ordinance itself.

The issuance of the circular had been expected since the talks between Dewantara and Kiewiet de Jonge in October. The consideration afforded Taman Siswa meant that it had been set apart from other private schools, even though Dewantara had announced during the talks that "Even if Taman Siswa is afforded an exceptional position whereby it is guaranteed special favor in the application of the ordinance, my opinion [about the ordinance] will not change."[120]

Taman Siswa's formal response to the notification was decided at the Second Taman Siswa Leaders' Conference (Konperensi Pemimpin Taman Siswa jang Ke II), held in Yogyakarta on 31 December 1932.[121] Together with other resolutions which will be mentioned shortly, the conference passed a resolution stating:

> By the "circular" and the "instruction," the government itself recognizes that the ordinance obstructed the People's educational movement and permitted the high-handedness of regional officials. While Taman Siswa holds in high regard the intentions of the government that issued these, it will in no way change the stance it has adopted from the outset.

WIRANATAKUSUMA'S LETTER OF INQUIRY

On 8 December 1932, the Volksraad delegate R. A. A. Wiranatakusuma sent a letter of inquiry to the colonial government.[122] The essence of his inquiry was whether or not, in view of the fierce resistance movement that was demanding the repeal of the ordinance, the government had made preparations to replace the licensing system of the ordinance with a system of notification.[123]

On 23 December an extraordinary meeting of the Council of the Indies (Raad van Nederlandsch Indië) was held under the chairmanship of Governor-General De Jonge. Also present were C. W. Boudenhausen, the vice-chairman of the council, P. A. A. Kusumo Judo, Prof. J. van Klan, W. Ch. Hardeman, and G. R. Erdbrink, all of whom were council members, and P. G. Gerke, the first government secretary.[124] Discussion centered on developments since the enforcement of the ordinance and what countermeasures the government should take. Specifically, this meant determining what policies the government should adopt to deal with the burgeoning resistance movement that had been sparked by Dewantara's telegram, the failure of the talks between Dewantara and Kiewiet de Jonge, the failure of the circular to save the situation, and Wiranatakusuma's letter of inquiry.

Opinion was divided between a hard-line stance favoring maintenance of the status quo, and a more flexible position from which a settlement would be sought along the lines suggested in Wiranatakusuma's letter. The view of the hard-liners, led by Boudenhausen, was also shared by Schrieke, the director of education and religion; but the moderates, including Gerke and Kusumo Judo, were in the majority in the council, and debate thus converged on the response to be made to Wiranatakusuma.

The gist of the government's reply, sent to Wiranatakusuma on the following day, 24 December, was that because the ordinance had already become law, the government could not repeal it on the grounds

stated by Wiranatakusuma; that because alteration of the provisions of
the ordinance had been rejected after debate in the Volksraad, there
was no room for reconsideration; and that the purposes of the ordinance were to prevent abuses by private schools and to raise their standards, and were in no way political.[125] That such a hard-line stance
should have emerged despite the debate in the council reflects the fact
that the debate was dominated by Boudenhausen and that the response
was drafted in line with his views and those of Schrieke (in practice,
together with Kiewiet de Jonge, Gobée, and Onnen).[126]

This response preceded by one week the Second Taman Siswa
Leaders' Conference, held on 31 December in Yogyakarta. Besides
clarifying its views on the circular, as discussed earlier, the conference
adopted three resolutions.[127] First, other educational organizations
that offered to join Taman Siswa in the struggle against the ordinance
would be accepted provided that they held pure (*sutji*) educational
aims, were organizationally ordered, and were nationalistic. Likewise,
other organizations offering to join the struggle would be accepted on
the same conditions. Second, Taman Siswa would actively accept
volunteers to become Taman Siswa teachers and step up its activities to
train them. Third, as the next stage in its "passive resistance," Taman
Siswa would aim for the abolition of the "Western colonial school
system."

All three of these resolutions represented a firming of Taman
Siswa's resistance. The first meant that Taman Siswa would increase
its cooperation with political parties and other groups. The second
meant the promotion of the tjantrik system, the most frequent bone of
contention with the authorities in the enforcement of the ordinance.
And the third meant that Taman Siswa would further push for an
educational system based on the national culture to replace the government-run system.

On this third point, Dewantara published in the December 1932
issue of *Pusara* an article calling for abolition of government-run education entitled, "National education will grow upon the grave of the
Western colonial school system."[128] The thrust of this was the call:
"Despite the educational ordinance, let us make every house a school
[*perguruan*]! Let everyone become a teacher [*djadi pengadjar*]!" This was
to be achieved by strengthening the tjantrik system and, through a
"national-intellectual mobilization" [*nationaal-intellectueele mobilisatie*]
reaching every *kampung* (urban area) and *desa* (rural village) by establishing *perguruan* and *pawijatan* schools in place of the colonial *sekolahan*.
In effect, this reiterated the rejection of Dutch culture contained in his
article of 1929 and in Soedyono's "Educate yourselves!"

THE VOLKSRAAD

With its response to Wiranatakusuma, the government may have thought it had settled the question of repealing the ordinance; but early in 1933 it suddenly found itself caught up in a flurry of activity in the Volksraad. Within the government, the conflict between the hard-liners and the moderates continued. Taman Siswa's view was that it was a conflict between Schrieke and Boudenhausen on one hand and Kiewiet de Jonge and Gerke on the other; and that the governor-general, because of his frequent contact with First Secretary Gerke, was tending to side with the moderates. It was also rumored that Schrieke had resigned and returned to Holland.[129]

To the hard-line Dutchmen like Schrieke, who had a thorough knowledge of Javanese society and culture, the colonial government's "order and tranquility" was achievable only through strong state measures; but to "well-intentioned" Dutchmen like Kiewiet de Jonge, who tried to show an understanding of Javanese society and culture, dialog and compromise still offered a path to "order and tranquility" in Javanese society. This difference between hard-liners and moderates mirrored the difference between the members of the Raad van Indië (Governor-General Idenburg and contemporary high colonial officials) during the Native Committee affair and Jonkman of the Indonesisch Verbond van Studeerenden (chapter 2). Now, Taman Siswa's opposition to the Wild Schools Ordinance had rallied the entire nationalist movement into Taman Siswa's camp and led to the emergence of moderates like Kiewiet de Jonge in the opposing camp.

It was in this situation that, on 11 January, having secured the agreement of Kasimo, De Dreu, Van Mook, Hadiwidjono, Joebhaar, Kan, and other members of the Volksraad, Wiranatakusuma put forward a proposal (*iniatief voorstel*) that the Volksraad initiate legislation on three points concerning the ordinance: that it be repealed for one year; that the old ordinance be revived for the same period; and that a committee be established to examine the ordinance during that period.[130]

Five days later, on January 16, the Dutch minister for colonies, De Graaff, sent an official note to the governor-general to the effect that, given the widespread unemployment created by the depression, it would not be in the government's best interests if the resistance movement were to grow further; that the objective of controlling the "wild schools" could be achieved through the old ordinance; and that Wiranatakusuma's proposal could be approved.[131]

With this impetus from the Dutch government, matters were soon settled. First, Wiranatakusuma's proposal was debated at a sectional meeting of the Volksraad, and as a result, on 23 January, the chairman of the Volksraad contacted the governor-general seeking official reconfirmation of the government's position.[132] In response, the first government secretary, while avoiding expressing an official opinion, noted that "the government is ever more firmly convinced that the only way to solve this situation is for amendment [of the ordinance] to be decided in the Volksraad." He also stated that "the governor-general has received word that the minister for colonies has sent a note, but this has not yet arrived."[133] Nevertheless, the substance of this response showed that the colonial government had started to move in the direction indicated by the minister.

Debate in the Volksraad on Wiranatakusuma's proposal began on 31 January, ran through a second session on 3 February, and concluded in a third session on 7 February, when, with slight modification, the proposal was adopted.[134]

With the promulgation of "1933 Ordinance No. 66" on 20 February, it was officially announced that enforcement of the 1932 ordinance would be suspended for one year and the old ordinance brought back into effect, and that during this period a new ordinance would be deliberated by the government and the Volksraad.[135]

Return to the Fields

DEWANTARAS OVERVIEW

On 9 February, following the Volksraad's adoption of Wiranatakusuma's proposal, Taman Siswa's Supreme Council responded with an announcement that "if the Volksraad's resolution is made effective, Taman Siswa's opposition to the ordinance will naturally disappear."[136] This was followed on 1 March by an announcement from Dewantara, published under the title "Opposition to the Wild Schools Ordinance and its conclusion."[137]

Dewantara's announcement confirmed that since the system of notification had been restored in place of the licensing system, the resistance movement would cease. It also confirmed that the purpose of the new educational ordinance that was to be debated was not "political" but to supervise "evil" private schools; but nevertheless a careful watch should be kept on the new ordinance. Dewantara then called upon the various supporting committees born during the struggle to join together in one association to promote "national education for the People" (*Perguruan Nasional untuk Rakjat*); he called upon the various institutions for national education to establish an association in which they could discuss common problems; and he called for such institutions to accept the principle of *gescheiden samengaan*, each going their own ways to the same end and respecting the "independence" of their component bodies.

Together with this announcement, which set forth his position for those outside of Taman Siswa, Dewantara wrote an article entitled, "Return to the fields," which was addressed to Taman Siswa's members.[138] In it he described fully his view of the struggle.

> In the past six months, we have left our homes, left our children, left our fields and farms. All these, we should rightfully nurture with the greatest possible care. . . . Since October, we have been doing the collective work [*gugur gunung*] that is the duty of the village [*desa*]. This was all in order to achieve peace for those who live in the same village. While our own homes have not themselves been visited by danger, nor our fields destroyed by the outflow of lava of the ordinance, out of our sense of duty as residents of the village we have helped each other and exerted our strength together to extinguish the danger that threatened to enter the village.

Dewantara again likened Taman Siswa to farmers working the fields, and compared the national resistance movement to the collective work of a village. He then went on:

> Having exerted ourselves fully in body and soul, we have repaired the broken fence and restored the ruined road. At the same time, in order to confront this danger, we have had to clear a new road. These roads have become very useful for us in visiting our friends of the same village.

Now that the danger had been averted, it was time for Taman Siswa to return to its primary duties.

> The fence and the roads we now hand over to those responsible [for their maintenance; *jang kewadjiban*]. That is, we hand them over to the People's Movement lead by the commanders [*hulu-hulubalang*]. Now they are gathering the strength to uphold [our] safety, and as a result, we farmers, whose task it is to work in the fields, can work in the same way as before. We can tend the fields, planting seedlings and nurturing them to produce a rich crop.
>
> Let us return to the fields. And let us continue our own work, which has been rather neglected due to the activities of the village.

Dewantara here depicted the People as bearers of the People's Movement and as troops guarding the farmers' (Taman Siswa's) "order and tranquility." The People's Movement was no longer amorphous and disordered but composed of "people with duties" (*jang kewadjiban*): Taman Siswa's ideology had come into full bloom through the struggle over the Wild Schools Ordinance. This was a time of remarkable concurrence (*gescheiden samengaan*) of Taman Siswa's pandita qualities, distilled in the words "farmers," "fence," and "fields," and the satria qualities of the People's Movement. The legitimacy of Taman Siswa's "order and tranquility" was clearly established in the People's Movement.

Dewantara's "Return to the fields" ended significantly:

> Let us put our heirloom weapons (*sendjata-pusaka*) safely away until that time we know not when, when we will need them again, . . . and go back to the order of the day.

Again Dewantara invokes perfectly the image of the pandita, the traditional intelligentsia of Java. As leader of a pondok (or asrama or pesantren), he was the first of several to announce impending danger and to appear in the midst of the political arena. Now, having ascertained the future of the situation, he returns to his pondok.

SOEDYONO'S OVERVIEW

The struggle over the Wild Schools Ordinance also brought out the satria side of Taman Siswa. As if to show this, Dewantara's articles in *Pusara* were followed by Soedyono's overview of the struggle in an article entitled, "Forward towards organization." Again writing under the pseudonym Gadjah Mada, he extended to the Wild Schools Ordinance struggle the ideas he had expounded in the "Educate yourselves!" series of 1931 and 1932.[139]

Soedyone began by asserting that through the struggle Taman Siswa had acquired an "honest and pure discipline" (*dicipline jang tulus dan sutji*), that the struggle had purified Taman Siswa. The energy Taman Siswa had displayed during the struggle must now be channeled into "organization" (*organisasi*). This meant, as Dewantara had stated, rejecting the "Western colonial school system" and the ideology that supported it, and replacing it with Taman Siswa's education system.

This was the focal point of Soedyono's argument. The colonial school system was the product of the grace and favor of the "colonial ethic," its ideology based upon a "*mission-sacre.*" It was, therefore, "entirely unable to harmonize with our ideology." He continued:

> Now, however, we have opened our eyes and come to understand that to copy [*mengopy*] the behavior of the colonists, to copy the manners, customs, and style of conduct of the Europeans, to copy the colonial-style schools, to copy their materialist-capitalist society, and so on, is daily to collect medicine for suicide and to make our People socially dead [*maatschappelijk dood*].

To accept the Dutch "mission" meant, in short, copying the model of Dutchmen and their society; but such an ideology had benefited the

People not the slightest. The most important thing was to seek "education for large numbers of the People."

Finally, Soedyono asked whether the education that Taman Siswa offered had created the kind of nationalist ideological spirit that could oppose colonial education and cited three reasons for concluding that it had failed entirely to do so (*sama sekali belum*). The first was that enrollment was severely restricted by Taman Siswa's tuition fees, which were unaffordable for most people. If this situation persisted, the children of lazy villagers would themselves be lazy, and it would probably be several centuries before such people could receive an education. Secondly, Taman Siswa's educational methods were old-fashioned (*kuno*). Teachers continued to give their lessons whether or not children showed any real interest; and children's interest was not sustained, because new subjects were taught little by little, one after another, according to a schedule. Children were then assessed, and those who could not keep up were allowed to fall by the wayside. They were thus imbued with the idea of gaining good grades and constantly comparing themselves with others. This was no different from the colonial education system. Finally, almost all of the textbooks used by Taman Siswa were identical to those used in the government schools.

Soedyono thus criticized the "Western colonial school system" as being contrary to the People's interests and old-fashioned; and he warned that by adopting this system, Taman Siswa was merely copying "Western colonial society." This Soedyono claimed was tantamount to amassing "poison for suicide." And only through "organization" (*organisasi*) could Taman Siswa quickly break away from this situation.

In effect, Soedyono was calling upon Taman Siswa to achieve "organizationally" the self-discipline that he had stressed earlier. Self-discipline meant suppression of pamrih, wholehearted devotion to the People, and becoming one with the People. The People were none other than Sang Hyang Tunggal, Lord of Universe; and Taman Siswa's mission should be to perceive (*rasa*) the will of this lord, become one (*manunggal*) with the lord, and bring his will to fruition.

As when he advocated "self-discipline," Soedyono again displayed in this article his fervor and his fighting spirit. This style of communication was diametrically opposite to the pandita's, which relies on mutual, spontaneous response to metaphor and simile between guru and murid. Rather, his style was always declaratory or imperative, and any similes used were direct and harsh. Dewantara had said, "Let us put our heirloom weapons safely away until that time . . . when we will need them again;" but Soedyono declared that "every day will be a struggle." This fighting spirit was, of course, an expression of his satria qualities, and the passion of his advocacy equaled that shown earlier by Tjipto Mangoenkoesoemo.

Dewantara's and Soedyono's overviews of the Wild Schools Ordinance struggle show not only that Taman Siswa's basic character was clearly expressed through the struggle, they also signify the fruition of the Selasa Kliwon group's idea of giving form and direction to the People's Movement in general. As a "pandita," Taman Siswa came to occupy the center of the People's Movement, and around it the diverse elements of the movement formed a protective "fence." By defending the "order and tranquility" of Taman Siswa, the People's Movement was for the first time given form by that center.

Encircled by this protective "fence," Taman Siswa reinforced its role as counterinstitution to the colonial system. Such indeed was the essence of "organization." This was achieved with the lever of apprehension that there was "still far to go" (*sama sekali belum*; Soedyono), by means of direct, simple "instructions" firmly issued. These "instructions" must have enhanced the centripetalism of the world within the "fence."

The "vitality" of this centripetalism derived from the "will of the sacred People." Taman Siswa saw it as its "mission" (*zendingsarbeid*) constantly to carry out the People's will, of which the ultimate embodiment was Dewantara, the "father" of the "great sacred family" of Taman Siswa. As the General Leader (Pemimpin Umum), Dewantara occupied the center of the world within the "fence," the pinnacle of the conical structure formed through the systematization of leadership.

Insofar as such an organization existed, the disorder of the flood of the People, the flood of democracy, by no means brought catastrophe: rather, it not only enhanced the tenacity and vitality of Taman Siswa as a counterinstitution, it also supported the "order and tranquility" of that counterinstitution.

NOTES

1. Mailr. 19743/A o.s. Afschrift. Verbaal 16 Jan. 1933, Lett. S. no. 2 (Director of Education and Religion B. J. O. Schrieke to Governor-General De Jonge, 13 June 1932; reproduced in S. L. van der Wal, comp., *Het Onderwijsbeleid in Nederlands-Indië*, (Groningen: J. B. Wolters, 1963), p. 510). See also Soekesi Soemoatmodjo, "Taman Siswa adalah salah satu aspek dari Perdjuangan Nasionalisme" (B. A. diss., Gajah Mada University, Yogyakarta, 1966), pp. 69–70.

2. Contemporary reports on "unsubsidized schools" include the following: Mailr. 250X/1922 (on Soewardi's school), Mailr. 329X/1922 (Soewardi's school), Mailr. 416X/1922 (SI schools with Communist Party links), Mailr. 750X/1922 and

Mailr. 1257X/1922 (supervision of native schools), Mailr. 1308X/1922 (presentation of teaching qualifications to Douwes Dekker), Mailr. 4X/1923 (supervision of native schools), Mailr. 112X/1923 (Communist Party schools), and Mailr. 755X/1923, Mailr. 829X/1923, and Mailr. 961X/1923 (unsubsidized native and Chinese schools).

3.   Mailr. 421/I. Geheim. Afschrift. Verbaal 12 Mar. 1923, no. 45 (Acting Director of Education and Religion J. F. W van der Meulen to Governor-General Fock, 27 July 1922; reproduced in Van der Wal, *Het Onderwijsbeleid*, pp. 364–373).

4.   No. 187ax. Geheim rondschrijven. Eigenhandig. Verbaal 4 Nov. 1925, Lt. V15 (Acting first government secretary to heads of regional government, 7 June 1925; reproduced in Van der Wal, *Het Onderwijsbeleid*, p. 385). The full text of the 1923 ordinance was also published in *Pusara*: "Staatsblad regeling toezicht bijzonder onderwijs 1923 no. 136," *Pusara* 1, no. 6–7 (December 1931): 53–54.

5.   Soekesi Soemoatmodjo, *Taman Siswa adalah*, pp. 71–72.

6.   No. 33338/I. Afschrift. Verbaal 19 Sept. 1930, no. 27 (Director of Education and Religion K. F. Creutzberg, 21 Sept. 1923; reproduced in Van der Wal, *Het Onderwijsbeleid*, pp. 373–374).

7.   Afschrift. Verbaal 19 Sept. 1930, no. 27 (Note from Director of Education and Religion J. F. W. van der Meulen, 6 Jan. 1925; reproduced in Van der Wal, *Het Onderwijsbeleid*, pp. 380–382).

8.   No. 187 ax. Geheim rondschrijven. Eigenhandig. Verbaal 4 Nov. 1925, Lt. V15 (Acting first government secretary to the heads of regional government, 7 June 1925; reproduced in Van der Wal, *Het Onderwijsbeleid*, pp. 387–338).

9.   No. A 19/1/1. Afschrift. Verbaal 19 Sept. 1930 (Director of Education and Religion J. Hardeman to Governor-General De Graeff, 23 April 1929; reproduced in Van der Wal, *Het Onderwijsbeleid*, pp. 463–464). One reason for the government's high regard for Taman Siswa was its approval of its slogan "order and tranquility" (*tertib-damai, tata-tentrem*), which was the same as the Dutch catchword for colonial rule (*rust en orde*). Ruth McVey, "Taman Siswa and the Indonesian National Awakening," *Indonesia*, no. 4 (October 1967): 146, n. 26.

10.   Afschrift (Recommendations of the Council of the Indies, 4 Oct. 1929, No. XXII; reproduced in Van der Wal, *Het Onderwijsbeleid*, pp. 467–472).

11.   No. 1974/A o.s. Afschrift. Verbaal 16 Jan. 1933. Lett. S. no. 2 (Director of Education and Religion B. J. O. Schrieke to Governor-General De Jonge, 13 June 1932; reproduced in Van der Wal, *Het Onderwijsbeleid*, pp. 508–520).

12.   The full text of the 1932 ordinance is published in *Pusara*: "*Toezicht-ordonnantie particulier onderwijs,*" *Pusara* 3, no. 2–3 (November–December 1932): 43–44.

13.   Team Studi Taman Siswa, *Laporan Studi Sejarah Pendidikan Swasta Taman Siswa* vol. 1 (Yogyakarta, 1974), p. 231.

14.   J. N. Pluvier, *Overzicht van de ontwikkeling der nationalistische beweging in Indonesië in de jaran 1930 to 1942* (The Hague: Van Hoeve, 1953), p. 52.

15.   K. H. Dewantara, "Tentang 'Wilde' Scholen," *Pusara* 1, no. 1–2 (October 1931): 16–17.

16.   Ibid., p.17.

17.   "Staatsblad regeling toezicht bijzonder onderwijs 1923 No. 136," *Pusara* 1, no 6–7 (December 1931): 53–54.

18.   "Ab. no. 254, Pertanjaan dan Djawab," *Pusara* 1, no. 1–2 (October 1931): 18.

19.   "Ab. no. 187, Pertanjaan dan Djawab," *Pusara* 1, no. 1–2 (October 1931): 17–18.

20.   Tjokrodirdjo, "Harus diperhatikan!" *Pusara* 1, no. 3–5 (November 1931): 21.

21.   "Diktatuur dilakukan," *Pusara* 1, no. 6 –7 (December 1931): 55.

22.   "Bukan Taman Siswa," *Pusara* 2, no. 5–6 (May 1932): 45.

23.   K. H. Dewantara, "Drukpers dan Moral," *Pusara* 2, no. 1–2 (March 1932): 2–3. Dewantara's claim was fully justified. The advertisements then carried by *Pusara* were mostly for books, with the odd ones for a pharmacy and a clothing shop in Yogyakarta. Almost every month advertisements appeared for the works of Soetatmo Soeriokoesoemo (particularly his drama *Astogini of Het Spel van Vif*) and for the

work by those involved in the 1913 incident, discussed in Chapter 2 (Douwes Dekker, Tjipto Mangoenkoesoemo, Soewardi Soerjaningrat, *Onze Verbanning*). There were also advertisements for Taman Siswa-related publications, the works of Dewantara, and a number of dictionaries.

24. K. H. Dewantara, "Tentang Sifat dan Maksud Pendidikan," *Pusara* 1, no. 6–7 (December 1931): 47–50; P. H. S., "Pendidik-pendidik di Eropa jang Ternama," *Pusara* 1, no. 6–7 (December 1931): 50–51; P. H. S., "Pendidik-pendidik di Eropa, Pokok dari 'De geschiedenis van onderwijs en opvoeding's Karangan tuan B. J. Douwes," *Pusara* 1, no. 11–12 (February 1932): 84–86; P. H. S., "Pendidik-pendidik di Eropa," *Pusara* 2. no. 3–4 (April 1932): 23–24: P. H. S., "Pendidik-pendidik di Eropa," *Pusara* 2, no. 5–6 (May 1932): 35–37; P. H. S., "Pendidik-pendidik di Eropa," *Pusara* 2, no. 9–10 (July 1932): 70. The fourteen "great European teachers" introduced in this series were: Quintilianus, Alcuin, Vittorino, Vives, Luther, Trotzendorf, De Loyola, Valcoogh, Rabelais, Montaigne, Bacon, Comenius, De La Salle, and Fenelon. The articles were stated to be intended for use as teaching materials for aspiring "assistant teachers" (*pembantu-guru*, probably tjantrik) in Taman Siswa schools.

25. S. Tirtosoepono, "Dr. Maria Montessori," *Pusara* 2, no. 1–2 (March 1932): 12–13; Bambang Soemantri, "Jean Jacques Rousseau," *Pusara* 2, no. 1–2 (March 1932): 13–15.

26. Helen Parkhurst and her Dalton System, for example, were discussed in the article: Tjokrodirdjo, "Dalton-systeem bukan barang baru bagi kita" [The Dalton system is nothing new to us], *Pusara* 3, no. 6 (March 1933): 84–85. As its title indicates, this articles sees this "latest system" as corresponding to educational ideas long cherished by the Javanese.

27. W. G. Soewandhi, "Taman Dewasa atau Mulo-Nasional, Zendings dan Reddingsarbeid," *Pusara* 1, no. 6–7 (December 1931): 41–42; and "Verslag Konperensi Taman Siswa Daerah Djawa-Tengah," *Wasita* 2, no. 3–6 (August 1931): 171.

28. Madjelis Luhur Harian, "Sikap Taman Siswa terhadap pada Ordonnantie Pengadjaran 1 Oktober," *Pusara* 3, no. 1 (October 1932): 11–12. The announcement by the working committee was immediately reported in *Sedio Tomo*, a daily newspaper published in Yogyakarta under the editorship of Hardjosoemitro. From October 1932, the activities of Taman Siswa and Ki Hadjar Dewantara were followed closely by a variety of newspapers. "Sedio Tomo, 28–30 Sept. 1932," *I. P. O.*, 1932, no. 40, p. 235.

29. "Tilgram dari K. H. Dewantara kepada G. G.," *Pusara* vol. 2, no. 12–vol. 3, no. 1 (September 1932): appendix.

30. Ibid. The full text of the telegram also appeared in *Utusan Indonesia*, a Yogyakarta daily, on 1 October 1932. *I.P.O.*, 1932, no. 40, p. 235.

31. An editorial in *Utusan Indonesia* of 27 September commented: "We are dissatisfied that the Taman Siswa leadership has raised not a word of protest against the new ordinance." From that day on, however, such dissatisfaction was rapidly dispelled. "Utusan Indonesia, 27 Sept. 1932," *I.P.O.*, 1932, no. 41, p. 249.

32. K. H. Dewantara, "Membatalkan Ordonnantie dengan seketikanja. Uraian Kepada sekalian Anggota Taman Siswa," *Pusara* 3, no. 1 (October 1932): 12–14; idem, "Persambutan Onderwijs-Ordonnantie, Maklumat kepada sekalian Pemimpin Pergerakan Ra'jat, Mataram, 3 Oktober 1932," *Pusara* 3, no. 1 (October 1932): pp. 14–15.

33. Dewantara, "Membatalkan Ordonnantie," p. 12.

34. Ibid., p. 13.

35. Ibid.

36. Ibid., p. 14.

37. Dewantara, "Persambutan Onderwijs-Ordonnantie," p. 14. I am grateful to Mr. Mohammad Said for information on the attitude of *nrima*, given in an interview in July 1975 in Jakarta. Mr. Said also stated that the meaning of this word and the attitude based on it were expounded by Sosrokartono, elder brother of Kartini, and

one-time head of the Taman Siswa school in Bandung.

38.   As if in response to this announcement by Dewantara, an editorial in *Sedio Tomo* of 5 October commented to the effect that since the enforcement of the ordinance Dewantara had returned to his former self, asserting himself as Soewardi Soerjaningrat once did. "Sedio Tomo, 5 Oct. 1932," *I.P.O.*, 1932, no. 41, p. 259. That Soewardi Soerjaningrat was here recalled as a satria who played a major role in the Native Committee incident of 1913 is a prime illustration of how Dewantara's part in the Wild Schools Ordinance struggle was understood.

39.   Dewantara, "Persambutan Onderwijs-Ordonnantie," pp. 14–15.

40.   Dewantara's "Announcement to all leaders of the People's Movement" was also published in *Utusan Indonesia* on 4 October (*I.P.O.*, 1932, no. 40, pp. 235–236). This declaration of "passive resistance" aroused various comments in the press, which, while differing slightly in emphasis, left no doubt that it was seen as a form of resistance. In *Sedio Tomo* of 5 October, a writer identified as A. S. D. commented: "This compares with *tapa brata* [*tapa*, asceticism], Java's traditional form of resistance, being an expression of a deeper and higher understanding, rather than yielding oneself to anger and passion" (*Ibid.*, no. 41, p. 250). On the same day, *Suara Umum*, a newspaper published three times weekly by Soetomo's Partai Bangsa Indonesia, opined: "Dewantara's passive resistance follows Gandhi's formula one hundred percent" (*Ibid.*, no. 41, p. 250). *Adil*, however, an Islamic daily published in Solo, expressed reservations in an edition of around 13 October: "Passive resistance in Indonesia is not prepared to go as far as to risk death. It lacks the ring of commitment of Gandhi's resistance movement" (*Ibid.*, no. 42, p. 269). Writing in *Siang Po*, a Batavia daily published in Malay and Dutch, however, one Saeroen warned: "Dewantara's plan of avoiding a direct clash with the government is related to Eastern philosophy. The government should regard the situation more seriously" (*Ibid.*, no. 42, p.270).

41.   "Tjabang Surabaja," *Pusara* vol. 2, no. 12–vol. 3, no. 1 (September 1932): 5.

42.   "Usul-usul tentang sikap terhadap Onderwijs Ordonnantie buat Konperensi Djawa Timur, Golongan Argopuro." *Pusara* 3, no. 1 (October 1932): 15: "Perslah dari Konperensi Golongan Argopuro Ke IX di Bondowoso pada 1–2 Okt. 1932," ibid., p. 25.

43.   Madjelis Daerah Djawa Timur, "Daerah Djawah Timur. no. 6. Hal Ordonnantie 'wilde scholen' " ibid., p. 15.

44.   "Usul-usul, tjabang Modjokerto," ibid., p. 15. This "carbon copy" idea accorded with the views expressed earlier by Soedyono.

45.   "Madjelis Daerah dan Golongan Semarang Berrapat," ibid., p. 16.

46.   "Rapat Besar Daerah Djawa Timur jang Ke IV," *Pusara* vol. 2, no. 12–vol. 3, no. 1 (September 1932): 5.

47.   "Putusan Madjelis Luhur Lengkap dari Taman Siswa di Tosari, 15/16 Oktober 1932," *Pusara* 3, no. 2 (November 1932): 18.

48.   Of secret government documents (Mailr. Geheim [X]) written between 1924 and 1931, no. 84x/1924, no. 108X/1930, and no. 561X/1931 deal solely with Taman Siswa, while scattered references may be found in "(unsubsidized) private schools inspection reports" and "Yogyakarta sultanate political reports."

49.   These are collected in Mailr. 1175X/19132. In addition to Kiewiet de Jonge's report (see note 50), they include the text of Dewantara's telegram to the governor-general, translations of Dewantara's "instruction" to Taman Siswa members and his "announcement to leaders of the People's Movement," and documents related to the authorities' subsequent negotiations.

50   H. J. Kiewiet de Jonge, "Opdracht met betrekking tot den Taman-Siswa leider Ki Adjar Dewantara," Mailr. 1175X/1932 (to Governor-General De Jonge, 26 Oct. 1932; reproduced in Van der Wal, *Het Onderwijsbeleid*, pp. 524–545).

51.   "Konpersensi antara Mr. Ir. Kiewiet de Jonge dengan Ki Hadjar Dewantara," *Pusara* 3, no. 2 (November 1932): 18.

52.   Kiewiet de Jonge, "Opdracht," p. 1 (Van der Wal, *Het Onderwijsbeleid*, p. 525).

53. *Bintang Timur*, a Malay-language daily published in Weltevreden under the editorship of Parada Harahap, commented on Kiewiet de Jonge's departure for Yogyakarta: "We believe this will not be used as part of the government's coercive measures against Taman Siswa." "Bintang Timur, [n.d.]," *I.P.O.*, 1932, no. 43, p. 284.

54. "Vertaling uit Pusara Taman Siswa van Oktober 1932," Afschrift no. 13, Mailr. 1175X/1932, p. 3.

55. Kiewiet de Jonge, "Opdracht," pp. 5–6 (Van der Wal, *Het Onderwijsbeleid*, p. 527).

56. Kiewiet de Jonge, "Opdracht," pp. 9–10 (Van der Wal, *Het Onderwijsbeleid*, pp. 529–530).

57. Kiewiet de Jonge, "Opdracht," p. 7 (Van der Wal, *Het Onderwijsbeleid*, p. 528).

58. Kiewiet de Jonge, "Opdracht," p. 10 (Van der Wal, *Het Onderwijsbeleid*, pp. 530).

59. Kiewiet de Jonge, "Opdracht," p.11 (Van der Wal, *Het Onderwijsbeleid*, pp. 530–531).

60. Kiewiet de Jonge, "Opdracht," pp. 13–14 (Van der Wal, *Het Onderwijsbeleid*, p. 532).

61. Kiewiet de Jonge, "Opdracht," p. 14 (Van der Wal, *Het Onderwijsbeleid*, p. 532).

62. Kiewiet de Jonge, "Opdracht," pp. 15–16 (Van der Wal, *Het Onderwijsbeleid*, p. 533).

63. Kiewiet de Jonge, "Opdracht," p. 20 (Van der Wal, *Het Onderwijsbeleid*, p. 535).

64. Kiewiet de Jonge, "Opdracht," p. 20 (Van der Wal, *Het Onderwijsbeleid*, pp. 535–536).

65. Mailr. 1175X/1932 (First government secretary to heads of regional government, "Rondschrijven. Uitvoering Toezicht-ordonnantie particulier onderwijs," Buitenzorg, 24 November 1932; reproduced in Van der Wal, *Het Onderwijsbeleid*, pp. 546–549).

66. Kiewiet de Jonge, "Opdracht," p. 22 (Van der Wal, *Het Onderwijsbeleid*, p. 537). Dewantara's emphasis of "an overall synthesis while each and every one remained himself" was in complete agreement with Soedyono's ideas in "Educate yourselves!"

67. Kiewiet de Jonge, "Opdracht," pp. 22–23 (Van der Wal, *Het Onderwijsbeleid*, pp. 537–538).

68. Kiewiet de Jonge, "Opdracht," p. 15 (Van der Wal, *Het Onderwijsbeleid*, p. 533).

69. Kiewiet de Jonge, "Opdracht," pp. 24–25 (Van del Wal, *Het Onderwijsbeleid*, pp. 538–539).

70. Kiewiet de Jonge, "Opdracht," p. 26 (Van der Wal, *Het Onderwijsbeleid*, p. 539).

71. Already evident here is the core idea of Dewantara's work of his later years, *Democracy and Leadership* (1949). Kiewiet de Jonge, "Opdracht," p. 29 (Van der Wal, comp., *Het Onderwijsbeleid*, p. 541).

72. Kiewiet de Jonge, "Opdracht," p. 30 (Van der Wal, *Het Onderwijsbeleid*, p. 542).

73. Kiewiet de Jonge, "Opdracht," pp. 32–33 (Van der Wal, *Het Onderwijsbeleid*, p. 543).

74. Soekardi, "Peringatan Korban-Ordonansi jang pertama dalam Taman Siswa," *Pusara* 3, no. 2 (November 1932): 26–29. The arrest was reported in *Bintang Timur* of 14 November 1932 under the heading, "Taman Siswa's first victim of the 'Wild Schools Ordinance.'" *I.P.O.*, 1932, no. 46, p. 33.

75. Soekardi, "Peringatan Korban-Ordonansi," p. 26.

76. Ibid.

77. Ibid., pp. 26–28.

78. Ibid., p. 28.

79. Ibid.

80. Ibid., pp. 28–29.

81. "Putusan dari Konperensi Pemimpin Taman siswa," *Pusara* 3, no. 2 (November 1932): 17–19.

82. "Besluit van de Leiders-Conferentie der Taman Siswa," *Pusara* 3, no. 2 (November 1932): 19–20.

83. "Putusan dari Konperensi," p. 19.
84. Mailr. 1175X/1932, Bijlagen 2 (November 1932), pp. 1–2.
85. Mailr. 1175X/1932, Bijlagen 3 (Weltevreden, 7 November 1932), pp. 1–4.
86. Badan Pemimpin Taman Siswa, "Orientatie," *Pusara* 3, no. 2 (November 1932): 17–18.
87. The "Ajat group" was centered on Ajat, a member of the Surabaya branch of Taman Siswa who published the bimonthly Javanese-language *Djenggala*. After his expulsion from Taman Siswa by resolution of the 1930 national congress, Ajat continued to publish, and was frequently critical of Taman Siswa and Dewantara. Having earlier censured Soetomo for failing to fight for the true interests of the People ["Djenggala, 13 September 1931," *I.P.O.*, 1931, no. 40, p. 34; and "Djenggala, 14 October, 1931," *ibid.*, no. 44, p. 213], he began to level similar criticisms against Dewantara. In the issue of 12 February 1932, for example, he stated that although Dewantara had renounced his title of nobility, he had adopted in its place a title of divinity (*goddelijkheid*) [*I.P.O.*, 1932, no. 7, p. 104]. Again, in the 22 November 1932 issue of the renamed publication *Panggugah Rakjat*, he criticized Dewantara's "passive resistance" and called Soetomo and Dewantara "scoundrels" (*badjingan*) as far as the People's Movement was concerned [*ibid.*, no. 49, p. 378].
88. This is identical to the idea expressed in Soedyono's article about "the one in whom the wahju resides."
89. Party Sjarikat Islam Indonesia, Abikoesono Tjokrosoejoso (vice-president), S. M. Kartosoewirjo (secretaris), "Menentang Ordonnantie Onderwijs Baru. Ma'lumat dari Pimpinan Ladjnah Tanfidzijah Party Sjarikat Islam Indonesia Kepada Segenap Ra'jat dan Pers Indonesia," *Pusara* 3, no. 1 (October 1932): 16.
90. "Sikap P.S.I.I. jang luas dan pasti," *Pusara* 3, no. 2 (November 1932): 32–33.
91. "Comite van Actie Wilde Scholen," *Pusara* 3, no. 1 (November 1932): 16. Further, in its edition of 5 October, *Sin Tit Po* reported that "Teachers at private schools in Surabaya have decided to form a committee to discuss the Wild Schools Ordinance." Chaired by Soerowijono and with Soeparnadi as secretary, this may have been the same body as the Wild Schools Action Committee mentioned earlier. *I.P.O.* 1932, no. 42, p. 267.
92. "Revolusi Isteri Sadar," *Pusara* 3, no. 2 (November 1932): 35; "Banteng Rajat, 5 October 1932," *I.P.O.*, 1932, no. 42, p. 267.
93. "P.G.H.B. Mengeluarkan Suaranja," *Pusara* 3, no. 2 (November 1932): 35.
94. "Rapat Umum Partai Indonesia," ibid., p. 35.
95. "Partai Indonesia dan O.O.," ibid., p. 41.
96. Madjelis Guru, "Perguruan Kebangsaan Indonesia," ibid., pp. 35–36.
97. "Adhaesie Betuiging, Tjabang Budi-Utama di Ngandjuk," ibid., pp. 36–37.
98. "Kommunike dari Onderwijs Commissie B.U.," ibid., p. 37. On the contents of this communiqué, the Solo daily *Darmo Kondo* commented in its 11 November 1932 edition that "The Wild Schools Ordinance allows a bureaucratic taint to permeate the academic world. Until this is repealed, the private schools are as good as under sentence of death." *I.P.O.*, 1932, no. 46, p. 330.
99. Komité Menentang Onderwijs Ordonnantie H. B. Malang, "Ma'lumat Kepada Sekalian Kaum Marhaen di Indonesia," *Pusara* 3, no. 2 (November 1932): 36.
100. "P.B.I.; Lijdelijk-Verzet," ibid., p. 36.
101. "Sikap P.P.P.L.S.I. di Blora," ibid., p.37.
102. "Mosi Pasundan," ibid.; "Sipatahunan, 11 November 1932," *I.P.O.*, 1932, no. 46, p. 331.
103. "Motie P.P.P.I. Bandung," *Pusara* 3, no. 2 (November 1932): 38.
104. "Putusan Konperensi P.P.P.K.I. h.b. 12 Nov. 1932 di Mataram," ibid., pp. 38–39. P.P.P.K.I. held a further meeting on 11 December in Surabaya. Attended by a thousand delegates representing twenty-five groups, this conference also adopted a resolution calling for abolition of the ordinance and support for Taman Siswa. "Mosi Rapat Umum P.P.P.K.I. di Surabaja," ibid., p. 42.

105. "Tiga Bangsa Berserikat Melawan Ordonnantie 'Liar' " ibid., p. 39.

106. "Ma'lumat dari Komite Penjokong Perguruan Kebangsaan," ibid.

107. Muhammadijah had also established schools across Java, but whether or not they accepted government subsidies depended on the situation in individual branches.

108. Aminuddin Rasyad, "Rahmah El Yunusiyyah," in *Manusia dalam Kemelut Sejarah,* ed. Taufik Abdullah (Jakarta: LP3ES [Lembaga Penelitian, Pendidikan dan Penerangan Ekonomi dan Sosial], 1978), pp. 219–243.

109. "Putusan Spoed Konferensi Persjarikatan Ulama di Madjalengka," *Pusara* 3, no. 2 (November 1932): 40.

110. "C.K.O. di Djember," ibid., pp. 40–41.

111. "O.O. dibatalkan di Blora," ibid., p. 50.

112. "Fihak Katoliek dengan O.O.," ibid., p. 42; "Comité Mentjapai Kebenaran," ibid., p. 41; "P.K.N. Tidak mau Ketinggalan," ibid., p. 50.

113. William Joseph O'Malley, "Indonesia in the Great Depression: A Study of East Sumatra and Jogjakarta in the 1930's" (Ph.D. diss., Cornell University, 1977), pp. 305–314.

114. "Persambutan Onderwijs-Ordonnantie dari Segenapnja Ra'jat," *Pusara* 3, no. 2 (November 1932): 20; "Ra'jat melawan 'wilde' ordonansi," ibid., p. 34; "J.I.B. dan O.O. Kutipan verslag dari pidato tuan Wiwoho dalam Rapat J.I.B. di Semarang," ibid.

     Contemporary newspapers also came out solidly in opposition to the ordinance and in support of Taman Siswa. On 20 October, *Aksi* claimed: "All the People of Indonesia are against the Wild Schools Ordinance (*I.P.O.* 1932, no. 43, p. 285); on the same day the Chinese daily *Pewarta Surabaja* commented: "Behind Taman Siswa's 'passive resistance,' a massive force is waiting" (*ibid.,* no. 43, p. 286); and on 25 October *Suara Umum* stated: "The people of Taman Siswa are continuing their 'passive resistance' prepared for imprisonment" (*ibid.,* no. 44, p. 297). Support for Dewantara was also voiced. "Strengthen Dewantara's influence further," asserted *Darmo Kondo* on 24 October (*ibid.,* no 43, p. 285); "The Indonesian People recognize Dewantara as a true leader for the 'life or death resistance' he is conducting," stated *Berita,* a Padang publication, in its 1 November issue (*ibid.,* no. 46, p. 330); "Everyone is captivated by the model of Dewantara," claimed M. Widjaja in the 3 November issue of *Bahagia,* a Semarang daily (*ibid.*).

115. Mailr. 1175X/1932, Bijlagen 3 (Kiewiet de Jonge to Governor-General, Weltevreden, 7 November 1932), p. 3.

116. Mailr. 1175X/1932(see note 65 above; reproduced in Van der Wal, *Het Onderwijsbeleid,* pp. 546–549); "Circulaire Pemerintah kepada Hoofdambtenaren," *Pusara* 3, no. 2 (November 1932): 44–46.

117. "Instructie v.d. Directeur v. O. en E. aan inspecteurs van onderwijs betreffende uitvoering van de Wilde Scholen Ordonnantie, *Pusara* 3, no. 2 (November 1932): 46–47.

118. Mailr. 1175X/1932, p. 3 (Van der Wal, *Het Onderwijsbeleid,* p. 547).

119. "Instructie v.d. Directeur," pp. 46–47.

120. Mailr. 1175X/1932, Bijlagen V, p. 19.

121. "Putusan Konperensi Pemimpin Taman Siswa jang Ke II. Di Mataram h.b. 31 Desember 1931," *Pusara* 3, no. 4–5 (January–February 1933): 51–52.

122. Wiranatakusuma was born on 8 August 1888 in Bandung. In 1910 he graduated from OSVIA, the training school for native officials, and for ten years served at various posts in West Java before being appointed *bupati* (regent) of Bandung in 1920. From 1921 to 1935 he also served as a member of the Volksraad. Gunsei Kanbu (Japanese Military Administration), *Orang Indonesia jang Terkemuka* (Jakarta, 1944), p. 110. He is also recorded as being a freemason. Paul W. van der Veur, *Freemasonry in Indonesia from Radermacher to Soekanto, 1762–1961,* Ohio University, Center for International Studies, Papers in International Studies, Southeast Asia Series No. 40 (1976), p. 36; H. Sutherland, "Pangreh Pradja" (Ph.D. diss., Yale University, 1973), pp. 361–363.

123. "Ordonnantie Liar dikembalikan kepada Pemerintah," *Pusara* 3, no. 4–5 (January–February 1932): 52.
124. Afschrift. Zeer geheim. Verbaal 17 Mar. 1933, Lt. W5 (Minutes of the extraordinary meeting of the Council of the Indies presided over by Governor-General De Jonge, 23 Dec. 1932; reproduced in Van der Wal, *Het Onderwijsbeleid*, p. 549).
125. Van der Wal, *Het Onderwijsbeleid*, p. 555.
126. "Ordonnantie Liar dikembalikan," p. 53.
127. "Putusan Konperensi Pemimpin Taman Siswa jang Ke II," pp. 51–52.
128. K. H. Dewantara, "Bertumbuhnja Perguruan Nasional diatas Kubur Westersch Koloniaal Schoolsysteem," *Pusara* 3, no. 2–3 (November–December 1932): 48–50.
129. "Ordonnantie Liar dikembalikan," p. 53.
130. Ibid., p. 54.
131. Lt. S. no. 2, Geheim (Minister for Colonies De Graaff to Governor-General De Jonge, 16 Jan. 1933; reproduced in Van der Wal, *Het Onderwijsbeleid*, pp. 555–558).
132. "Persediaan Pembitjaraan dalam Volksraad Afdeelingsverslag," *Pusara* 3, no. 4–5 (January–February 1933): 54–55.
133. "Keterangan Pemerintah," ibid., pp. 55–56.
134. "O.O. kembali kedalam Volksraad," ibid., pp. 56–65.
135. K. H. Dewantara, "Penentangen O.O. Liar dan Kesudahannja," *Pusara* 3, no. 6 (March 1933): 75–76.
136. "Putusan Madjelis Luhur," *Pusara* 3. no. 4–5 (January–February 1933): 65.
137. Dewantara, "Penentangen O.O. Liar," pp. 75–76.
138. K. H. Dewantara, "Kembali ke Ladang," *Pusara* 3, no. 6 (March 1933): 76–77.
139. Gadjah Mada, "Madju ke Organisasi," *Pusara* 3, no. 6 (March 1933): 77–78.

7

DEMOCRACY AND LEADERSHIP

In the preceding chapters we have detailed the origins and development of the Taman Siswa movement, which climaxed with its fight against the Wild Schools Ordinance. In the stiff and persistent resistance it mounted to the ordinance, Taman Siswa showed itself fully able to function as a "counterinstitution."

Since that time, the Taman Siswa movement has braved the vicissitudes of the colonial era, the Japanese military occupation, the struggle for independence, and the establishment of the Republic, to survive to the present day. The name of Ki Hadjar Dewantara, who died in 1959, lives on in the memory of the Republic as an outstanding educator, and has been added to the roll of its "saints."

To detail Taman Siswa's history in the half century since the Wild Schools Ordinance struggle would require more space than is available here. In this final chapter, I wish merely to examine this later period in the context of the years covered by the earlier chapters and consider how Taman Siswa provided a basis for the legitimating principle of the Republic.

Of particular concern is the idea of Guided Democracy, for this did not simply rest on the charismatic qualities of Sukarno the individual but can be fixed in the framework of the modern Indonesian understanding of culture and politics that was discussed in earlier chapters.

Here we shall first survey the disturbance of Taman Siswa's "order and tranquility" following the Wild Schools Ordinance struggle and examine how Dewantara tackled the situation. Next we shall examine the concept of "democracy with leadership" that was Dewantara's "legacy." Lastly, we shall look briefly at the ideological structure of Sukarno's Guided Democracy.

THE DISTURBANCE OF "ORDER AND TRANQUILITY"

Internal and External Troubles

Although the Wild Schools Ordinance was repealed in 1933, never to be restored, the colonial government thereafter stepped up its repression of the noncooperationist parties, including Partindo, PNI-Baru, and PSII; and Taman Siswa teachers believed to belong to these parties were disqualified from teaching. Almost monthly, their names appeared in the "Berita Keluarga" (Family news) section of *Pusara*, which normally reported births, marriages and deaths, transfers, and appointments; and from December 1933 a "Disqualified teachers" column was added to this section.

In December 1933 twelve disqualifications were recorded, by February 1937 the number had risen to fifty-six, and between March and August 1937, twenty-six more names were added to the list.[1] Among those disqualified were such influential leaders as Safioedin, Soerjopoetro, and Ngoesoemandji. Each time the government acted, Taman Siswa protested in the pages of *Pusara*. But against such forceful oppression it was unable to organize the kind of resistance that it had against the Wild Schools Ordinance.

To make matters worse, this external attack was compounded by internal dissent. One reason for the effectiveness of Dewantara's leadership had been his frequent visits to Taman Siswa branches, particularly in the late 1920s and early 1930s, when his travels accounted for most of the expenditures from the central fund. For almost two years, however, from 1934–1936, sickness confined him to Yogyakarta.[2]

The Faces of Conflict

In the same period, Taman Siswa's "order and tranquility" was severely threatened by various internal conflicts in certain branch schools and more seriously, by overt opposition to the Supreme Council by the Jenggala branch. The trouble began with a spate of disputes that could not be resolved through the guidance and advice of Dewantara and the Taman Siswa leadership based at headquarters in Yogyakarta. Though mostly rooted in personal confrontations, sometimes trifling, their exposure led to the graver threat to "order and tranquility" of factionalism. The inability of Taman Siswa headquarters to resolve these disputes, moreover, cast doubt upon its own legitimacy and diminished its authority in dealing with the Jenggala branch's challenge over matters of principle.

Internal dissension began to surface from the middle of June 1933, stemming from a variety of causes and taking a variety of forms. In that month, several teachers were ordered to resign from the council of the

Medan branch in North Sumatra, while in November of the same year, a whole class was expelled from the teacher-training course at the Jakarta branch.[3]

The Jakarta branch had an enrollment of 519 students in 1935, surpassing Yogyakarta's (356) and second only to Surabaya's (662).[4] It was headed by Sarmidi Mangoensarkoro, a member of Sukarno's Partindo (who from April 1949 to September 1950 was to serve as minister of education in the Republic).[5] Together with his wife, who was president of the women's association, Wanita Taman Siswa, he exercised firm control over the branch. Such strong leadership, however, continued to provoke internal dissension, and in october 1934 several teachers resigned.[6]

By August 1935, the situation had grown more serious following the expulsion of four students for defying the branch rule—set by Sarmidi himself—that students should clean their own classrooms. Eight of their fellow students sent a demand to Taman Siswa headquarters (the Supreme Council) that the branch decision be overturned, with notice that if their demand was not met they would leave the school.[7] After deliberation, headquarters decided that the punishment had been too severe and urged Sarmidi to reconsider. But in a detailed and tightly-argued article published in *Pusara*, Sarmidi justified his decision and rejected the demand for its reversal.[8]

During August and September there followed several exchanges of opinion among Taman Siswa headquarters, Sarmidi (and the Jakarta executive), and the anti-Sarmidi faction of the Jakarta branch, but no path could be found to a settlement. In September, seeing the situation as dangerous, Mr. S (Sartono) of B branch (Bandung) took upon himself the task of conciliation between headquarters and the Jakarta branch, but also without success.[9] Ultimately, the affair was shelved "to protect the honor" of both Taman Siswa and Sarmidi, leaving the expellees and their sympathizers out in the cold.[10]

The dissension in the Jakarta branch followed a typical pattern. Antagonisms within the branch spilled over to Taman Siswa headquarters and, as a result of exposure, led to confrontation between headquarters and the branch.

Troubles in the same mold, though with different causes, were reported at a number of branches. In January 1935, for example, when Taman Siswa headquarters suspended the leader of A branch from office, teachers and students who supported him repeatedly appealed to headquarters to rescind the decision. Ultimately relations were severed between A branch and Taman Siswa. At M branch and G branch, factional disputes were brought to headquarters, and although headquarters dispatched arbitrators, the dissension was not quelled. Similar troubles arose at S, R, and P branches. At T branch, trouble began when the branch head expelled from the staff accommodation teachers who were playing bridge there.[11] Because gambling had been taking place at branches other than this one, in late November 1935 the Supreme Council issued a proclamation forbidding gambling at teachers' residences and the loan of staff accommodation for purposes unrelated to education.[12]

The problem with the Jenggala branch stemmed from a proclamation, issued by Taman Siswa headquarters following a meeting of the Supreme Council on 9–10 August 1935, prohibiting Taman Siswa teachers from joining the Indonesian youth movement.[13] In response, Taman Siswa's youth group, Pemuda Taman Siswa, and others involved in the youth movement wrote to headquarters asking the reason for the proclamation. In September, headquarters explained that this measure had been taken because of the fear that the special bonds formed between pupils and teachers belonging to the same youth group would not be educationally desirable. It stressed that the ban had been imposed purely on educational grounds, not because of government pressure, particularly pressure related to the "child allowance" (*kindertoelage*), or because of fear that the youth group would become politically involved.[14]

This "child allowance" was an educational subsidy for the children of officials, granted under an ordinance of February 1935 to three classes of schools: public schools, government-subsidized schools, and private schools meeting the same requirements as public schools. Taman Siswa belonged to the third class, but the government was demanding the right to enter every Taman Siswa school to examine whether Taman Siswa qualified. This problem was to remain a source of tension between Taman Siswa and the government for three years, until it was settled through a meeting between Dewantara and the governor-general late in 1937, as a result of which, from 1938, all public employees sending children to school became entitled to a grant irrespective of the kind of school.[15]

That the Supreme Council specifically mentioned government pressure in its proclamation was because of certain criticisms that had been submitted to *Pusara*. One of these, made by Soetomo's Partai Bangsa Indonesia, was that Taman Siswa had yielded to the government in accepting the *kindertoelage*; and a second, more severe criticism charged that Taman Siswa could "no longer be called an educational institution of the People."[16]

Although the announcement of September 1935 appeared to have answered these criticisms, in December of that year the Jenggala branch sent a leaflet to other branches in East Java refuting the Supreme Council's decision. The leaflet charged that the decision was related to the government's repression of the previous year, and that the Supreme Council had contravened the principles of independence (*kemerdekaan*) and self-determination (*zelfbeschikkingsrecht*).[17] The editors of *Pusara* responded with an article stating that the Jenggala branch's claims were spurred by outside influences; that as far as contravention of principles went, their argument overlooked the fundamental principle of the welfare of the pupils (*sang anak*); and that the Jenggala branch should accept responsibility for the consequences of having circulated the leaflet.[18] The Supreme Council, on the other hand, made no formal response to the leaflet since it had not been sent directly to Taman Siswa headquarters. But because of the betrayal of confidence implicit in the Jenggala branch's circulation of this leaflet without notifying it, the Supreme Council suggested that the branch should reshuffle its administration.[19]

As the foregoing summary indicates, in the mid–1930s Taman Siswa faced a grave threat to its "order and tranquility" from the internal dissension and opposition to the center that resulted from the interaction between its quantitative expansion and its qualitative diversification. How Dewantara handled this situation will become clear from the following examination of the congress of 1936.

The 1936 Congress: Crisis Averted

Immediately before the annual congress of 1936, *Pusara* carried an article entitled, "The coming congress: A final call from K. H. Dewantara," in which Dewantara explained his view of the danger to Taman Siswa's "order and tranquility."[20] Essentially, the danger lay in the major deviation of present circumstances from "the spirit of Taman Siswa" (*ke-Taman Siswa-an*), which Dewantara attributed to the introduction of certain alien principles into Taman Siswa. Specifically, these were "Western democracy based on numbers of votes" and its attendant intellectualism. These external factors had acted on Taman Siswa's essentially "extremely pure principle" of self-determination at a time when that principle was not resting upon "pure foundations," giving rise to individualism and selfishness which sapped Taman Siswa's strength (*kekuatan*) and destroyed "order and tranquility." Dewantara went on to hint that, because the present state of Taman Siswa represented not only a departure from the principles he embraced but also a loss of faith in him, he might have to step down as leader; and he envisioned that the forthcoming congress would expose his leadership to a severe test.

The annual congress of 1936 took place from 19–24 April at Taman Siswa headquarters in Yogyakarta. It comprised a plenary session of the Supreme Council (19–20), the congress proper (20–22), and a second plenary session of the Supreme Council (23–24).

The Plenary Supreme Council (Madjelis Luhur Lengkap) debated several pressing matters, the most serious of which was the question of Dewantara's resignation. As well as announcing his intention to resign at the congress, Dewantara had also tabled proposals for revision of Taman Siswa regulations, which could normally only be debated at a national congress. Although the present congress had not been so convened, the Plenary Supreme Council decided that under the present circumstances debate would be allowed as an emergency measure, and that after adoption by the congress the new regulations would become effective through a "vote of confidence."

Discussion then turned to the question of Dewantara's resignation, on which Dewantara's views were broadly as follows.[21] (1) Leadership was unassailable (*onaantastbaar*) and stood above statutes (*statuten*). If he was distrusted (*wantrouwen*), the leader should resign. (2) The relationship between the leader and the masses should be one of trust and should not be subject to "haggling" (*njang-njangen*). For this reason, Dewantara declared that he would not be present at the congress when the revised regulations were debated. (3) The wheel of Taman Siswa would continue to turn without him; and when there was open rebellion against him, as there was in the Jenggala incident, the leader should step down in accordance with the principles stated in (1) and (2). (4) The major reason for his inability to deal effectively with this situation was a lack of systematic guarantees that would allow him to display his leadership.

These views of Dewantara's became clear in the course of his exchanges with the members of the Supreme Council. And while no further details of their discussions are available, the council eventually reached the following conclusion.[22]

> The Supreme Council appeals to Dewantara not to abandon the position of General Leader even for one minute before his proposals for revision of regulations are rejected. In this connection, this council agrees fully with Dewantara's proposals and will recommend to the congress that it should actively accept these proposals. If the congress should reject these proposals, Dewantara and the members of the Supreme Council will resign.

Having heard an explanation of Dewantara's proposals and a situational report by the Supreme Council, the main congress then debated the proposed revisions, the essence of which was to increase the powers of the Supreme Council, in particular by vesting in it the power to appoint personnel in other sections of the organization, and to define clearly its duties. Through the power of appointment, the chain of command from the General Leader to the Supreme Council, the heads of branches, and the branch leadership councils would be strengthened, and the organizational alignment of the branches around the center in Yogyakarta would be renewed.[23]

Dewantara's explanation of his proposals at the congress was a repetition of the substance of his precongress appeal combined with a statement of the views that had emerged at the Supreme Council.[24] In particular, he stressed the inseparability of Taman Siswa's educational ideals from the principles of leadership and the principle that a leader should be able to decide guidelines independently of regulations.[25]

As a result of the ensuing debate, the details of which are unclear, the congress confirmed Dewantara's position as General Leader and adopted his proposed amendments.[26] For the moment, the internal problems were resolved and "order and tranquility" restored. And at the national congress held two years later Dewantara's leadership was further consolidated when the position of General Leader was formally separated from the Supreme Council and placed above it.[27]

DEMOCRACY AND LEADERSHIP

Dewantara's exposition of the relationship between leadership and regulations, expressed at the 1936 annual congress, was in effect a reaffirmation of the concept of kebidjaksanaan, which had been central to Taman Siswa since its founding, and of the principle that, as discussed in chapter 1, should conflict arise between kebidjaksanaan and "Western-style regulations," the former should prevail.

More than two decades later, just before his death on 26 April 1959 at the age of seventy, Dewantara again argued the validity of this principle in the context of Javanese culture in an article entitled "Democracy and leadership."[28] This was at a time when, two months later, President Sukarno would abolish the provisional constitution of 1950 and restore the constitution of 1945, and when the idea of Guided Democracy (*Demokrasi Terpimpin*), two years after first seeing the light of day, was being proclaimed nationwide as the official ideology. As the "pioneers" of Guided Democracy, it was natural that Taman Siswa should remain among its strongest proponents.

As Dewantara's "legacy" (*warisan*), "Democracy and leadership" formulated the ideas of leadership that had evolved to near completion within Taman Siswa.[29] In its title it suggested an Indonesian translation of Soetatmo's "Democratie en Wijsheid;" and its substance was in fact Dewantara's development of the ideas of the friend who had died thirty-five years earlier. It was, in sum, a modification of Soetatmo's thesis that "democracy without wisdom is a catastrophe" into a form that was subsumable with Soedyono's injunction to "become one with the children who are the prospective People of the future" and with the idea of "equality and solidarity" (*sama rasa sama rata*). Its thrust was as follows.[30]

The idea of "democracy and leadership" had developed in Taman Siswa in response to two requirements of the age.[31] One was the urgent need to establish a different form of democracy from Western-style democracy (*demokrasi setjara Barat*), which, because of the principle of majority decision and the concomitant process of canvassing for that majority, always disturbed overall "order and tranquility," caused factionalism and discord, and ultimately invited rule by the strong. The second requirement was to realize the ideal of *sama rasa sama rata*. Even if the idea of "equality" (*sama rata*) could be derived from Western democratic principles, the ideal of "equal well-being" (*bahagiaan sama*) could not be achieved through their operation.

Dewantara's task was to marry these two requirements with educational ideology and organizational principles. In education, this was accomplished through the Javanese principle of *tut wuri andayani*, "leading from behind." This was democratic in that pupils were free to choose their own path; but the teacher followed closely behind to give guidance when his "discernment" (kebidjaksanaan) told him this was needed. Such a relationship between pupil and teacher allowed the idea of "democracy and leadership" to be formulated.

Organizationally, these two requirements could be met through the functions of the "family organization" (*organisasi keluarga*). These were implicit in the origin of *keluarga* in the words *kawula* and *warga*. *Kawula* meant "servant" (*abdi*), one whose duty was total devotion to the one he regarded as his "master" (*tuan*). *Warga* meant "member" (*anggota*), one who bore the responsibility to take decisions and guide their execution. The union of these two functions of devotion and sharing of responsibility allowed family members simultaneously to be *abdi* and *tuan*. The goal of their devotion was to achieve the unity of kawula and gusti, that is, the "happiness and well-being" (*keselamatan dan kebahagiaan*) of the whole family, and through this to realize sama rasa sama rata in the "family organization."

To bring about the "social justice" (*keadilan sosial*) of sama rasa sama rata within this organization, there must be a leader in whose ability to comprehend this "justice" and point the way to its realization members could trust (*kepertjajaan*). Without such a leader, the organization would soon collapse into anarchy. Ultimately, it was through the leader's "discernment" (kebidjaksanaan) that sama rasa could be realized, and that the "family" could function not simply as an organization (*organisatoris*) but as a living organism (*organis*).

SUKARNO'S GUIDED DEMOCRACY

Dewantara's "Democracy and leadership" displayed a logic for the creation and maintenance of order in the nation-state that was a reformulation, without changing the paradigm, of the traditional conceptual system of witjaksana and Manunggal Kawula lan Gusti. Witjaksana was reinterpreted as the kebidjaksanaan (wijsheid) of the leader; manunggal became achievable through the People's kebidjaksanaan, which was manifested in their perception (*rasa*) of the leader's kebidjaksanaan; and in becoming one with the People, the leader also perceived their "divine will."

This line of political thinking had the corollary that "men's minds" are manifested as the "voice of God," independently of "Western democratic" processes involving the election of representatives. This in turn supported the claims that Western democracy as a legitimating principle runs counter to Javanese (Indonesian) methods, and that Western domocracy only brings the disorder of individualism, egoism, and materialism.

A similar ideology also underlay the *Pantja Sila*, the five principles that Sukarno advanced as the basis for independent Indonesia. The principle of belief in one God (Tuhan jang Maha Esa) irrespective of one's religion accorded with the theosophical teaching of the unity of God; and the principles of nationalism, internationalism, democracy, and social justice were to be pursued through a structure which concentrated on "one divine point" from where they were again expressed. Sukarno expressed the essence of the Pantja Sila in the concept of *gotong rojong* (mutual cooperation) and this meant that the state was seen as an expanded, ideal type of village community. In such a community, sama rasa sama rata was always realized; and at the same time it was considered to come about through the principles that functioned in what Dewantara called the "family."

The full development of such principles in the political arena gave rise to "the Sukarno system," an ideological structure centered on Sukarno, on whom all heterogeneous elements would converge and in whom they would unite.[32] The motto, *Bhinneke Tunggal Ika* (Unity in Diversity), would be realized in the person of Sukarno. This meant that all elements would be ordered and given a mode of existence by the center; and as a result, various hierarchies emerged, each with Sukarno at its apex.[33]

The functions of these hierarchies rested on the abilities of their members to judge their own distance from the apex of power and the sphere of authority vested in them by the apex. At each level within a hierarchy, moreover, were formed subhierarchies: smaller cones of authority likewise functioning through sensibility of distance from the apex. Such sensibility was, of course, nothing other than kebidjaksanaan. And however much this "system of kebidjaksanaan" may have been attired in the trappings of modern bureaucracy, what circulated therein bore not the slightest resemblance to zakelijkheid, to "conducting business without anger or excitement;" rather, it was kebidjaksanaan, manifested in such qualities as "implemental skill," "discernment," "perspicacity," "mutual complementarity," "adaptability," and "resourcefulness."

Conceptually, the People were separated from the hierarchies; their contact with them was to be through Sukarno—the apex and "the People's mouthpiece" (*penjambung lidah rakjat*).[34] His relationship with the People was one-to-one and mutually responsive. What he perceived of the People, Sukarno would circulate to the hierarchies as "the People's will." In this way, the People subsumed the hierarchies, and at the same time were linked directly to them "from above" through the apex.

That Sukarno could be "the People's mouthpiece" was because he was seen to be able, by virtue of his kebidjaksanaan, to perceive the People's will. The legitimacy of his authority, in other words, rested entirely on his "power of perception." This was a divine power which, in its pure form, was expressed as the existence of the People within Sukarno, as Sukarno becoming the People. In the traditional schema, this was equivalent to "Manunggal Sukarno lan Rakjat."

Sukarno himself relates in his Independence Day speech of 17 August 1964 that it was by entering a state akin to religious ecstasy that he acquired knowledge of "the People's will." The following passage from this speech, delivered at a time when Guided Democracy was reaching its peak, depicts clearly the ideological structure of Guided Democracy: that it was democracy (*ke-Rakjat-an*) in that it embodied the concept of the People's voice as the voice of God; and that it was guided through the agency of Sukarno's kebidjaksanaan.[35]

> [Every year on 17 August] I hold a dialogue. A dialogue with whom? A dialogue with the People. A two-way conversation between myself and the

People, between my Ego and my Alter-Ego. A two-way conversation between Sukarno-the-man [Sukarno-*manusia*] and Sukarno-the-People [*Sukarno-Rakjat*], a two-way conversation between comrade-in-arms and comrade-in-arms. A two-way conversation between two comrades who in reality are One!

That is why, every time I prepare a 17 August address, whether in Yogyakarta, in Jakarta, in Bogor, or in Tampak Sirin, I become like a person possessed. Everything that is non-material in my body overflows! Thoughts overflow, feelings overflow, nerves overflow, emotions overflow. Everything that belongs to the spirit that is in my body is as though quivering and blazing and raging, and then for me it is as though fire is not hot enough, as though ocean is not deep enough, as though the stars in the heavens are not high enough.

For me, these 17 August addresses must be a dialogue with you. In these 17 August addresses I must become the mouthpiece of those who live in hovels, those who trade from roadside stalls, those who work in the fields, those who cannot speak for themselves.

This passage depicts vividly Sukarno's view that his legitimacy as Great Leader (*Pemimpin Besar*) rested on his kebidjaksanaan, his paramount ability to perceive the People's will and to be the "mouthpiece" of "those who cannot speak for themselves." Equally clearly, it depicts that, for Sukarno, the People really existed within him ("two comrades who in reality are one"); and that it was only possible for him to reach them by entering a kind of religious trance.[36]

Sukarno's concept of Guided Democracy shows a clear structural resemblance to Dewantara's "democracy and leadership," which, as we have seen, was itself a reformulation of a classical paradigm of Javanese culture. There were, of course, differences between Dewantara and Sukarno. Dewantara saw the People in terms of "family" principles for the creation of order; Sukarno saw them as "dynamic" and "revolutionary," a divine will that ordered him constantly to destroy and constantly to create. Also called Great Leader of the Revolution, Sukarno was the center of the sphere of the People, directing, as their mouthpiece, its perpetual revolution.[37] Such must have been Sukarno's view of the People that had been created through the process of the People's Movement.

Despite these differences, the ideologies of Dewantara and Sukarno shared the same conceptual structure. And inasmuch as they were consonant with the "structures of understanding" of Javanese culture, these ideological systems that were permeated by kebidjaksanaan had tremendous potentiality and great durability.

NOTES

1. "Ditjabut haknja mengadjar," *Pusara* 4, no. 3 (December 1933): 48; 7 no. 4 (February 1937): 48; 7, no. 9–10 (July–August 1937): 149.
2. "Kundjungan K. H. D. pada Tjabang-tjabang," *Pusara* 6, no. 11 (September 1936): 231.
3. Sajoga, "Riwajat Perdjuangan Taman-Siswa" *Buku Taman Siswa 30 Tahun* (Yogyakarta, 1937), p. 239.
4. "Statistik Guru-guru dan Murid-murid Taman Siswa 1935/1936," *Pusara* 6, no. 7 (May 1936): 162.
5. On the leading role played by Sarmidi Mangoensarkoro in the PNI in the early period of independence, see Benedict R. O'G. Anderson *Java in a Time of Revolution: Occupation and Resistance, 1944–1946* (Ithaca, N.Y. and London: Cornell University Press, 1972), pp. 226–230.
6. Sajoga, "Riwajat Perdjuangan," p. 240.
7. "Tentang Perkara jang timbul di Tjabang-tjabang," *Pusara* 6, no. 7 (May 1936): 136–137.
8. Sarmidi Mangunsarkoro, "Apakah arti menjapu kelas sendiri, sebagai alat Pendidikan di Taman Siswa," *Pusara* 6, no. 3 (January 1936): 36–42; no. 4 (February 1936): 69–72.
9. The internal troubles of this time were reported by the Supreme Council of Taman Siswa at the annual congress of 1936. Only the initial letters of the names of branches and individuals are given, however, and in some cases these cannot be confirmed. That B and S represent Bogor and Sartono I inferred from Taman Siswa's obituary to Sartono: "In Memoriam Mr. Sartono," *Pusara* 24, no. 12 (December 1968): 22. And this was confirmed by Mr. Sajoga in an interview in Yogyakarta, May 1975.
10. "Tentang Perkara jang timbul di Tjabang-Tjabang," *Pusara* 6, no. 7 (May 1936): 137–138.
11. Ibid., pp. 135, 138–141.
12. "Perumuman Madjelis Luhur Pusat," *Pusara* 5, no. 12 (October 1935): 286; K. H. Dewantara, "Pertanjaan dan Djawabnja," *Pusara* 6, no. 1 (November 1936): 13–14. After independence, Taman Siswa was to face another period of internal struggle from the mid-1950s to the mid-1960s, which centered on the political factionalism that accompanied the remarkable inroads into Taman Siswa made by the PKI. The confrontations of this period are analyzed in Lee Kam Hang, "The Taman Siswa in Postwar Indonesia," *Indonesia* no. 25 (April 1978): 41–59.
13. Madjelis Luhur Pusat tertanda Soedarminta (Ketua), S. Djojopraitno (Panitera), "Perumuman Madjelis Luhur," *Pusara* 5, no. 10 (August 1935): 231–232.
14. "Guru-guru Taman Siswa dengan Pergerakan Pemuda," *Pusara* 5, no. 11 (September 1935): 269–271.
15. Sajoga, "Riwajat Perdjuangan," pp. 240–243.
16. Ki Banijak, "Geniepig . . . ," *Pusara* 5, no. 11 (September 1935): 266–267; "Kritik à la P. B. I.," ibid., 267–268; "Taman Siswa dan Protest-Lurik," ibid., pp. 268–269. Centered in Surabaya, and with support in East Java, Soetomo's Partai Bangsa Indonesia began in the early 1930s openly to criticize Taman Siswa, which was even more influential in East Java. On this confrontation, see Soekesi Soemoatmodjo, "Taman Siswa adalah salah satu aspek dari perdjuangan nasionalisme" (B.A. diss., Gajah Mada University, Yogyakarta, 1966) pp. 39ff.
17. Sdm., "Motie Taman Siswa Daerah Djenggala, Tumapel, Desember 1935," *Pusara* 6, no. 2 (December 1935): 25–27.
18. Red. Pusara, "Tambahan," *Pusara* 6, no. 2 (December 1935): 27; Sdm., "Motie Taman Siswa," pp. 25–26.
19. "Tentang Guru T. S. dan Pergerakan Pemuda," *Pusara* 6, no. 7 (May 1936): 134.
20. K. H. Dewantara, "Rapat Besar jang akan datang: Seruan jang terachir dari K. H.

Dewantara," *Pusara* 6, no. 3 (January 1936): 48–52.

21. "Verslag Lengkap Rapat Besar Ke IV, 19–23 April 1936 di Mataram: Rapat Madjelis Luhur Lengkap," *Pusara* 6, no. 7 (May 1936): 142–144.

22. Ibid., p. 145.

23. The full text of this regulation can be found in: K. H. Dewantara, "Rentjana Peraturan Besar Taman Siswa," *Pusara* 6, no. 6 (April 1936): 101–109.

24. K. H. Dewantara, "Keterangan 'Rentjana' Perubahan," ibid., pp. 109–116.

25. Dewantara pointed out that the inseparability of educational principles from "leadership" and "control" derived from the educational ideal of the *amongsysteem*, that "while children should be allowed freedom to develop, they should be guided so that they do not stray from the right path" (as will be discussed shortly, this was the Javanese principle of *tut wuri andayani*). Ibid., p. 112. On the leader's freedom from regulations, see ibid., p. 111, and chapter 1.

26. "Putusan-Putusan Rapat Besar Ke IV," *Pusara* 6, no. 6 (April 1936): 118.

27. "Verslag Rapat Besar Umum Ke III dari Persatuan Taman Siswa, 16–22 November 1938 di Mataram," *Pusara* 8, no. 13 (December 1938): 237–239.

28. Ki Hadjar Dewantara, "Demokrasi dan Leiderschap," *Pusara* 20, no. 4 (April 1959): 31–33; ibid., no. 5 (May 1959): 44–52, 55. Soon thereafter, the article was published separately by Taman Siswa: Ki Hadjar Dewantara, *Demokrasi dan Leiderschap* (Yogyakarta, 1959).

29. In a preface lamenting Dewantara's death, *Pusara* described this article as a "legacy" of value not just to Taman Siswa but to the Indonesian People. *Pusara* 20, no. 4 (April 1959): 1.

30. Dewantara, *Demokrasi dan Leiderschap*, pp. 4–16.

31. Dewantara attributes the first of these two requirements to Soetatmo, the second to Mas Marco. Ibid., pp. 5, 8.

32. See, for example, Clifford Geertz, "The Politics of Meaning," in *Culture and Politics in Indonesia*, ed. Claire Holt, Benedict R. O'G. Anderson, and James Siegel (Ithaca, N.Y. and London: Cornell University Press, 1972), pp. 321–322.

33. As president, Sukarno headed the military, the bureaucracy, and the political party.

34. Sukarno is said to have wanted his gravestone to bear the simple epithet, "Mouthpiece of the Indonesian People." *Sukarno, An Autobiography as Told to Cindy Adams* (Indianapolis IN., Kansas City, and New York N.Y.: The Bobbs-Merrill Company, 1965), p. 312.

35. Sukarno, *Dibawah Bendera Revolusi*, vol. 2 (Jakarta: Panitya Penerbit Dibawah Bendera, 1965), pp. 525–526. The English translation is taken in part from J. D. Legge, *Sukarno: A Political Biography* (London: Allen Lane, 1972), p. 2.

36. Sukarno began using the word *Rakjat* frequently as a sacred image at virtually the same time as he began advocating Guided Democracy. In the fifteen-year period from 1950–1964, the numbers of times be used the word in his Independence Day speeches (excluding its appearance in the names of specific institutions, such as Dewan Perwakilan Rakjat) were as follows: 1950, 1; 1951, 3; 152, 4; 1953, 2; 1954, 2; 1955, 8; 1956, 29; 1957, 6; 1958, 31; 1959, 60; 1960, 67; 1961, 117; 1962, 63; 1963, 56; and 1964, 103. Though this is simply an enumeration without regard to the context in which the word was used, it does show that Sukarno's use of the word Rakjat increased sharply from the late 1950s. (In compilation of these figures, I am grateful for the assistance of Mr. Noriaki Oshikawa. The text used was Sukarno, *Dibawah Bendera revolusi*, vol. 2, pp. 99–598.)

37. The concept of revolution about a center was also expressed by Dewantara in 1936, when he said "the wheel of Taman Siswa will turn without me." (See section 2, this chapter.)

APPENDIX
The Situation in Taman Siswa Schools, 1935–1936

NO.	BRANCH NAME	DATE FOUNDED	STUDENTS F	STUDENTS M	STUDENTS TOTAL	NO. OF CLASSES	TEACHERS F	TEACHERS M	TUITION FEES TOTAL	TUITION FEES AVG/STUDENT	TUITION-EXEMPT STUDENTS
2	Srono	1930 10/ 2	14	34	48	8	0	3	45	0.96	1
3	Glenmore	1930 10/31	5	17	22	5	0	2	17.50	0.79	2
5	Banyuwangi	1930 9/ 1	22	45	67	7	0	4	110	1.64	6
6	Kalibaru	1930 10/ 1	15	32	47	8	0	2	30	0.63	7
7	Cluring	1929 7/ 1	2	8	10	4	0	2	10.50	1.05	1
8	Jember	1928 7/ 9	27	55	82	9	1	4	130	1.60	5
9	Tanggul	1927 7/ ?	6	40	46	8	0	4	40	0.87	3
10	Pamekasan	1931 3/28	35	107	142	10	0	8	210	1.50	0
11	Situbondo	1931 3/ 4	21	132	153	8	1	4	181.50	1.18	10
12	Bondowoso	1931 3/ 1	20	53	73	7	0	3	100	1.37	0
13	Kalisat	1931 4/ 7	23	60	83	7	0	3	95	1.14	8
16	Klakah	1931 7/ 1	15	29	44	6	0	3	60	1.36	0
17	Lumajang	1930 ?/ ?	5	20	25	7	0	2	35	1.40	2
18	Probolinggo	1930 7/ 1	44	113	157	12	1	6	180	1.17	9
19	Kraksaan	1928 8/ ?	46	42	88	8	0	5	100	1.25	9
20	Malang	?	98	245	343	12	1	17	535	1.56	20
21	Turen	1930 1/ 1	16	40	56	8	0	3	75	1.34	0
22	Dampit	1930 9/ 8	6	18	24	6	0	3	18	0.75	6
23	Surabaya	1922 11/11	155	507	662	11	0	19	900	1.36	?
24	Wonokramo	1923 7/ 1	31	73	104	7	0	6	80	1.75	3
25	Porrong	1952 7/ 1	14	29	43	6	0	2	53	1.24	6
26	Bojonegora	1930 7/ 1	15	97	112	8	0	5	116	1.03	3
27	Bangkalan	1929 10/ 1	14	36	50	8	0	3	40	0.80	14
28	Mojokerto	1925 5/ ?	30	67	97	10	0	10	184.50	1.90	15

30	Plosso	1927	10/31	5	27	32	8	1	3	35	1.09	3
32	Jombang	1929	7/ 1	11	43	54	11	0	5	110	2.03	10
33	Tulungagung	1931	5/ 1	12	85	97	10	1	6	150	1.54	15
34	Blitar	1930	12/ 1	12	55	67	8	1	6	120	1.79	4
35	Kertosono	1930	1/ 1	14	24	38	7	0	3	46	1.21	8
36	Kesamben	1931	4/ 3	28	56	84	7	0	3	32.50	0.39	26
37	Talun	1929	5/ ?	6	16	22	9	0	2	11	0.50	1
38	Tosari	1931	1/ 1	15	25	40	6	1	2	30	0.75	2
40	Kediri	1931	7/ 1	4	54	58	7	0	3	85	1.46	3
41	Ngoro	1931	9/ 2	11	28	39	9	0	3	41.50	1.06	1
42	Sampang	1932	7/ 3	10	56	66	6	1	4	90	1.36	4
43	Sukowono	1932	9/19	8	22	30	5	1	1	32.50	1.08	0
45	Mojosari	1932	5/ 1	12	30	42	7	1	1	50	1.19	3
47	Wates-Kediri	1929	?/ ?	10	17	27	8	0	2	29	1.07	0
48	Nganjuk	1931	7/ 1	14	70	84	10	1	4	70	0.83	0
49	Kasian	1932	7/29	18	28	46	8	1	2	37.50	0.81	4
50	Balung	1932	7/24	24	58	82	7	0	4	90	1.09	3
52	Tumpang	1932	4/ 7	19	42	61	7	1	3	50	0.82	5
53	Donomulyo	1932	3/ 1	39	56	95	9	1	4	50	0.52	4
54	Maron	1932	5/ 2	8	18	26	5	0	2	18	0.69	3
55	Tuban	1931	10/12	11	44	55	7	0	2	65	1.19	?
56	Pare	1931	7/ 1	14	28	42	5	0	2	56	1.33	4
	Pare sore	?		50	4	54	1	?	?	?	?	?
57	Gurah	1931	11/15	3	21	24	6	0	2	15	0.63	0
58	Trenggalek	1931	7/ 3	9	47	56	7	1	3	60	1.07	0
59	Ngunut	1931	8/ 1	4	29	33	6	0	2	27.50	0.83	2
60	Rogojampi	1932	4/ 2	13	39	52	8	0	3	50	0.96	4
61	Madiun	1929	?/ ?	28	169	197	14	2	11	300	1.52	19
62	Ngawi	1930	6/ 1	26	70	96	8	0	4	103	0.17	11
63	Ponorogo	1931	?/ ?	7	37	44	6	1	2	50	1.13	4

The Situation in Taman Siswa Schools, 1935–1936

NO.	BRANCH NAME	DATE FOUNDED	STUDENTS			NO. OF CLASSES	TEACHERS		TUITION FEES†		TUITION-EXEMPT STUDENTS
			F	M	TOTAL		F	M	TOTAL	AVG/STUDENT	
64	Solo	1930 9/ 9	36	99	135	12	2	8	235	1.74	5
65	Pedan	1930 7/ 1	16	58	74	8	0	4	54	0.73	7
66	Prambanan	1931 7/ 1	17	75	92	9	0	6	65	0.70	19
67	Mataram	1922 7/ 3	101	255	356	18	7	14	700	1.96	34
	T. G. Persatuan	?	3	35	38	3	do.	do.	140	3.69	0
68	Godean	1930 7/14	7	26	33	5	0	3	32.50	0.98	3
69	Magelang	1930 7/ 7	15	85	100	9	0	6	100	1.00	13
71	Blabak	1930 9/ 1	23	64	87	8	0	3	35	0.40	7
72	Kedu	1930 11/ 4	2	17	19	3	0	2	12.50	0.65	0
73	Salaman	1931 1/ 6	17	49	66	6	0	3	78.25	1.18	9
74	Purworejo	1931 7/ 5	46	141	187	10	1	7	200	1.70	7
75	Karanganyar	1931 7/15	31	96	127	7	2	4	150	1.19	11
77	Purwokerto	?	61	254	315	20	?	?	300	0.95	14
78	Sumpyuh	1930 9/ 7	18	29	47	8	0	3	40	0.85	6
79	Kroya	1930 1/ 1	22	59	81	8	1	3	80	0.98	16
80	Cilacap	1930 9/ 4	10	40	50	8	1	3	55	1.10	7
81	Purbolinggo	1930 10/10	9	78	87	11	1	5	55	0.63	2
83	Kasugihan	1931 7/ 1	4	9	13	5	1	1	15	1.15	1
84	Slawi	1924 5/18	17	43	60	9	1	3	60	1.00	6
89	Pekalongan	1930 10/ 3	24	124	148	14	2	6	250	1.75	14
88	Brebes	1932 7/ 4	16	51	67	8	2	2	105	1.56	3
89	Margasari	1932 7/ 1	17	30	47	6	0	2	65	1.38	1
90	Ngadirejo	1931 8/ 1	31	37	68	7	2	3	87.50	1.28	2
91	Wonosobo	1931 8/ 3	6	28	34	7	0	5	30	0.88	8

No.	Name	Year	Date									
93	Semarang	1932	7/ 1	42	117	159	12	4	5	370	2.32	9
94	Salatiga	1932	7/ 1	21	50	71	8	1	3	82.50	1.16	2
95	Cepu	1932	1/15	35	90	125	10	3	3	208	1.66	?
96	Ngawen	1932	7/ 1	25	55	80	6	1	3	75	0.94	3
197	Juwana	1932	4/10	10	39	49	5	0	2	80	1.63	0
102	Pacitan	1932	7/ 1	24	70	94	8	0	5	120	1.26	7
104	Boja	1932	7/ 1	16	40	56	5	0	3	50	0.89	?
105	Kutowinangun	1932	7/ 4	118	38	56	7	6	3	60	1.07	?
106	Jakarta	1929	7/15	63	356	519	33	3	31	1232	2.37	30
107	Bandung	?		87	65	172	15	4	10	261	1.52	17
108	Cirebon	1923	7/ 6	38	114	152	12	1	6	300	2.11	12
110	Cianjur	1928	11/ 4	41	79	120	8	3	5	200	1.66	3
111	Sukabumi	1931	3/ 1	13	53	66	8	1	3	60	0.90	3
113	Banjar	1931	8/10	45	77	122	9	0	4	100	0.82	12
114	Parigi	1932	3/ 1	5	18	23	4	0	2	14	0.77	2
115	Ciamis	1931	12/ 3	16	61	77	6	0	3	32	0.42	12
116	Subang	1931	11/ 1	6	25	31	8	0	2	40	1.30	0
117	Kalijati	1931	11/ 1	5	15	20	4	1	1	30	1.50	0
118	Cikoneng	1932	2/15	16	49	65	5	0	2	20	0.30	7
120	Pamanukan	1932	8/ 7	16	28	44	7	0	1	29	0.66	0
124	Bakumpai	1930	3/ 1	1	19	20	3	0	1	17	0.85	1
125	Banjarmasin	1930	12/ 1	4	55	59	9	4	4	92	1.56	1
130	Matur	1933	5/ 1	41	63	104	8	4	4	95	0.91	5
131	Palembang	1932	7/ 3	29	147	176	10	1	5	375	2.13	2
133	Pabang	1932	7/ 1	35	19	54	5	0	2	110	2.04	4
134	Selatpanjang	1932	8/ 1	5	34	39	7	1	2	108	2.77	0
136	Tg. Karang	1933	4/ 1	21	76	97	8	0	4	150	1.55	3
137	Galang	1934	6/ ?	13	92	105	7	1	2	140	1.33	1
138	Meulaboh	1933	7/15	14	76	90	7	0	3	130	1.44	7
139	Mangkasara	1933	7/ 1	34	198	232	14	2	9	445	1.49	5

APPENDIX (*continued*)

THE SITUATION IN TAMAN SISWA SCHOOLS, 1935–1936

| BRANCH | | DATE FOUNDED | STUDENTS | | | NO. OF CLASSES | TEACHERS | | TUITION FEES† | | TUITION-EXEMPT STUDENTS |
NO.	NAME		F	M	TOTAL		F	M	TOTAL	AVG/STUDENT	
140	Kepanjen	1933 7/ 1	19	34	53	7	0	3	50	0.94	1
141	Kandangar	1932 7/ 1	5	22	27	6	0	2	25	0.93	2
142	Kebumen	1933 7/ 8	9	21	30	5	0	2	22	0.73	4
143	Babad	1933 7/ 1	16	35	51	5	1	2	55	1.08	2
144	Teluketung	1934 9/ ?	17	95	112	?	1	8	120–150	1.20	3
145	Kalianda	?	3	21	24	?	?	?	30–35	1.35	1
146	Comal	1933 7/15	7	25	32	6	1	2	28.50	0.89	11
147	Sipirok	1933 7/ 1	14	72	86	6	1	4	120	1.40	4
150	Talangpadang	1933 7/11	9	40	49	5	0	3	60	1.22	2
155	Badung	1933 9/ 9	57	42	47*	6	0	3	90	1.91	5
158	Sepanjang	1933 10/25	2	59	86*	7	1	2	60	0.69	10
159	Pematangsiantar	1934 2/ 2	21	90	111	5	0	4	180	1.62	0
160	Tarakan	1934 2/25	14	79	93	10	0	3	140	1.50	0
162	Krawang	1934 2/ 1	15	26	41	6	1	1	33	0.80	0
163	Kalanggret	1932 7/ 1	4	6	10	4	1	1	15	1.50	1
164	Cibadak	1933 7/ 3	30	44	74	6	0	3	70	0.96	0
166	Bukittinggi	1934 6/ 5	31	117	148	7	0	6	260	1.75	1
169	Batang	1934 8/ 6	2	45	47	6	0	2	35.50	0.75	2
171	Padang	1934 9/ 3	19	72	91	6	1	4	125	1.37	2
172	Tanjung	1934 8/ 1	6	4	10	5	0	1	19	1.90	0
173	Batu	?	15	51	66	7	1	3	58.25	0.88	1
174	Besuki	1935 1/ 1	10	11	21	4	0	1	17.50	0.88	1
175	Ketanggungan	1935 3/ ?	5	22	27	5	0	2	?	?	1
176	Puger	?	7	38	45	8	0	2	42	0.93	6

No.	Branch											
178	Bandung T. Agung	1931	8/ 3	4	15	19	6	0	1	11	0.58	0
182	Batusangkar	1935	7/20	9	64	73	3	0	2	90	1.23	0
183	Talu	1935	7/ 2	9	36	45	3	0	2	40	0.87	0
184	Wonosari	1935	7/ ?	0	22	22	2	0	1	5.50	0.25	3
186	Gedungtatakan	1935	8/ 5	10	21	31	6	0	2	35	1.13	0
187	Gunungtua	1935	8/ 1	1	34	35	3	0	1	30	0.82	1
	TOTALS (136 branches)			2,855	8,380	11,235	1,037	88	514	15,188	1.36	696

Source: *Pusara* 6, no. 7 (May 1936). The above table was compiled by Taman Siswa headquarters from reports made by individual branches. Branches failing to submit reports were stated to include the following:

1. Genteng	9. Tegal	17. Tebingtinggi
2. Rambipuji	10. Pemalang	18. Pg. Brandan
3. Cukir	11. Ambarawa	19. Kisaran
4. Sidoarjo	12. Bogor	20. Kutoarjo
5. Wlingi	13. Garut	21. Tangerang
6. Ngadiluwih	14. Padalarang	22. Klaten
7. Grabag	15. Cibatu	23. Pd. Sidempuan
8. Sidareja	16. Medan	24. Jeunib
		25. Pg. Pinang

* These figures are apparently erroneous.
† Tuition fees are paid monthly in guilders.

INDEX